Samuel Beckett

Critical Studies in the Humanities
Victor E. Taylor, Series Editor

This open-ended series provides a unique publishing venue by combining single volumes issuing from landmark scholarship with pedagogy-related interdisciplinary collections of readings. This principle of cross-publishing, placing scholarship and pedagogy side by side within a single series, creates a wider horizon for specialized research and more general intellectual discovery. In the broad field of the humanities, the Critical Studies in the Humanities Series is committed to preserving key monographs, encouraging new perspectives, and developing important connections to pedagogical issues.

Proposals for submission should be directed to the Series Editor, Victor E. Taylor, Department of English and Humanities, York College of Pennsylvania, York, PA 17405-7199.

Sander L. Gilman, *Nietzschean Parody*
Sharyn Clough, Ed., *Siblings Under the Skin: Feminism, Social Justice and Analytic Philosophy*
Dominick LaCapra, *Emile Durkheim: Sociologist and Philosopher*
Gregg Lambert, *Report to the Academy*
Michael Strysick, Ed., *The Politics of Community*
Dennis Weiss, Ed., *Interpreting Man*
Jonathan Culler, Flaubert: *The Uses of Uncertainty*
Geoffrey Galt Harpham, *On the Grotesque*
Steven Connor, *Samuel Beckett: Repetition, Theory and Text*
Gregg Lambert, *The Return of the Baroque in Modern Culture*
David D. Roberts, *Nothing But History*
Gregg Lambert, *The Return of the Baroque in Modern Culture*
Julia Reinhard Lupton and Kenneth Reinhard, *After Oedipus*
Neil Hertz, *The End of the Line*

Samuel Beckett

Repetition, Theory and Text

Steven Connor

A volume in the series
Critical Studies in the Humanities
Victor E. Taylor, Series Editor

The Davies Group, Publishers
Aurora, Colorado USA

Address all requests to: The Davies Group, Publishers
PO Box 440140 Aurora, CO 80044-0140   USA

Library of Congress Cataloging-in-Publication Data

Connor, Steven, 1955-
  Samuel Beckett : repetition, theory, and text / Steven Connor.
    p. cm. -- (Critical studies in the humanities)
  Includes bibliographical references and index.
  ISBN-13: 978-1-888570-88-5 (alk. paper)
  ISBN-10: 1-888570-88-1 (alk. paper)
  1. Beckett, Samuel, 1906-1989--Technique. 2. Repetition (Rhetoric)
I. Title.
  PR6003.E282Z62116 2006
  842'.914--dc22
                              2006034064

Printed in the United States of America
Published 2006. The Davies Group Publishers, Aurora, Colorado

                    1 2 3 4 5 6 7 8 9 0

To my mother,
Vivien Connor (1922–1985)
in memory of her love and courage.

Contents

Preface

You return to a book you have written a long time ago with a mixture of elation and precaution, a little as one prepares to return to a childhood home. It is touching to see how much remains just as you left it (even if everything that seemed so big and scary then now seems so pitiably miniature now). But it's also humiliating to see how easy it has been for subsequent owners to live without so much that at the time seemed so necessary and unbudgeable.

Indulging myself in this hindsight reminds me that that the book was written blind, I mean with no definite prospect of publication. It is so far the only book that I have written in that way. I wrote it, over the course of a few months, from beginning to end, without having sent anyone a proposal, circulating drafts, or having the benefit of readers' reports. This is not usually the way in which books are written nowadays, and certainly not anything I would advise a younger academic colleague to do. Normally, in academic and other circles, one has, if not a firm contract, then some kind of indication that somebody is interested in publishing the book. I wouldn't say that the book lacks purpose or coherence because of that: indeed, it may be that I seem to have surrendered to the opposite temptation, what the Director in Beckett's play *Catastrophe* calls the 'rage for explicitation'. Certainly it could do with a certain looseness in the joints here and there. But it's also clear that, in many ways, it is a book in which the idea of repetition is so much to the fore because it allowed me to write about everything in the work of this writer that so mesmerised and mattered to me. Fortunately, Blackwell thought well enough of the product to offer me a contract for it. But when my editor Stephan Chambers suggested to me, in a tone of tentative complicity (whatever that sounds like), that, rather than using any of the preeningly exquisite titles I had in mind, I might just call the book 'Samuel Beckett', it may have been partly in recognition of this, rather than as a canny piece of dragnetting for keywords, which were not yet of great importance.

There is always a kind of edginess in writing any critical book of this kind about a writer whom one has admired for as long as I had admired

Beckett. Obviously, in one sense, it gave me the opportunity to share the limelight, to get to see my words on the same page as Beckett's – a bit like those fan photos where you go cheek-to-cheek with your idol in a pretended intimacy that can then be captioned 'Tori and me at the Wembley Arena'. On the other hand, I felt the usual crude and competitive urge to upstage, dummy and outdo my subject. In my original acknowledgements to the book, I thanked Jim Knowlson for his courtesy in the face of the 'loutishness of learning', using a phrase from Beckett's poem 'Gnome'. Reading this book has shown me that I still had a lot of that loutishness to unlearn.

When I first reread the book, I was seized with the desire to repossess it, to make it the book I would write now if I were called upon to write a book about repetition. So repeating myself would mean having to do it all differently. This would be like retouching a photograph, not in order to make one's present self look younger, but in order to make one's younger self seem more like the older self one takes oneself to have turned out (so far) to be. I came unstuck with this when I got to the chapter dealing with the ways in which Beckett revisited and reconstructed himself in self-translation. For here I found myself being sagely instructed by my younger self about Beckett's strange attempts both to catch up with himself, and to push his earlier works even further away into the past. I found my book teaching me about a repetition strangely blent with resenting, repenting and retention.

In fact, the book was full of this kind of booby trap for the second comer I now was. I was particularly looking forward to reading the chapter on *Krapp's Last Tape*, a play about an old man listening to tapes made earlier in his life. Krapp is bored and disgusted by the earnest self-regard of the writer who feels he is at the turning point of his life, when he is about to come into his own. Older (oldest?) Krapp knows now that his real life has been lived, more intensely and more irretrievably, elsewhere, elsewhen, than in the triumphant moment when he seemed to be taking the helm of his life. One of the best jokes in the play, and one that sniggered the most at my own archival exercise, occurs as Krapp is listening to the scornfully self-confident retrospections of his younger self: 'The voice! Jesus! And the aspirations! [*Brief laugh in which Krapp joins.*] And the resolutions! [*Brief laugh in which Krapp joins.*] To drink less in particular. [*Brief laugh of Krapp alone.*]'. I sometimes felt, like Krapp himself, that I wanted to listen to another tape, or to try to make out something else on the tape, than the official record.

The book seems to me to divide into two, asymmetrical parts. The first seven chapters move through Beckett's work, trying to show that it is held together by an intense impulse to and curiosity about repetition. I show how the predicament of repetition, both desired for its consecrating and consummating power and disdained for its redundancy, is much more than a linguistic issue. Saying again is bound up with Krapp's unconvincingly disavowed desire to 'be again'. Repetition is at the heart of living in time. Beckett's turn to theatre, which might have seemed to offer the chance to see and be seen directly, in the immediacy of presence, unshadowed by repetition, in fact turned the screw on this predicament, especially in the work that he undertook for radio and TV, which seemed to allow Beckett to fold theatre on itself, doubling it over in recording and mediation. The theatre that promised to deliver a definite, delimited, self-evident world loses its remedying immediacy in re-mediation.

The last chapter broaches a rather different perspective. Here I found myself writing, not about Beckett, but about the empire of 'Beckett studies', that reports, repeats and deports him. Beckett's centenary year, which, as I write, is still only half-expired, has provided many occasions to reflect on what has changed and what continues to repeat itself in that world.

In 1987, it seemed to me that Beckett studies was (the singular is requisite) in a kind of reverential stupor. To the harsh, hurrying tyro I was, the world of Beckett studies was dominated by people who knew or had known 'Sam', and depended for their authority on a kind of apostolic succession. Having been In the Presence, or had hands laid upon them, they were the only ones entitled to carry on the benediction business. It seemed strange to me, and, as it would turn out, to others of my age and unforgiving inclination, that, where Joyce's work had provided a roaring free market of interpretative opportunity, Beckett studies was so austerely protectionist, sheltering its subject from the manifold possibilities of new kinds of reading — feminist, postcolonial, psychoanalytic, deconstructive — that were sprouting everywhere. What made this seem even more perverse was the fact that, on close inspection, Beckett's work seemed more than most authors to validate, thematise and even to anticipate these new forms of reading. What I hoped to do was not just to write about the particular insistence of repetition in Beckett's work but, more generally, to wrest that work away from its association with Descartes, Sartre, existentialism and the Theatre of the Absurd and into the vicinity of writers like Deleuze, Derrida and Foucault, who not only excited me, but also seemed, without saying so (or not very often), to have Beckett in mind in everything they wrote. I wanted to show, not just that Beckett was unusually alive to the powers of repetition in his work, but that the theory used to bring that to light itself repeated Beckett's explorations and discoveries.

The passing of time has proved the usual truth: just when it seems like things can never change, they are in fact on the point of never being the same again. A number of other writers, Thomas Trezise, Leslie Hill, Sylvie Debevec Henning, Mary Bryden, Anna MacMullan, Carla Locatelli among them, had very similar ideas at around the same time, and *Repetition, Theory and Text* quickly formed part of a new dispensation in Beckett studies. Far from being an eccentric Irish gloomist, Beckett became your theorist's only man.

Beckett himself died in the year following the appearance of my book, though I do not flatter myself that it was the last straw. One of the mournful duties I had in revising this book was to change the present perfect tenses into completed past tenses, oxymoronic though this notion is for Beckett, for whom tenses are so often a cause of tension. Beckett's death was followed by a simultaneous contraction and diffusion of Beckett studies, a sort of reculer pour mieux sauter. On the one hand, the figure of Beckett was baked by his mortality into even more of a colossus than ever, remote and chiselled, with his admirers and officiants teeming emmet-like about it. The Estate has made itself grimly steadfast in acting in Beckett's stead, to ensure that none of his works will ever look or sound any different from the ways in which they looked and sounded in the days when Sam still walked the earth. But, at the same time, among literary critics, his work has also been subject to a huge effort of what anthologies and essay-collections called 'revisiting', reconstructing', 'rethinking'. Over the last twenty-five years, Beckett's work has become extravagantly and compulsorily open to every conceivable kind of approach and interpretation. He has become a writer to think with, as well as about.

That final chapter now seems to me to contain not a few overstatements, and also in some respects to have become an historical document. I complained in it that 'the discourse of Beckett criticism has a special representative place within discourses of culture as a whole, for it is a site in which cultural values of great importance may be repeated and recirculated with authority'. I don't think that Beckett represents such conservative or traditional values as he did. The current centenary has shown how fantastically easy for the name, face, idiom and idea of 'Beckett' to be turned to account, by all and any - critic, artist, publisher, director, cartoonist, adapter, advertiser, broadcaster. Under such circumstances, it may no longer seem as urgent as it once did to liberate Beckett from the dead hand of uniformity. There now seems to me to be an equally urgent need to put a spoke or two in the frantic freewheel in which it seems that 'Beckett' can be anything and everything we choose to coin from it, even as it remains authentically and unfalsifiably Beckettian as ever. In the face of Beckett Unlimited, the principle of illimitability asserted in the final chapter of *Repetition Theory and Text* might need revisiting.

For a long time, this book has been an unobtainable exotic. Blackwell, the original publisher, rang me up in the mid 1990s to say that, as they were not planning to reprint the book, I could have the rights back (and me thinking that, like Vladimir and Estragon I had 'got rid of them') and by the way would I consider relieving them of the last bale of copies that people kept tripping over in the warehouse? So I took the orphans in, and, whenever people contacted me asking how to obtain a copy, posted them out to putatively good homes for a tenner, or a fiver, or for free. By the time that The Davies Group approached me with the idea of a reprint, I was down to my last specimen.

This new edition of the book has been subject to a very detailed revision. I have taken the opportunity to remedy grogginess, pomposity, fuss and nagging where they seemed to be intolerable or remediable. Though the book's main arguments have had to be left to fend for themselves, I hope that, as a result, their exposition may now seem clearer, more candid and more lenient.

Writing a preface of this kind is a frankly self-indulgent thing to be allowed to do. One does not often have the chance of acting as one's own resurrectionist in this way and I am very grateful to Victor Taylor as series editor and The Davies Group, Publishers for offering this book the chance to be read and written again. Sure enough, I find myself having planted in the book itself a motto for this whole procedure. 'Repetition always leaves some active residue; in coming full circle, the book ends up in a different place from where it had begun, leaving the desire to begin again as strong as ever.' So then: from the top.

Acknowledgements

I must record my gratitude to the staffs of the Washington University Library, St Louis, the Humanities Research Center at Austin, Texas, the New York Public Library and the Yale University Library for their courtesy and helpfulness during my visits from 1984 to 1986. My thanks also go to John Edwards and Jim Knowlson of the Reading University Beckett Archive. Samuel Beckett showed his usual patience, courtesy and goodwill in the face of the loutishness of learning.

Throughout the writing of this book, I have been lucky to have had the advice, shrewd and generous at once, of my colleague Barbara Hardy. Ruby Cohn, Jim Knowlson and Katherine Worth all responded kindly and helpfully to versions of the chapters which they heard in the form of papers, while John Pilling read the typescript with a friendly, expert eye and saved me from many blunders. I am grateful, too, for the helpful comments of Andrew Gibson and stimulating conversations with Dennis Foster, Alan Astro and my research students, Stephen Barfield, Yolande Cantu and David Green. But nobody could have contributed more to the writing of the book than Lynn Nead, whose attentive, sceptical reading of all the drafts of the chapters showed me the limits of my approach and encouraged me to go beyond them; she changed this book no less than she changed my life.

Thanks are due to the following for permission to quote at length from already published sources: Jacques Derrida, Routledge and Kegan Paul and the University of Chicago Press for extracts from *Writing and Difference*; English translations from Gilles Deleuze, *Différence et Répétition*, © Gilles Deleuze 1968 by permission of Athlone Press and Columbia University Press; extracts from Beckett's fiction by permission of John Calder and Grove Press Inc.; from Beckett's poetry and dramatic writings by permission of Faber and Faber and Grove Press Inc.; extracts from Beckett's writings in French by permission of Editions de Minuit. I am very grateful, too, to Samuel Beckett for permission to quote from the manuscripts of *Mercier and Camier* in the Reading Beckett Archive, *Watt* and *Premier Amour* in the Humanities Research Center at Austin and *Le Dépeupleur* in the Berg Collection of the New York Public Library.

Abbreviations and Editions Cited

References to Beckett's works in English are to the following editions:

Murphy	(London: Calder and Boyars, 1969)
Watt	(London: Calder and Boyars, 1963)
Mercier and Camier	(London: John Calder, 1973)
T	*Molloy, Malone Dies, The Unnamable* (London: Calder and Boyars, 1959)
How It Is	(London: John Calder, 1964)
CSP	Collected Shorter Prose 1945–1980 (London: John Calder, 1984)
Company	(London: John Calder, 1980)
Ill Seen Ill Said	(London: John Calder, 1982)
Worstward Ho	(London: John Calder, 1983)
CDW	Complete Dramatic Works (London: Faber and Faber, 1986)
CPEF	Complete Poems in English and French (London: John Calder, 1977)
Our Exag	'Dante...Bruno. Vieo...Joyce', in *Our Exagmination Round His Factification for Incamination of Work in Progress*, first published 1929 (London: Faber and Faber, 1962)
PTD	*Proust and Three Dialogues With Georges Duthuit* (London: John Calder, 1965)
Disjecta	*Disjecta: Miscellaneous Writings and a Dramatic Fragment,* ed. Ruby Cohn (London: John Calder, 1983)

References to the following works are also abbreviated:

Bair	Deirdre Bair, *Samuel Beckett: A Biography* (London: Jonathan Cape, 1978)
Admussen:	Richard L. Admussen, *The Samuel Beckett Manuscripts: A Study* (Boston: G.K. Hall and Co., 1979)
WD	Jacques Derrida, *Writing and Difference,* trans. Alan Bass (London: Routledge and Kegan Paul, 1978)
DR	Gilles Deleuze, *Différence et Répétition* (Paris: Presses Universitaires de France, 1968).

All translations from this text are my own.

Chapter 1

Difference and Repetition

It will be the argument of this book that repetition is a central and necessary concept within all attempts to understand individual and social being and representation. While to a large extent repetition determines and fixes our sense of our experience and representations of that experience, it is also the place where certain radical instabilities in these operations can reveal themselves. It is therefore no accident that Samuel Beckett, the writer who in this century has most single-mindedly dedicated himself to the exploration of what is meant by such things as being, identity and representation, should have at the centre of his work so strong and continuous a preoccupation with repetition. His early works show the hopeless, habitual wanderings of characters struggling to escape from habit, even though they are themselves constitutively enslaved by it. Subsequent characters go on to repeat with variations what these early characters say and do, to such an extent, in the end, that our sense of the individuality of characters in Beckett's work is very difficult to sustain. Malone is a version of Molloy, crippled, desperate and playful, just as Molloy is a version of Moran, and all of them have family resemblances to the shuffling moribunds in the novellas. Later, the bedridden solipsist will be relocated to the ditch of *Texts for Nothing* and the mire of *How It Is,* and will subsequently come in from the cold to occupy the closed spaces of *The Lost Ones, Ping* and *All Strange Away.* There are, to be sure, significant breaks in the chain of repetitions, moments when Beckett seems to achieve some real novelty amid the nothing new, but even these are liable to reversions - as when, for instance, the inhabitant of closed space who begins *Company* ends up crawling, like the inhabitant of the mud in *How It Is.*

Beckett's world is one of linguistic repetitions, too. His earlier works, *Dream of Fair to Middling Women* and *More Pricks Than Kicks,* are characterized by an enormous density of allusions, which continually send the reader outside to the other texts which they repeat or ironically repudiate. As Beckett's work develops, these external allusions are progressively outweighed by internal allusions to and citations from his own texts. As John Pilling has suggested, one of his last pieces, *Company,* can be seen very largely as a compendium or palimpsest of citations from previous works.[1]

Beckett's prose work therefore shows a self-constraining movement in which sameness always inhabits or inhibits what may initially present itself as novelty. A similar ratio of sameness and difference seems to be enacted in Beckett's move to the theatre. Although Beckett has frequently indicated that he turned to the theatre as a form of relief from the impasse that the writing of fiction had led him to, it seems as though his project in the drama is really to find new avenues of approach to the same impasse. Characters and situations, ideas and phrases, recur irresistibly between the fiction and drama, as well as between the different forms of drama that Beckett has produced since the 1960s.

This obsessive concern with repetition in all its forms within his texts is curiously echoed in the necessity that Beckett has faced since his turn to the French language during the Second World War to repeat himself in self-translation. This necessity has its origin, of course, in factors other than internal, aesthetic ones; but the different pressures, commercial and psychological at once, which leave Beckett unable or unwilling to entrust the translation of his works to others, intersect very curiously with the recurrent themes of his works, and in particular the compulsion that so many of his characters feel to make and remake themselves in narratives and languages not their own.

Extraordinary though Beckett's concern is with repetition in all its forms, it is by no means unique in this century. Other modern writers and artists, James Joyce, Gertrude Stein, Georges Bataille and other surrealists, Alain Robbe-Grillet and other *nouveau romanciers,* have given repetition a new centrality in their work. The principle of repetition seems to have acquired a particular power in the cultural era we have come to know as the 'postmodern'; in painting, writing and film, the modernist imperative to 'make it new' has been superseded by a desire to recirculate the old or the already known, if only in the attempt to subvert the grounds of familiar knowledge. It would surely be a mistake to see this as merely the emptying of life or urgency from cultural activity, however, since what underlies modernist and postmodernist experiments with the forms of repetition is not so much a movement between the fixed polarities of creative originality on the one hand, and plagiarizing imposture on the other, as an attempt to shift and complicate the fixity of each of those positions, and to explore the problematic interrelationship that exists between originality and repetition.[2]

This awareness has not been confined to literary or artistic spheres. In philosophy, linguistics, sociology and other human sciences, the relationship of originality and repetition has become an obsessive theme. But it is perhaps in the work of the two contemporary French philosophers, Gilles Deleuze and Jacques Derrida, that the operations of repetition have come under the closest scrutiny.

Repetition has a double nature in the work of Derrida. Repetition is at one and the same time that which stabilizes and guarantees the Platonic model of original and copy and that which threatens to undermine it. Repetition must always repeat originality, must always depend on some thing or idea that is by definition preexisting, autonomous and self-identical. Repetition is therefore subordinated to the idea of the original, as something secondary and inessential. For this reason, repetition is conventionally condemned in Western culture as parasitic, threatening and negative. But if repetition is dependent upon a preexisting originality, it is also possible to turn this round and argue that originality is also dependent upon repetition. If repetition requires something that is already fixed and finished, already constituted as an essence, then it is equally true that originality or essence can never be apprehended as such unless the possibility exists for it to be copied or reiterated. The question 'How can you have a repetition without an original?' brings with it the less obvious question 'How can you have an original which it would be impossible to represent or duplicate?'

Derrida argues this mutual dependence of original and repetition in terms of his well-known speech/writing dichotomy. A sacred text such as the Jewish Torah represents itself as the infallible Word of God, a sacred 'speech' that, despite its actual condition as writing or scripture, predates and resists the distortions and falsifications of writing. But if writing, and the possibility of every form of reproduction which writing exemplifies, is antagonistic to the immediacy and self-evidence of speech, then this speech is also to a degree dependent upon writing, or at least the possibility of being written down or reproduced in some other form than its original. What is original, in other words, is not the autonomous Word of God, but its instantaneous and continuing possibility of being repeated, just as in ordinary language, what is most important is not what a word originally means, but its capacity to be reused to mean the same thing in different contexts.[3] So, in a curious way, the principle of repetition should really be seen as primary and original:

> Repetition does not reissue the book, but describes its origin from the vantage of a writing which does not yet belong to it, or no longer belongs to it, a writing which feigns, by repeating the book, inclusion in the book. Far from letting itself be oppressed or enveloped within the volume, this repetition is the first writing. The writing of the origin, the writing that retraces the origin, tracking down the signs of its disappearance, the lost writing of the origin.
>
> (*WD*, 295)

Repetition is different, of course, from simple copying or imitation, for repetition aims to cut out every vestige of difference between itself and its original. Repetition aspires to the condition of an invisible membrane that encloses its original, without impeding access to it in any way, or interfering with its nature. But even this close, self-effacing servitude displaces the authority of the original. Like a circle which is traced twice, argues Derrida, nothing changes with a repetition, but at the same time, an imperceptible difference emerges:

> Once the circle turns, once the volume rolls itself up, once the book is repeated, its identification with itself gathers an imperceptible difference which permits us efficaciously, rigorously, that is, discreetly, to exit from closure. In redoubling the closure of the book, one cuts it in half. One then furtively escapes from it, between two passageways through the same book, the same line, along the same ring, '*vigil of writing in the interval of limits*'. The exit from the identical into the same remains very slight, weighs nothing itself, thinks and weighs the book *as such*.
>
> (*WD*, 295)

This difference is essential to the nature of the sign, though it constitutes that essential nature not as a protrusive fullness, but as a lack, and a non-self-identity: 'the same line is no longer exactly the same, the ring no longer has exactly the same center, *the origin has played*' (WD, 296). Obviously, seen in this way, the origin is secondary to, or an epiphenomenon of the repetition, is, in fact always missing from the repetition and constituted as a magnetic point of desire within it: 'the book has lived on this lure: to have given us to believe that passion, having originally been impassioned by *something*, could in the end be appeased by return of that something' (*WD*, 295).

The result of this adjustment of priority is not a simple inversion, a perverse preference for copies over originals, which would leave the terms of the opposition between them unaffected. Rather, origin and repetition are to be understood as moments in an unending process of mutual definition and redefinition. It is for this reason that Derrida refuses to see origin and repetition in a relationship of simple presence and simple absence, the original being defined as a presence by the absent, potential repetition. Repetition, Derrida says, 'is not absence instead of presence, but a trace which replaces a presence which has never been present'. He therefore protests against that form of 'atheology' which 'pronounces the absence of a center, when it is play that should be affirmed' (*WD*, 297).

The work of Gilles Deleuze, though proceeding along a path similar to that of Derrida, has had much less influence on Anglo-American literary studies, perhaps because so little of his work before *Anti-Oedipus* has been translated. Nevertheless, the close re-examination in his work of the concepts of difference and repetition and the strange links between them makes Deleuze a very important and representative figure in the history of twentieth-century reimaginations of repetition.

For Deleuze, as for Derrida, repetition plays a crucial part in reinforcing the Platonic sense of essence and identity. A large part of his *Différence et Répétition* is given over to a critical examination of the ways in which repetition and difference have cooperated in this function throughout Western philosophy. We are unable, says Deleuze, to conceive of difference *as such,* needing always to see difference as a variation of an identity, difference made *to* something preexisting, or difference *from* something else. Identities are similarly defined by the differences which place and constitute them, but the effect of perceiving difference is always to reinstate the sense of an original identity. Even when difference takes the form of negativity or contradiction, the originating concept still controls and delimits the forms of the contradiction, contradiction being the shadow behind which identity is confirmed (*DR*, 342–3).

Deleuze distinguishes two different forms of repetition. Repetition which is humbly obedient to its original, which merely and simply reproduces it without any addition or distortion, Deleuze calls 'mechanical' or 'naked' repetition. Distinct from this is the 'clothed' or 'disguised' repetition which adds something to its original and seems to impart a difference to it:

> The first repetition is repetition of the Same, explicable by the identity of the concept or representation; the second repetition comprehends difference, and comprehends itself as the alterity of the Idea, in the heterogeneity of an 'appresentation'. The first is negation, in the absence of the concept, the second, affirmation, due to its excess over the Idea...the first is committed to equality, commensurability, symmetry, the second is founded on inequality, incommensurability, dissymmetry. The first is material, the second spiritual.... The first is inanimate, the second the secret of our deaths and lives, our slaveries and liberations, the demonic and the divine. The first is a 'naked' repetition, the other a clothed repetition, which comes into being in clothing itself, in masking and disguise.
>
> (*DR*, 36–7)

However, by the end of his analysis, Deleuze has abandoned the clear relationship between the two kinds of repetition, the one identical with the original, the other in excess of it:

> Living, clothed, vertical repetition, which comprehends difference, must be seen as the cause which brings about horizontal, material, naked repetition. The clothed lies beneath the naked, produces it, secretes it, as the effect of its secretion ... repetition comprehends difference not as an accidental or extrinsic variation, but as its heart, in the essential variation which forms it, the displacement and disguise which constitute it as a difference itself divergent and displaced.
>
> (*DR*, 370)

So, if repetition marks the place where difference most conspicuously confirms identity, the place where difference reduces to its absolute minimum to become almost invisible, it is a category that is both self-evident and deeply problematic; for repetition shows the fact of difference without our being able to say in what the difference consists. In repetition — as, perhaps, in the figure of Derrida's twice-described circle — we confront the form of invisible but irreducible difference, the form, perhaps of 'pure' difference, ungoverned by preexisting categories of representation.

Deleuze's intention is to liberate philosophy from the grip of systematized and preconceived structures of difference, and to suggest to it ways of thinking 'nomadic' difference, that is, difference unconstrained by the horizons of conceptual regulation. In order to do this, Deleuze brings together *différence libre,* or nomadic difference, and *répétition complexe,* repetition which resists its subordination to the function of mechanical reproduction of the same (*DR,* 2). For there can never be any such thing as pure or exact repetition. In order to be recognizable as such, a repetition must, in however small a degree, be different from its original. This 'difference' is invisible except in the fact of its pure differentiality. Functioning in this way, repetition becomes a kind of weak point in the principle of identity. If the Same attempts to stabilize itself by capturing and controlling the forms of the Other, and subordinating them to itself, then repetition marks the point where the confirming presence of difference melts away, leaving identity only itself to confirm itself. Repetition is difference without force — or without force to guarantee identity — and therefore a principle which can force identity apart. As Michel Foucault describes it in his essay on Deleuze's work, repetition is simultaneously a point of weakness and of deconstructive strength:

> Repetition betrays the weakness of similarity at a moment when it can no longer negate itself in the other, when it can no longer recapture itself in the other. Repetition, at one time pure exteriority and a pure figure of the origin, has been transformed into an internal weakness, a deficiency of finitude, a sort of stuttering of the repetition: the neurosis of dialectics.[4]

Repetition is therefore the key to affirming 'nomadic' difference 'as such'. In the work of Deleuze and of his associates, Foucault perhaps chief among them, nomadic difference is seen as a liberation from the constricting untruth of difference and repetition in the service of the Same. The orgiastic play of this kind of difference even dissolves the difference between difference and repetition, that is to say, the difference between difference and nondifference, since, as Foucault explains it, repetition 'would cease to function as the dreary succession of the identical, and would become displaced difference' (p. 182). Deleuze looks forward to a Nietzschean 'eternal recurrence' which, he argues, is really the form of absolute differentiality. Eternal recurrence is the regime of the 'simulacrum', in which the very opposition between original and copy is done away with:

> Simulacra are systems in which different things are related to each other simply *by difference* itself. The essential thing is that in such systems there is no *preexisting identity*, no *interior resemblance* to be found. There is nothing but difference in the series, and difference of difference in the communication of the series. What is displaced and disguised in the series cannot and must not be identified, but exists and functions as the differentiation of difference.
>
> (*DR*, 383)

Repetition turns out to be the motive principle of this vision of difference, for pure difference implies and relies upon the unhierarchized interdependence of different elements, in what can be seen as an incessant mutual recall or repetition. So it becomes possible to free repetition from its role as the slave or mirror of identity and to see it as a liberating principle within an eternal recurrence which is also absolute difference:

> Repetition in eternal recurrence presents itself under all its aspects as the essential power of difference; and the displacement and disguise of that which repeats itself act only to reproduce the divergence and decentring of the different, in a single movement which is the *diaphora* or transport. Eternal recurrence affirms difference, affirms dissemblance and disparity, chance, multiplicity and becoming.
>
> (*DR*, 383)

In *Différence et Répétition* as well as in subsequent works, Deleuze sees the lifting of servitude to the Same as a revolutionary liberation. Art has an important part to play in this liberation. Art depends upon repetitions of various kinds, but can never itself be reduced to mere repetition. Rather, Deleuze argues, by setting different sorts of repetition in play against each other, art (and especially modern art) can highlight the principle of pure difference, and therefore 'point out to philosophy the path that leads to the abandonment of representation' *(DR,* 94) and free us from our contemporary servitude to the social forms of repetition in standardization, routine and consumption:

> The more standardized our everyday life seems, the more stereotyped, the more subordinated to the accelerated reproduction of objects for consumption, the more art must fix upon and draw out that tiny difference that plays elsewhere and simultaneously between the different levels of repetition.... Every art has its techniques of imbricated repetition whose critical and revolutionary power can attain the highest point in leading us from the dreary repetitions of habit towards the profound repetitions of memory, and to the ultimate repetition of death where our liberty plays.
>
> *(DR,* 375)

The effect of Derrida's and Deleuze's work is to show the radical duality of repetition, its involvement simultaneously with two contradictory models of being and representation.[5] A similar duality emerges in the work of another influential twentieth-century theorist of repetition. As is well-known, Freud's work on repetition drew him 'beyond the pleasure principle' to the discovery of the death-drive, the 'urge inherent in organic life to restore an earlier state of things'.[6] The repetition compulsion, he writes, is an expression of this 'inertia inherent in organic life', and therefore stands against the pleasure principle, or the sexual drives, which project the organism forwards to encounter the 'vital differences' of life *(BPP,* 55). But this is not a simple opposition. For Freud, it is not enough for the death-drive simply to oppose the life-instincts. Rather, its function is to bind and control excitations *(BPP,* 30), in order that the individual can pass through life, taking 'ever more complicated *detours'* on the way to death *(BPP,* 39), experiencing difference in order to bend it back towards death:

Seen in this light, the theoretical importance of the instincts of self-preservation, of self-assertion and of mastery greatly diminishes. They are component instincts whose function it is to assure that the organism shall follow its own path to death, and to ward off any possible ways of returning to inorganic existence other than those which are immanent in the organism itself. We have no longer to reckon with the organism's puzzling determination (so hard to fit into any context) to maintain its own existence in the face of every obstacle. What we are left with is the fact that the organism wishes to die only in its own fashion.

(*BPP*, 39)

As Deleuze observes, the binding force of habit and repetition is not secondary to the pleasure principle; rather, pleasure must be seen as the product of repetition *(DR,* 129–30). Pleasure and unpleasure are therefore bound together, depending upon and successively producing each other, and providing another instance of the complex junction of difference and repetition discussed by Deleuze. This may offer an important insight into Beckett's writing practice. As many have argued, Beckett's works are attempts to deny or negate by means of the complex detours of affirmation, to efface by means of repetition. Time and again his writing throws up formulae "which seem to re-enact Freud's conception of the union of affirmation and negation in the repetition-compulsion: 'This time, then once more I think, then perhaps a last time, then I think it'll be over' as Molloy writes *(T,* 8) or, as the voice in *The Unnamable* puts it, more bitterly, 'first dirty then make clean' *(T,* 302). In order to have done, it is always necessary for Beckett to begin again: 'Imagination dead imagine. A place, that again. Never another question. A place, then someone in it, that again. Crawl out of the frowsy deathbed and drag it to a place to die in' *(All Strange Away, CSP,* 117).

Finality is often associated for Beckett with structures of alternation, as, for example, in the game that Watt plays while he watches the light diminish from a range in the kitchen 'covering the lamp, less and less, more and more, with his hat, watching the ashes greyen, redden, greyen, redden, in the grate, of the range' *(Watt,* 36), or the game played by the narrator of *First Love* with the cries receding behind him after he leaves Anna's house:

> I began playing with the cries, a little in the same way as I had played with the song, on, back, on, back, if that may be called playing. As long as I kept walking I didn't hear them, because of the footsteps. But as soon as I halted I heard them again, a little fainter each time, admittedly, but what does it matter, faint or loud, cry is cry, all that matters is that it should cease.
>
> (*CSP*, 19)

In both these cases, the move towards ending is accompanied by a repetitive rhythm of psychic control and release, which resembles very strikingly the famous 'fort/da' game described at the beginning of *Beyond the Pleasure Principle,* in which a child who repeatedly threw away a wooden reel and drew it back on a piece of string suggested to Freud the dialectic of mastery and loss, pleasure and unpleasure, involved in the repetition compulsion (*BPP*, 9–13).

Beckett's work therefore repeatedly produces that duality demonstrated in Freud's work in which repetition and the death-instinct do not stand against the pleasure principle in simple opposition, but enfold the pleasure principle within them, affirming life at the very moment of death, openness within the jaws of closure. At the end of *Ill Seen Ill Said,* for example, finality is held back momentarily to allow the imminence of the ending to be relished. The text ends by repeating the fact of death in advance, ends by not ending:

> Farewell to farewell. Then in that perfect dark foreknell darling sound pip for end begun. First last moment. Grant only enough remain to devour all. Moment by glutton moment. Sky earth the whole kit and boodle. Not another crumb of carrion left. Lick chops and basta. No. One moment more. One last. Grace to breathe that void. Know happiness. (p. 59)

Time and again, Beckett's work, with its asymptotic approaches to zero, enacts this complex play between reduction and addition, in which to repeat oneself, and therefore to say progressively less, seems, uncannily, always to involve saying more. Beckett himself spoke of this division between excess and minimality, drawing a contrast between his work and the expansive inclusiveness of Joyce and Proust: 'Il suffit, remarque-t-il, d'examiner leurs manuscrits ou les épreuves qu'ils ont corrigées. Ils n'en finissaient pas d'ajouter et de surajouter. Lui il va dans l'autre sens, vers le rien, en comprimant son texte toujours davantage.'[7]

But there is a sense in which the proliferation of minima in Beckett's work begins to resemble the superabundance of Joyce and Proust, as he seems to acknowledge a moment later, saying that 'quelque part, les deux manières doivent se rejoindre.'[8] For Beckett, we will see, the centrality of death and the repetition compulsion which draws near to it is not a matter of a simple instinct for negation. The forms of repetition that proliferate in his work establish death not as the mere absence of life, but rather as the place where the natures of life, death, difference and repetition are concentrated and problematized. As Deleuze writes, criticizing the simple opposition of life and death which he finds at work in Freud:

> Death is reducible neither to the negation of opposition nor the negation of limitation. It is neither limitation of mortal life by matter, nor the opposition between immortal life and matter, which gives death its nature. Rather, death is the last form of the problematic, the source of problems and questions, the mark of their persistence underneath every answer, the Where? and When? which designates this (non)being where every affirmation grows.
>
> (*DR*, 148)

Most accounts of repetition in Beckett's work have stressed what one might call its metaphysical aspect, rather than the junction of difference and repetition. Rubin Rabinovitz, for example, argues for the unifying or centring effect of repetition in *Murphy:* 'Like a leitmotif', he writes, 'the reiterated formula adds significance and intensity'.[9] The varieties and complexities of repetition provide for Rabinovitz a guarantee that diversity will always be drawn into unity: 'as the work's diverse elements coalesce into a unified pattern, its beauty is revealed' (p. 71). Repetition is associated with the pairings and symmetries which, Rabinovitz argues, makes the novel a balanced, aesthetic whole (p. 93). And repetition is secondary, that is to say, it stands always in a subsidiary relationship to what it repeats, so that repetition appears as the expression on the surface of the 'the novel's hidden meanings' (p. 76).

For Ruby Cohn, too, repetition functions as a constructive, centring principle. The metaphor which expresses this sense for her is above all that of weaving: *Waiting for Godot,* she writes, is 'woven with repetitions ... the refrains form a warp for the woof of less pervasive repetitive devices.'[10] This metaphor again allows the multiplicity of repetitive effects to be seen as subordinated to and structurally expressive of the essential unity of the text. Repetition is above all intensification and magnification of a centre, so that, in the end it is a metaphorical device which collapses art and life into unity: 'rather than increase "the stale churn of words" in subsequent plays, Beckett explores new avenues of repetition, that substantive that embraces theater rehearsal and life process' (p. 115). Though Cohn does point to the polysemic, metonymic effects of repetition as well as its 'liquid erosive action' in *That Time,* she concludes in the end that 'verbal repetition serves Beckett as music, meaning, metaphor' (p. 139).

In both these formulations, repetition is conceived of as naked, rather than clothed, in Deleuze's terms, and therefore expressive of the principles of 'equality, commensurability and symmetry'. Repetition is subordinated to the return of the Same and guarantees the inviolable selfhood and particularity of each text as well as the essential unity of Beckett's oeuvre as a whole. Though both accounts point to the variety of functions performed by repetition, what they undervalue is the complexity of the displacements effected by repetition in Beckett's work, the challenges which it proposes to notions of essential unity.

Bruce Kawin's work depends on a rather more developed model of repetition. Kawin opposes the 'destructive repetition' of habit and compulsion to the two forms of 'constructive repetition' to be found in film and writing. The first of these Kawin calls 'building time': 'involved with the concepts of past and future, and believing in the integrity of memory, [it] builds repetitions one on the other toward some total effect.' The second, 'continuing time', considers the present to be the only apprehensible tense and 'deals with each instant and subject as a new thing, to such an extent that the sympathetic reader is aware less of repetition than of continuity'.[11] These two conceptions seem to correspond to the two 'passive syntheses' of time which, Deleuze argues, are made by memory and habit. 'Habit is the original synthesis of time, which constitutes the life of the passing present; Memory is the fundamental synthesis, in time (which allows this present to pass)' (*DR*, 109).

Where Deleuze gives priority to the repetitive synthesis effected by memory, in which past and present are blended in the totality of something like Bergsonian *durée*, Kawin sees the principle of 'continuing time' as more valuably life-affirming. For Kawin, Beckett's works are examples of this principle, and the representative character in Beckett's work is therefore the speaker in *The Unnamable*, who 'exists in one continuing time where it is always present — the time of consciousness — and in one nonplace' (p. 141). Beckett's writing for the theatre similarly emphasizes the amnesiac condition of 'the continuous present, without consciousness of repetition' (p. 151). Kawin praises Beckett's work as exemplifying that intense being-in-the-present which can free us from the dead repetitions of habit:

> It is the strength of assertion, the assurance of identity, that is the force of repetition; . it is the apologetic consciousness squeezed between past and future, unsure of itself and its intentions, wavering, faltering, that gives the sense of the repetitious to recurrence. The present is eternal, and eternity is repetition. (p. 185)

Kawin's analysis is subtle and powerful, but it ends up, like those of Rabinovitz and Cohn, undervaluing or denying that principle of difference which repetition brings. In fixing on the 'continuing present' as a principle of identity and permanence, Kawin disallows that perverse dynamism of difference which repetition always activates, a difference that always prevents the sedimentation of full being or identity. The chapters that follow will be concerned with the ways in which Beckett's work activates and explores, within and against each other, the principles of difference and repetition. But if repetition is by its nature dual, concerned with relationship rather than essence, then to restrain analysis to the effects of repetition *within* texts is to run the risk of reinstating the subordination of repetition to the Same, creating of Beckett's oeuvre a closed system which both permits and precludes the play of repetition. For this reason, we will need to move towards a consideration of the principle of repetition as it operates *upon* Beckett's texts, as well as within them, in the work of displacement involved in the production and reproduction of dramatic texts, and the displacements and reappropriations effected by criticism and commentary. At this point, repetition will emerge as something more than a principle of inert, indifferent plurality, and become visible as a principle of power, embodying authority, subordination, conflict and resistance. This displacing repetition, in which questions of knowledge and interpretation within literary texts return as questions of control and authority in critical discourse, will not leave those texts unchanged, for they themselves will now seem to require a rereading in the new terms of repetition as power.

Chapter 2

Economies of Repetition

Murphy

Repetition in Beckett's work does not just involve the mirroring or duplication of situation, incident and character. From the beginning, repetition has been the dominating principle of his language; repetition of words, of sounds, of phrases, of syntactic and grammatical forms. And as the consciousness of language as a distorting or constricting force tightens its hold on Beckett, so repetition seems to become more and more necessary in his work. We will see that where repetition begins as a supplementary feature of language, secondary to and derived from the uniqueness of particular utterances, it comes to occupy the centre of his work. Repetition will come to be all there is, the only novelty available being the variation in the forms of sameness.

It is repetition, more than any other trope, that draws the attention of the reader to the medium of language. 'Natural', non-literary language is characterized by its flowing irreversibility, moving too fast for us to be conscious of the process of signification. It is at the moment when we recognize that a repetition has taken place that language begins to bulk in our apprehension as arbitrary, systematic and material. To hear or read the same word twice or more is to catch ourselves in the act of hearing or speaking, or to read ourselves reading. And, as many have believed, it is this self-designation which characterizes the literary, the 'set towards the message', as Jakobson expresses it.[1] The work of art overlooks or overhears itself, the reader always aware of the fact of his or her reading, and so art is constituted upon a sort of primordial doubling. It is only in life that we suspend our disbelief in the fictions that we live; in literature we always know that we are reading — even if that knowledge is not possessed as personal awareness it is a structural knowledge, built into the activity of reading itself.

Beckett seems to take this principle even further. For him repetition governs not just literary language, but language as such. In this he is close to Derrida, who has argued that language is defined and enabled by its capacity for reuse. Because a word is inescapably different from what it names, the word is available at any time for communication of a meaning, in the absence of what it names — though it also communicates the fact of that absence. The abstraction of language from the world which it names, and its capacity for repetition, are therefore aspects of the same thing[2]

But if repetition is the enabling principle of all language, then it is also inimical to language. The recurrence of the Same seems to us to offer a threat to the principle in language of difference among its elements. So repetition threatens language even as it constitutes its possibility. It is impossible to say anything in a language in which there is no repetition, but it is equally impossible to say anything if one merely repeats oneself. When Murphy expresses his sense of the mutually reflecting bond between him and Mr Endon, his motto dramatizes the life and death which repetition brings to meaning:

> the last at last seen of him
> himself unseen by him
> and of himself.

> (p. 171)

The possibility of meaning is demonstrated in the play of contrast, identity and discrimination in these words, even though the density of their repetitions retards and confuses meaning.

Beckett's work explores all the implications of life-in-death and death-in-life that are focused in repetition. In Beckett's work, repetition is what enables characters to survive and carry on speaking, even when there is nothing to say, though the possibility that one may be merely repeating oneself is at the same time resisted desperately. As we are told repeatedly in Beckett's work from *Murphy* onwards, the purpose of speaking is to have done, to be able to stop speaking; the purpose of the endless reiterations of the narrator of *The Unnamable* is to find the right 'pensum' which, once repeated, will close off utterance for good. The narrator seeks through reiteration an 'ur-reiteration' that will cancel language out. So repetition is not only a form of survival in language, it is a way of negating it, for, if repetition is the sign of the endlessness of language (it is always possible to say something again), then repetition is a strategy for turning language against itself, using words to erase other words. The young Beckett's destructive ambitions with regard to language are set out well in his letter to Axel Kaun of 1937:

> It is indeed becoming more and more difficult, even senseless, for me to write an official English. And more and more my own language appears to me like a veil that must be tom apart in order to get at the things (or the Nothingness) behind it. Grammar and Style. To me they seem to have become as irrelevant as a Victorian bathing suit or the imperturbability of a true gentleman. A mask. Let us hope the time will come, thank God that in certain circles it has already come, when language is most efficiently used where it is being most efficiently misused. As we cannot eliminate language all at once, we should at least leave nothing undone that might contribute to its falling into disrepute. To bore one hole after another in it, until what lurks behind it — be it something or nothing — begins to seep through; I cannot imagine a higher goal for a writer today.
>
> (*Disjecta*, 171–2)

A contemporary reader might have taken this statement as a modish assertion of the need to develop new forms of expression, to further that 'revolution of the word' urged by Eugene Jolas. But Beckett is not looking for a new language which is more supply responsive to the task of representing a higher reality. He wants instead to have done with language because it is inherently falsifying. The problem is that one has to stay inside language even as one tries to sabotage it: 'Of course, for the time being we must be satisfied with little. At first it can only be a matter of somehow finding a method by which we can represent this mocking attitude towards the word, through words' (*Disjecta*, 172).

By the time of *The Unnamable,* this destructive desire has become an ordeal, a need to bring language to an end without the possibility of doing so without or outside language. There, as in his earlier work, it is by various kinds of repetition that Beckett seeks to perform this feat. In a way, Beckett's characters resemble Krook, in Dickens's *Bleak House,* who writes words on the wall that he does not fully understand, but erases each letter as he goes along, before inscribing the next. Molloy imagines a similar kind of autonegation of the name of his mother:

> I called her Mag, when I had to call her something. And I called her Mag because for me, without my knowing why, the letter g abolished the syllable Ma, and as it were spat on it, better than any other letter would have done. And at the same time I satisfied a deep and doubtless unacknowledged need, the need to have a Ma, that is a mother, and to proclaim it, audibly. For before you say mag, you say ma, inevitably.
>
> (*T,* 17)

The dig at psychoanalytic cliché apart, Molloy seems to have become aware of one form of the strange economy between affirmation and negation that can be induced by repetition; the letter 'g' both abolishes the syllable 'ma', and allows it to be proclaimed. As Beckett's work proceeds, the overlapping and conflict of these two principles of repetition grow more and more marked. But the economy is visible from the start, in the resounding opening words of *Murphy:* 'The sun shone, having no alternative, on the nothing new' (p. 5). The reader of this novel is denied the possibility of any novelty in what is to follow — in this 'novel', there is nothing new. What is surprising is the way that subsequent sentences manage nevertheless to generate some unpredictability out of the closure of repetition:

> Murphy sat out of it, as though he were free, in a mew in West Brompton. Here for what might have been six months he had eaten, drunk, slept, and put his clothes on and off, in a medium-sized cage of north-western aspect commanding an unbroken view of medium-sized cages of south-eastern aspect. Soon he

would have to make other arrangements, for the mew had been condemned. Soon he would have to buckle to and start eating, drinking, sleeping, and putting his clothes on and off, in quite alien surroundings. (p. 5)

Here, the vacuous repetitiveness of Murphy's life is physically enacted in the text's verbal repetitions. But if there is a comic spurt of energy derived from the repetition, it is an energy which is very quickly expended. First, there is the mirroring relationship of the medium-sized cages of northwestern and southeastern aspect. The phrase about the 'unbroken view' suggests that the eye may be about to be led out of this *endroit,* but it is of course unbroken only in the sense that it is unrelieved. This repetition is itself repeated in the next sentence, though there is a minimal variation in the way that it is constructed. Here, the parallelism of syntax 'Soon he would have to.... Soon he would have to' makes us expect intensification, with a consequent opening out, but gives us only exact repetition; it is clear that the 'other arrangements' will consist of the same old routine. So repetition here seems to induce a double movement. The two halves of the antithesis are opened before us, like the recto and verso of a book; but, having been opened, are slapped shut, flattening the pages together indistinguishably. Opening this book, the repetition seems to promise, is just like closing it, or never having picked it up.

This relationship between openness and closure is acted out in the very smallest details of the language of the passage. The first and second sentences consist of propositions interrupted by parentheses; 'The sun shone, having no alternative.... Murphy sat out of it, as though he were free.' In the first case, 'having no alternative' could mean either that the sun has no alternative but to shine (that is what a sun has to do though, if it had any choice, it probably wouldn't bother), or that the sun has no alternative but to shine on the nothing new (how nice to be able to shine on something different, something new, for a change). It is odd, and entirely typical of this passage, that the phrase 'having no alternative' should actually give the reader this sort of alternative. The chink of light opened up by this phrase is also shut out in advance; by the time the reader has become aware of the alternatives contained in the words, she is already aware that neither exists; in both cases the sun is compelled to shine.

The next sentence introduces another possible alternative: 'Murphy sat out of it, as though he were free.' Does this mean that Murphy might not be part of the nothing new, might be original, autonomous and individual? It does not. The possibility is denied as soon as affirmed by the little proviso 'as though he were free'; Murphy may sit out of the sun, but he is not out of the nothing new. (We ought to note, by the way, that it is the proviso cancelling the possibility of Murphy's freedom that also suggests that freedom in the first place.) The deadening effect of the repetition is heightened by the syntactic similarity between the two opening sentences and their negating clauses. The French version seems to heighten the repetitive effect by moving the negation back in the sentence, thereby increasing the sense of a possibility being annulled at the very moment of its utterance: 'Murphy, comme s'il était libre, s'en tenait à l'écart.'[3]

Of course, the lines contain another repetition, in the recapitulation of the phrase from Ecclesiastes, 'There is no new thing under the sun' (Ecc. 1:9). Beckett's slight misappropriation of the phrase induces another little disappointment for the reader. For, where the Authorized Version uses what we may call the negative version of the negative, which stresses what isn't there, Beckett uses a positive term to signify the absence. If Ecclesiastes suggests that everything the sun shines on is old, then Beckett's form suggests that the sun shines, not just on monotony, but on nothingness, even though it may be an endlessly-renewed nothingness.[4] The capacity which language possesses to make negatives out of positives is something which amuses and irritates Beckett. In a letter to Axel Kaun about the poet Ringelnatz, Beckett quotes Goethe's ironic remark that 'it is better to write NOTHING than not write at all' (*Disjecta*, 171), and in *Watt* he observes similarly that 'the only way one can speak of nothing is to speak of it as though it were something' (p. 74).

Reading these opening sentences, one may be struck by the way that negation and repetition entwine in Beckett's writing.

Encountering the proviso, one has to hold it in suspense, until the end of the sentence is reached, at which point the proviso can be understood, reread, and used to reread the following phrase, and to bankrupt the rest of the sentence. This operation is described well by the formula proposed by the narrator in *The Unnamable* — 'affirmations and negations invalidated as uttered, or sooner or later' (*T,* 293).

But the opening paragraphs require more than this local rereading; we are invited to reread them in the light of what happens, or fails to happen, in the rest of the book. This would activate, for example, another layer of meaning for the phrase 'out of it'. For the greater part of the novel, Murphy pins his hopes upon the stars, seeing his microcosmic system as linked to and reflecting the macrocosmic system of the zodiac. By the end of the novel, he has reversed this priority. Withdrawing to his garret in the Magdalen Mental Mercyseat, he has come to believe that he is 'the prior system', that the stars are his projection (p. 126). Events seem rather brutally to contradict this view when he is blown up (apparently twice, once in the garret and once in the form of ashes in the pub) and his 'body, mind and soul' swept away with the leavings. So the book seems to demonstrate at some length what has been implied by the proviso in the second sentence — that Murphy is by no means 'out of it'. This doesn't mean that he is under the influence of the stars, for the book repudiates such mysticism. But he isn't free of the desperate, repetitive cycle of disaster and destruction that is human life, by no means 'out of' the nothing new. So, in rereading this sentence, we see how in its turn it reads in advance what is to come in the novel.

There are other kinds of anticipation in the passage. The mirroring enclosure of the two rows of cages which stare at each other is repeated in the look that is exchanged between Murphy and Mr Endon, a look which is structured about a self-cancelling repetition (Murphy sees the reflection of himself, unseen by Mr Endon, in Mr Endon's eyes). This is repeated in other details of the text, like the sound of the cuckoo clock which mingles with street cries to form the mirroring sound *'Quid pro quo! Quid pro quo!'* (p. 5), or Neary's view of the 'closed system' of life, in which the 'quantum of wantum cannot vary' (p. 43), this view perhaps being a gloss on the formula of conservation provided in Ecclesiastes: 'whatsoever God doeth, it shall be for ever: nothing can be put to it, nor anything taken from it' (Ecc. 3:14).

For all its breadth and abundance of comic detail, *Murphy* is built around repetitions. Its narrative structure is so designed as to disappoint the sense of progression, and to persuade us that, as the book plays out towards its 'only possible' conclusion, it does so in fulfillment of what has been prefigured in its opening paragraph. This structural doubling is reproduced throughout the language of the book, which can be seen continually echoing and mirroring itself. When, towards the end, Murphy settles himself in his chair to rock himself into oblivion, the language reproduces almost word for word the description given in chapter 1 (p. 9):

> Slowly he felt better, astir in his mind, in the freedom of that light and dark that did not clash, nor alternate, nor fade nor lighten except to their communion. The rock got faster and faster, shorter and shorter, the gleam was gone, the grin was gone, the starlessness was gone, soon his body would be quiet. Most things under the moon got slower and slower and then stopped, a rock got faster and faster and then stopped. Soon his body would be quiet, soon he would be free. (pp. 172–3)

Naturally, the repetition opens up an irony here. Murphy's body will indeed be quiet, not because he is about to achieve the oblivion of trance, but because he will soon be dead. But the ironic divergence of meaning seems to close again almost immediately; perhaps the only real quietness, all along, for Murphy, is that of death, and has only ever been quietness in that it simulates death.

Repetitions similarly help to suggest that the complicated double-crossings of Neary, Wylie and Miss Counihan all come in the end to much the same thing:

> If the worst comes to the worst, thought Wylie, if Murphy cannot be found, if Neary turns nasty, there is always the Cox.

If the worst comes to the worst, thought Miss Counihan, if my love cannot be found, if Wylie turns nasty, there is always Neary. (p. 91)

Neary's duplicate letters to Miss Counihan and Wylie offer only a little more variety (p. 126). These verbal re-enactments clearly reinforce the narrative repetitions which the narrator takes care to point out to us: Miss Counihan sitting on Neary's bed reminds the narrator of Celia sitting on Mr Kelly's bed and on Murphy's ('though Mr Kelly had had his shirt on', p. 142). A similar sense of closure results from the series of repetitions generated from a moment in Celia's and Mr Kelly's interchange in chapter 2: '"You are all I have in the world," said Celia. Mr Kelly nestled. "You," said Celia, "and possibly Murphy"' (p. 12). The phrase is recalled by Celia at the end of the chapter ('Now I have no one, thought Celia, except possibly Murphy' [p. 21]), again in chapter 3 ('Now she had nobody, except possibly Mr Kelly' [p. 28]) and by Mr Kelly in chapter 7 ('Now I have no one, said Mr Kelly, not even Celia' [p. 82].) Each repetition is, indeed, also a variation, but the persistence of the form of the utterance through all the changes of its elements suggests that the elements themselves are arbitrary and meaningless. The whole series seems to suggest just that constancy of relationship between dependence, relationship and lack which is articulated in Neary's formula for the unvarying 'quantum of wantum'.

Other repetitions in the novel activate and complicate this economy of lack and superfluity. The account of how Celia's narrative has been 'expurgated, accelerated, improved and reduced' (p. 12), squanders rather than saves time, and when the phrase is repeated with regard to Neary and Cooper (pp. 37, 84) the impression of redundancy is increased. Other repetitions suggest an insufficiency of narrative means, as with the weary formula 'So all things hobble together for the only possible' (p. 155) and its near-repetition a few pages later: 'So all things limp together for the only possible' (p. 160) (Is limping an advance on hobbling or a retreat from it?). Sometimes, the recycling of narrative materials brings about an obstruction in meaning: Celia's story of how she met Murphy is very difficult to disentangle from the narrator's account of her telling the story to Mr Kelly (pp. 12–21). Mr Kelly's gaze is as intermittent as Murphy's, Mr Kelly's because he cannot lie back in the bed without his eyes closing and Murphy's because his gaze is divided between the sky and the sheet of paper with his horoscope on it (the word 'sheet' associates him with Mr Kelly, too). When Mr Kelly purloins the words of a Chelsea pensioner within Celia's narrative ('Hell roast this weather, I shill niver fergit it') for his comment on Celia's circumstantiality ('"Hell roast this story," said Mr Kelly, 'I shall never remember it"' [p. 14]) the sense of the indigence of language grows more acute. More local repetitions set language against itself in the way suggested by Beckett's 1937 letter, as when Murphy's uncle is described as 'a well-to-do ne'er-do-well' (p. 16), or in Cooper's self-consuming telegram 'LOST STOP STOP WHERE YOU ARE STOP COOPER' (p. 43), or the evocation of Murphy's bliss in the chair — 'such pleasure that pleasure was not the word' (p. 6).[5]

If all these repetitions give the sense of a parsimony, or even of exhaustion of linguistic resources, then this is in conflict with the language of the book as a whole, which tends to *exceed* its objects in various ways. Simple, squalid objects and events are described in a language which is formal, allusive, and elaborately patterned, its register lying somewhere between the summing-up of an exceptionally profuse and opinionated High Court judge and a philosophical dissertation of more than usual barrenness. It is a language which has a life of its own; and it takes the disabling effects of repetition to highlight its arbitrariness and self-enclosure. We can say that, once again, repetition enacts a doubleness, asserting both the freedom of the language from referential constraints and its internal emptiness and exhaustion. Faced with this apparent determination to cancel out language as quickly as it is produced, the reader feels at times like Celia listening to Murphy: 'She felt, as she felt so often with Murphy, splattered with words that went dead as soon as they sounded; each word obliterated, before it had time to make sense, by the word that came next; so that in the end she did not know what had been said' (pp. 31–2).

In most cases, repetition is the chief factor in making us suddenly, disablingly aware of the functioning of language. Such self-consciousness often manifests itself in the presence of the metaphorical language with which *Murphy* bulges. Metaphor is one of the means used most often to mark the disproportion between the language of the book and its subject. Usually, there is a knowing cast towards metaphor which prevents it functioning properly, and sometimes this involves the elaboration or mixing of metaphors to the point where they become nearly incomprehensible, as when Neary complains about the backside of Cuchulain's statue that 'the Red Branch bum was the camel's back' (p. 36). Metaphor is made redundant in other ways, as well. A good example occurs in the first paragraph of the book, when we are told that Murphy would soon have to 'buckle to and start eating, drinking, sleeping, and putting his clothes on and off in quite alien surroundings' (p. 5). For the purposes of mock-heroic, 'buckle to' here revives some of its primary meaning of martial preparation, and the metaphor measures the gulf between the grandeur of 'buckling to' and the trivial readjustment in Murphy's routine. What slightly interferes with this mock-heroic, however, is the overlapping of the associations of 'buckling to' and 'putting his clothes on and off'. Though in one way this overlapping of the figurative and the literal increases the force of the metaphor, in another way it actually lames it. And, of course, this is an example of the insistence of the repetitive principle in Beckett's writing; instead of superseding or substituting for the literal reality, the metaphor seems merely to reproduce it.

Such deliberate disabling is to be found elsewhere in *Murphy*, most memorably perhaps in the remark that Cooper's 'acathisia' (fear of sitting down) is 'deep-seated and of long standing' (p. 84). Something similar, though less elaborate, can be found in the description of the padded cell in the Magdalen Mental Mercyseat: 'The tender luminous oyster-grey of the pneumatic upholstery, cushioning every square inch of ceiling, walls, floor and door, lent colour to the truth, that one was a prisoner of air' (p. 125). The joke would have worked quite well if the cell had been painted yellow, but the fact that it is greyness which 'lends colour' to an idea intensifies the redundant duplication.

Murphy himself seems to toy with this kind of metaphor, as he speculates about his continuing inability even in the MMM to cut himself off from desire for things in the outside world:

> These dispositions and others ancillary, pressing every available means (e.g. the rocking-chair) into their service, could sway the issue in the desired direction, but not clinch it. It continued to divide him, as witness his deplorable susceptibility to Celia, ginger, and so on. The means of clinching it were lacking. Suppose he were to clinch it now, in the service of the Clinch clan! That would indeed be very pretty. (p. 124)

The doubling effect here occurs in the reference to the rocking chair 'swaying the issue', and this is reinforced by another punning overlay: Murphy hopes to 'clinch' his solipsistic separation from the world in the service of those who would keep him firmly in the 'clinch' of the world (the homosexual associations of the Clinch clan should not be forgotten either).

Such self-doubling metaphors are not unique to *Murphy*. One of the darkest occurs at the beginning of *First Love*, where the narrator declares, 'Personally I have no bone to pick with graveyards' (*CSP*, 1). In *The Expelled*, the passage dealing with the narrator's eccentric, stiff-legged gait yields a couple of good examples: his precipitative carriage is due, he says 'to a certain leaning from which I have never been able to free myself completely' (*CSP*, 25). A moment later the narrator speculates that his gait derives from youthful incontinence when, having soiled his trousers, he is obliged to walk 'with legs stiff and wide apart' and to roll his chest to make people think he is full of gaiety, the latter 'no doubt intended to put people off the scent' (ibid.).

We can see at work in this undermining of metaphor a larger principle. For metaphor traditionally functions in Western culture as the figure of unity and transcendent knowledge. The metaphorical vehicle is seen as a repetition of the original meaning, but a repetition that allows the true nature of the original meaning to be known. Metaphor stands therefore as a guarantee of the power of literary language and of language in general: as Jonathan Culler has argued, the privileging of metaphor grounds rhetoric 'in the perception of resemblances in experience, in intuitions of essential qualities' and associates it with those defences of poetry which argue that 'poetry presents human experience to us in a new way, giving us not scientific truth but a higher imaginative truth, the perception of fundamental connexions and relationships.'[6] Beckett's practice undermines metaphor's claims by emphasizing the artificial and contingent nature of metaphor. In fact, his self-consuming metaphors rely upon the principle of metonymy, the figure of chance rather than necessity, for they draw upon accidental relationships between words and ideas in close proximity. For all the careful design of these encounters between metaphor and metonymy in Beckett's writing, the result is to assert the openness of process against the closure of design.[7]

This has a structural dimension, too. For, if metaphor is the 'figure of figurality',[8] it also embodies the totalizing function. In its offering of fundamental metaphorical relationships, a literary text offers itself as a self-identical whole. If repetitions seem to assist the affirmation of this unity, then the metonymic drift of the repetitions in *Murphy* resist the attempt to close or centre the book around the unified statement of fundamental truth.

And, in *Murphy,* not even the 'erasing' effect of repetitions is left wholly intact. For all its repetitions, *Murphy* is not just a grimly self-annulling anti-novel. What is so remarkable about the book is the tension between its linguistic improvidence and its niggardly desire to withdraw language as it is uttered. For all the disclaimer of novelty in the first paragraph, the book is never able completely to cover its tracks by repetitive erasure. Repetition always leaves some active residue; in coming full circle, the book ends up in a different place from where it had begun, leaving the desire to begin again as strong as ever.

Watt

It is perhaps the desire to balance the books between affirmation and negation that accounts for the extraordinary change which comes over Beckett's writing in *Watt*. Throughout this book, the purse strings are drawn much tighter, and expenditure of resources in language much more carefully controlled, while, as in *Murphy,* repetition seems to be the central principle of its language. The book begins with what seems like an exercise in the manner of *Murphy,* the conversation between Hackett and Mr and Mrs Nixon. But as a repetition or pastiche of the style of *Murphy,* the passage involves necessarily a slight shift of level, to include an element of self-conscious repudiation. Like *Murphy* in its whimsicality, its sudden and arbitrary shifts of time and place and in the comic stateliness of its characters' speech, the narration is already unlike *Murphy* in its baldness, the absence of authorial intervention and the unnerving obsessiveness of the enquiry conducted by the characters into why Watt has descended from the tram at this particular stop. This repetition-with-repudiation cannot last for very long. The novel very quickly abandons the pastiche of *Murphy* and falls into the insistent repetitive sequences which make it so exhausting to read and difficult to categorize.

Repetition first becomes apparent in *Watt* in the form of argumentative intensification, or clarification. Sentences in the book have a tendency to advance in a series of jumps, alternating with retrogressions which are intended to consolidate or to qualify a point that has already been made:

> Watt had watched people smile and thought he understood how it was done. And it was true that Watt's smile, when he smiled, resembled more a smile than a sneer, for example, or a yawn. But there was something wanting to Watt's smile, some little thing was lacking, and people who saw it for the first time, and most people who saw it saw it for the first time, were sometimes in doubt as to what expression exactly was intended. To many it seemed a simple sucking of the teeth.
> Watt used this smile sparingly. (p. 23)

When, the reader might ask, might there be a smile on Watt's face, except 'when he smiled'? One might expect a tautologous repetition like this to have an effect of lulling reassurance, but this is not the case. For the split between the noun and the verb ('Watt's smile, when he smiled') insists perplexingly on the difference between the activity and the result of smiling (and there certainly is a difference in Watt's case). The repetition reveals itself therefore as a differentiation. What is more, repetition seems to stimulate more repetition, for there is another 'smile' to be reckoned with: 'Watt's *smile,* when he *smiled,* resembled more a *smile* than a sneer'; though both nouns, the first and third 'smile's, clearly refer to different things — Watt's 'smile' (= attempt at a smile) and a 'smile' (= what we recognize as a smile, smiling as a category of facial expression). The second sentence, on the other hand, seems to open up distinctions only to abolish them. The phrase 'people who saw it for the first time' suggests that there may be plenty of people who have seen it more than once, have got used to the smile and are able to recognize it for what it is. But the qualification which follows suggests that there is rarely a second chance to see the smile, maybe because Watt doesn't like to risk it twice, or because he wishes to economize with it (or to 'spare' people the sight of it), or, most likely, because, having seen the ghastly sight of Watt smiling once, most people try to avoid setting eyes on him again. If the set of 'all people who have seen Watt's smile' and the set of 'those who have seen it only once' coincide nearly exactly, the point of the distinction is lost.

Soon, much longer repetitive sequences begin to appear in the narrative of *Watt.* One of the earliest is the description of Watt's way of walking:

> Watt's way of advancing due east, for example, was to turn his bust as far as possible towards the north and at the same time to fling out his right leg as far as possible towards the south, and then to turn his bust as far as possible towards the south and at the same time to fling out his left leg as far as possible towards the north, and then again to turn his bust as far as possible towards the north and to fling out his right leg as far as possible towards the south, and then again to turn his bust as far as possible towards the south and to fling out his left leg as far as possible towards the north, and so on, over and over again, many many times, until he reached his destination, and could sit down. So, standing first on one leg, and then on the other, he moved forward, a headlong tardigrade, in a straight line. The

knees, on these occasions, did not bend. They could have, but they did not. No knees could better bend than Watt's, when they chose, there was nothing the matter with Watt's knees, as may appear. But when out walking they did not bend, for some obscure reason. Notwithstanding this, the feet fell, heel and sole together, flat upon the ground, and left it, for the air's uncharted ways, with manifest repugnancy. The arms were content to dangle, in perfect equipendency. (pp. 28–9)

This description demonstrates a number of important things about the nature of repetition. The first is the sense of excess that it gives. Strictly speaking, there is no need to repeat the description of the simultaneous movements of the bust and leg, just because Watt repeats the actual movements. In one sense, the narrative becomes as automatic as Watt himself, a mechanism that runs on without supervision. But, at the same time, this repetition induces a sense of anxiety, a sense that the narrative must shadow Watt's movements in case, the next time he goes through the sequence, he might do it differently. Even when the narrative tears itself away from its own repetitions and substitutes the formula 'and so on', this too must be supplemented by a compulsive redoubling: 'and so on, over and over again, many many times'.

But the sense of excess in the language, its unwillingness to economize, coexists with a strange parsimony. The surprising exactness of the description comes from its inspired choreographic synecdoche. Beckett mentions only the bust, legs, knees and arms (and indeed gives them an independent life, for the arms are 'content to dangle' while the knees are apparently able to go out walking on their own); but we are nevertheless made aware of the splay-legged contortions of Watt's gait. So the fanatically intense description both exceeds its object and also lags behind it. Though apparently exhaustive, it is marked by holes which further repetitions would be needed to fill — what about the movements of Watt's head, his hands, or of his feet? The repetition comes from and induces a desire to meet every narrative eventuality, but the very assiduity of the repetition opens up of itself spaces for uncertainty, which can be cleared up only by more repetition.

This passage also displays a curious relationship between movement and stasis. The repetition, along with the paratactic syntax, enforces a sense of remorseless onward movement, step-by-step, word by word. The reader seems condemned to an absolute linearity, incapable of detaching himself from the contingent series of words. But because every new thing that happens has already happened before, this absolute motion becomes an absolute stillness — it is difficult to imagine Watt 'advancing' at all with the series of exclusively lateral movements which are described here.

Although these kinds of repetitive sequence are common in the early part of *Watt,* they still give the sense of an aberration from or interruption of the main business of the narrative. The reader can dismiss them as a kind of stammer after which the narrative may be resumed. Such is the case with Arsene's speech; he periodically finds himself locked into repetitive sequences, as when he contrasts ordinary eating habits with those of the maid Mary:

> The ordinary person eats a meal, then rests from eating for a space, then eats again, then rests again, then eats again, then rests again, then eats again, then rests again, then eats again, then rests again, then eats again, then rests again, then eats again, then rests again, and, in this way, now eating, and now resting from eating, he deals with the difficult problem of hunger, and indeed I think I may add thirst, to the best of his ability and according to the state of his fortune. (p. 51)

There seems no real reason why the sequence should ever stop, and there is a consequent sense of relief when it finally does; in fact, there may also be a flicker of apprehension in the reader with the phrases that immediately follow, for it's perfectly possible that they too might be lengthened into the same kind of mesmeric repetitions. Repetition seems to be necessary for Arsene, as it has been for the narrator describing Watt's manner of walking, because of his fear lest words should fail to match exactly what they designate. A moment later, Arsene gets caught up in another metonymic current of repetition, one from which it proves even more difficult to detach himself. Mary, he says, sits 'quietly eating onions and peppermints turn and turn about, I mean first an onion, then a peppermint, then another onion, then another peppermint... ' (pp. 49–50). Again, the sequence is both closed and open; the recognition of repetition is the recognition that there is no progression, that there is no point in spelling out the elements of the sequence, even while there is an irresistible urge to keep moving on to the next element. Repetition forces together openness and closure, because the desire for closure is actually the principle which drives repetition onwards.

After Watt moves into Mr Knott's house, these sequences of repetition become more sustained, and the tension between the rigidity of structure and the openness of sequence grows all the more marked.

As we have seen, this represents a division between the 'metaphorical' or paradigmatic dimension and the 'metonymic' or syntagmatic dimension. Indeed, there seem to be two kinds of sequence in the book, which in some sense match these two dimensions. The first is the finite permutation, which allows the exhaustion of all the possible combinations of and relationships between elements in a given structure. An example of this is the passage which itemizes the voices in Watt's head, which sing, cry, state and murmur, in different combinations. These elements can yield only a certain number of permutations and they are dutifully gone through (all except for one — the combination 'sang and stated and murmured' is omitted in both the English and the French).[9] Other examples of closed sequence are the twelve possibilities that occur to Watt regarding Mr Knott's food arrangements (pp. 86–7), the range of different relationships possible between the centre and the circle depicted in the painting in Erskine's pantry (p. 127), the musical distribution of the frogs' croaking (pp. 135–7), the different combinations of clothes worn by Mr Knott (pp. 200–1) and the variations in his appearance (pp. 209–10).

All these repetitive sequences can and do come to an end. But other combinations cannot. Examples of this in Arsene's speech are his praise of the earth, which has been his mother's

and his father's and his mother's mother's and his father's father's, and his father's mother's etc. (p. 45), the sequence of ser-
vants previously employed in Mr Knott's house (pp. 58–9) and,
of course, the endless sequences of alternatives, like the onions
and peppermints.

Naturally, the closed sequences are much more reassuring
for the reader than these open ones. In the closed sequence, the
possibility of an ending bounds and controls the unruly life of
the repetitions, while the open sequence has no such bounding
frame; in the one structure predominates over sequence, in the
other, sequence asserts itself beyond the control of structure. But
Beckett has a way of making even the closed sequences seem arbitrary and unfinished. At the end of the tabulation of voices
in Watt's head, we are told unnervingly that this has been 'to
mention only these four kinds of voices, for there were others'
(p. 27). This opens up the possibility of further repetitive series,
repetitions of this repetition with every other conceivable kind of
utterance or phonetic expression. The same applies to other sequences, the elements of which are often made to seem arbitrary,
so that the act of repetition becomes infinitely renewable.

This has important implications for our sense of *Watt* as a
whole. If we see the book as duplicating a structure of finite sequence then this makes it self-enclosed, and, on its own terms,
exhaustive. But we might also want to see the book as an infinite
series, or rather as part of an infinite series of arrangements of every possible group of elements. There is no possibility of closure
for such a book, only abandonment.

That such is the view Beckett himself may have taken of
Watt is suggested by its' Addenda' section. This material stands
outside the work and yet obviously also forms a part of it. In this
it seems to open up areas of incompleteness, if only because we
cannot resist trying to find the right places to incorporate the
appended material. The incisions that we would need to make in
the text of *Watt* might make us think of the novel as itself just an
arbitrary incision within a series which is endlessly open. Not the
least disturbing of the addenda is the passage describing Arthur's
discovery that Mr Knott is a member of a family. We may well

share Watt's dismay at the thought 'that Mr Knott was serial, in a vermicular series' (p. 254), and the consequent possibility that this 'centre' of the novel is not a centre at all, but part of a line or circumference.

Reading *Watt* is, of course, a slow and painful process. There can be few readers who can claim to have attended to every word of the novel in one reading, following through every permutative sequence without gliding to the end of the page or over a number of pages to the end of the sequence. There are plenty of rewards for persisting with the reading, it is true, but the longing for relief can be unbearable. It may be that these lists are so agonizing because they suggest a language which is out of control, or only remotely controlled; once the series has been generated we no longer need the presence of a writer injecting meaning at every moment, for the language can be relied upon to carry on without him.

But this does not fully account for the effects of the repetition in the book. Far from being absolutely predictable, the lists and permutations are intermittent, and seem in fact to fall away from the last sections of the book. What is more, Beckett gradually educates the reader in the repetitive compulsion. Always, mixed with a longing for the series to stop, there must also be a a kind of fear that it *will* stop. It is this which brings about the repetition of repetition itself in Beckett's writing, as when, for example, Arsene finds himself involuntarily repeating the repetitive sequence of previous retainers in Mr Knott's house (pp. 58–9) or when Molloy tries to accelerate or summarize the series of sucks and transfers in his sucking-routine, only to be forced into actual repetition (pp. 72–3). So repetition doesn't even give the composure of the automatic. Writer and reader are in the position of the circus performer who, in order to keep all the plates spinning on the tops of their poles, must keep returning to them to impart more speed to the individual plates. Even infinite mobility cannot be relied on to work without human supervision. We are forced to participate imaginatively in the repetitions which repel and alienate us in Beckett's work.

The economy of openness and closure which repetition generates is accompanied by a parallel economy of excess and deficiency. One of the most obvious features of repetitive lists and sequences is the way that they insist on their linguistic materiality. I mean this in the most literal way. The effort of getting through many of Beckett's repetitions, either reading silently, or, more especially, reading aloud, imparts an agonizing strain on the eye, cramps the tongue and paralyses the lips. In the end, such extreme consciousness of the shape and sound of language leads to the well-known phenomenon of the draining of meaning from the words, so that they do indeed become simply inert noises or shapes. Repetition is therefore a particularly effective means for enacting the arbitrariness and emptiness of language. The desperation of the reader, faced with an unparagraphed block of repetitious prose as she often is in *Watt* or *The Unnamable,* involves a particularly acute sense of the weary impenetrability of words; as she struggles down the page, she is likely to lose her place, lose the sense, and to become, like the disembodied voice of *The Unnamable,* adrift in the words which speak remorselessly through her.

But if repetition asserts the resistant materiality of language, we have seen that Beckett also thinks of repetition as an annulment, as one of the weapons which he will use to combat 'that terrible arbitrary materiality of the word surface' (*Disjecta,* 53). Repetition is language which has lost its substance, made redundant by its very nature in being the mere shadow of previous utterance. As such, repetition can sometimes involve the attempt to efface the signifier, so as to collapse the distinction between it and the signified. The compulsive repetitions of the child's demands for food, or of the language of pornography, both testify to the desire to make of the sign a substance, identical with what it signifies.

This results in a curious doubling. Repetition can involve both the promotion of the materiality of a sign and the erasure of that materiality. Repetition can often be read as an attempt to close the gap between word and thing, even though it is repetition which insistently opens up that gap. A localized example of this occurs in the description of the dog's dish in *Watt,* which has a lid 'that could be fastened down, by means of clasps, of clasps that clasped tight the sides, of the dish' (p. 111). The repetition expresses a desire not to let any particle of the meaning get away, to clasp tightly the meaning of the words in the words; but the repetition, and more especially the consciousness of the repetition, actually prises open the crevice between word and thing. In forcing signifier and signified together, repetition opens up semantic gaps at a different level; buttoned up tightly at the front, language splits its seams at the back.

This is just the difficulty that Watt encounters when he attempts to reunite signifier and signified in the word 'pot'. Despite all Watt's repetitions of the word, an irreducible difference remains:

> Looking at a pot, for example, or thinking of a pot, at one of Mr Knott's pots, of one of Mr Knott's pots, it was in vain that Watt said, Pot, pot. Well, perhaps not quite in vain, but very nearly. For it was not a pot, the more he looked, the more he reflected, the more he felt sure of that, that it was not a pot at all. It resembled a pot, it was almost a pot, but it was not a pot of which one could say, Pot, pot, and be comforted. It was in vain that it answered, with unexceptionable adequacy, all the purposes, and performed all the offices, of a pot, it was not a pot. And it was just this hairbreadth departure from the nature of a true pot that so excruciated Watt. (p. 78)

The attempts to close the gap between the word 'pot' and the 'true nature' of the pot only highlight the fact that there will always be a repetition involved, not just between signifier and signified, but also within the 'true nature' of the pot: in so far as the pot must be attested to by consciousness it becomes a sign, and therefore a repetition of itself. The self-identity of things can only be assured by a repetition that builds a delay or discontinuity into that self-identity. Derrida has commented on the tiny but radical unsettling that this apprehension of primordial repetition brings about:

> Something invisible is missing in the grammar of this repetition. As this lack is invisible and undeterminable, as it completely redoubles and reconsecrates the book, once more passing through

each point along its circuit, nothing has budged. And yet all
meaning is altered by this lack. Repeated, the same line is no
longer exactly the same, the ring no longer has exactly the same
center, *the origin has played.*

(WD, 296)

Repetition means that language must always be supplementary to what it designates, even as it gives the sense of falling short
of it. The more language is added on to its meaning, the greater
seems to be the debt that language runs up to its meaning. This is
demonstrated in the returning and cumulative doubts that Watt
has about the affair of the piano-tuners. Watt wants to be able to
acknowledge and freeze the episode into fixed meaning on each
occasion when the scene begins 'to unroll its sequences' (p. 71), but
this is impossible; for the scene comes to *consist* in its ramifications,
in its additions to itself. Nor is it even possible to put a limit on
the process of interpretative supplementation. Even specifying the
things that remain to be said about the Galls leaves an excess:

> Not that many things remain to be said, on the subject of the
> Galls father and son, for they do not. For only three or four things
> remain to be said, in this connexion. And three or four things are
> not really many, in comparison with the number of things that
> might have been known, and said, on this subject, and now never
> shall. (p. 73)

The tendency of interpretation to produce supplementarity
rather than translation is parodied in a footnote to the passage
dealing with Mr Knott's clothing:

> For the guidance of the attentive reader, at a loss to understand
> how these repeated investments, and divestments, of the night-
> dress, did not finally reveal to Watt Mr Knott's veritable aspect, it
> is perhaps not superfluous here to note, that Mr Knott's attitude
> to his nightdress was not that generally in vogue. For Mr Knott
> did not do as most men, and many women, do, who, before
> putting on their nightclothes, at night, take off their dayclothes,
> and again, when morning comes, once again, before they dream
> of putting on their dayclothes are careful to pull off their soiled

nightclothes, no, but he went to bed with his nightclothes over his dayclothes, and he rose with his dayclothes over his nightclothes. (p.211)

This extraordinary note makes nothing clear. Mr Knott is never revealed directly to Watt's enquiring gaze because he has always unaccountably got another layer of clothes beneath the surface layer. The reader is left to choose between addition or inversion as an explanation of this — either Mr Knott changes his clothes in bed, or more likely keeps adding layers of clothes at each retirement and reveille. We may begin to wonder whether Mr Knott has a 'veritable aspect' at all, beneath the repeated 'investments', or whether the multiple layers of supplementation do not constitute his being. It is characteristic of *Watt* that this disturbing information, like that regarding Mr Knott's family, should be given in a footnote, an inessential addition to the text, which nevertheless throws it off balance.

For a great deal of the book, it seems as though Watt and the narrator are trying to render nothingness in a language which cannot but misrepresent it by making it seem like a positive. Watt's solution to the problem of 'weighing absence in a scale' is to try to do away with language. Watt opts, not for silence, but for negation, that semiotic form which compounds absence and presence; negation is always secondary, always dependent upon a statement or sequence that has come before it and that must implicitly be re-invoked before it can be annulled. Like repetition, of which it is a form, negation runs together effacement and proliferation.[10]

The dependence on repetition of Watt's negation-by-inversion is very clear. In order to produce his passages of inverted speech, Watt has to go over his words, or reread them. We then have to reread this text, first 'forwards' and then 'backwards' to reconstitute the meaning. All this is quite apart from another level of repetition involved in the fact that Sam is repeating Watt's words for us. The effect is one of accretive concealment. The text doesn't really exist in any one of its embodiments, but in the very process of unrolling its stages. Nor does Watt really succeed in negating his language. In the inversions which leave the actual words intact, much of the sense of the 'original' is retained:

> Of nought. To the source. To the teacher. To the temple. To him I brought. This emptied heart. These emptied hands. This mind ignoring. This body homeless. To love him my little reviled. My little rejected to have him. My little to learn him forgot. Abandoned my little to find him. (p. 164)

Even when the order of the letters is inverted, meaning refuses to desert the utterance completely. Though the result looks and sounds like some curious Sino-Scandinavian hybrid, it strikes echoes from other languages. 'Ton vila, ton deda' (not alive, not dead) sounds like a commentary on the dead tone of Watt's own language; 'kup' becomes 'puk' (puke?) in a digestive recoil which matches semantically the inversion of the letters; 'Dis yb dis' (side by side) conjures up the ghosts of the hellish Dis and maybe even 'Charybdis'; and 'no' becomes that powerful and dreadful word, so common in Beckett's later texts, 'on' (pp. 165–7). In the French version too, considerations of euphony and orthography prevail with the inverted forms, to persuade meaning from meaninglessness.[11]

We need to remember, of course, that everything we are reading in the text of *Watt* is an inversion of Watt's original words, as spoken to and presumably reconstituted by Sam. We should therefore presumably read the whole book backwards to discover what Watt 'originally' said. It is true that we are able to forget about the text's origin in inversion for most of the time, but this makes it disturbing to find an allusion to it in the text:

> Yes, nothing changed, in Mr Knott's establishment, because nothing remained, and nothing came or went, because all was a coming and a going.
> Watt seemed highly pleased with this tenth-rate xenium. Spoken as he spoke it, back to front, it had a certain air, it is true. (p. 130)

Watt's words do attain a kind of fluency in reverse, and, indeed, it is striking how much of the writing in *Watt* does survive this sort of inversion. But of course it would be impossible to invert the book consistently, since we do not know what principle or principles of inversion Watt may have been using at any particular time. The sense remains, therefore, that *Watt* is not the 'actual' text of itself, but a derivation or repetition, which can never be translated back into the original.

Watt's attempts in the asylum to dissolve or efface language from within are not the only ones to be found in the book. As many have observed, Watt's own name, and the title of the book, are probably best understood as initiating the question 'what?' which is continually answered by Mr Knott's 'not'. These two words, especially the latter, are scattered throughout the book, and keep the ceaseless play of question and denial going. As with Watt's systems, 'not' is never strong enough to prevail over 'what', and the attempt at metaphorical substitution sustains an endless metonymic sequence. This sequence often seems to gather other phonemic elements to itself, as in the little rhyme in the addenda:

> Watt will not
> abate one jot
> but of what
>
> of the coming to
> of the being at
> of the going from
> Knott's habitat.
>
> (p. 250)[12]

Similarly, if we read Knott's name as 'know not', then the repetitions or near-repetitions of his name grow much thicker — at every occurrence, for instance, of the phrase 'not to know'. A passage quoted a little earlier seems to encode a particularly insistent series of such repetitions: 'It is perhaps *not* superfluous here to *note*, that Mr *Knott's* attitude was *not* that generally in vogue.' Some of Watt's difficulty with the word 'pot' might equally be seen to stem from its worrying closeness to the sound of his name and that of his employer.[13]

Given the tenuousness of the hold that language has on the world and the indistinctness of its differentiating units, it seems surprising that the book should itself bear a name so confidently. The title *Watt* seems as if it ought to be the simplest of references; it announces that the book is to be about the adventures of Watt, just as *Tom Jones* is about Tom Jones, *Emma* about Emma and *Murphy* about Murphy. We normally think of the title of the book as standing outside it, as a summation and interpretation of it. It stands on the threshold of the book, marking it off and setting its limits, even as it leads the reader into it. The title therefore marks the boundary of the book as well as marking its centre. Both centre and boundary are necessary to our sense of unity, and essential features of repetition, too (if I ask you to repeat something after me, you cannot do so until I have finished saying it, nor until you've decided what I've actually said). But the title of *Watt,* in repeating the name of its hero, may actually take us back into its text in disconcerting ways. If we take the title as a repetition (or repetition in-advance) of the phoneme 'Watt', considered as an element in the dissolving play of dialogue which we've just been looking at, initiating a question which is to be asked and answered again many times through the text, the title may come to seem as incomplete as the phonemic units which are scattered through the novel.

This is to say that *'Watt'* (the title) is in two different ways a repetition of the book it designates. Certainly it repeats the novel in the sense that it stands in for it, as a convenient substitute ('Have you read *Watt?'*) and has a metaphorical equivalence with what it names, even as that naming involves a move to a meta-level. But if we conceive the word *'Watt'* as initiating the kind of play of negation and difference which is enacted in the novel, then it has a different kind of equivalence with its signified; instead of repeating by naming it, it repeats by enactment and is therefore at the same linguistic level as the text that follows. Seen in this way, as a metonymic repetition, *Watt* functions as a synecdochic cue for the rest of the novel, rather than a substitute for it.

The conjunction of these two kinds of repetition means that the title is both more and less than the text it names, being outside and inside it. Like Watt the character, on his first appearance in the novel, it is 'disclosed' against the text it designates, as figure against ground, but, on closer scrutiny, becomes much harder to distinguish from it, just as the solitary figure of Watt is 'lit less and less by the receding lights, until it was scarcely to be distinguished from the dim wall behind it' (p. 14).[14]

Another metaphor which the book seems to provide for the relationship of title to text is the painting that Watt sees on Erskine's wall (and later inherits). The painting represents a circle and a point, separated from each other, which Watt thinks of, illogically enough, as a circle and a centre, either its centre, or the centre of another circle. But a centre cannot exist without a circle, because the concept of a centre has no meaning in itself, without the idea that there may be a circle, or some other spatial structure, for it to be the centre of. However, in the strange topology of *Watt,* such a divorce between centre and circle seems to be possible, even necessary. The divorce acts out Watt's feeling of alienation from, and desire to be fully within, himself — Arsene promises him that, in Knott's house, he will find himself 'in his midst at last, after so many tedious years spent clinging to the perimeter' (p. 39). But it also reproduces the strange irresolution of title and text. Centre and circle are as impossible to conceive without each other as text and title, but are also separated by an irreducible gap. As a result of this displacement of its centre, which refuses to be either inside or outside, the text is breached or hollowed, like the circle in the painting with the gap in its circumference. But if the painting is a sort of commentary on Watt himself, or on *Watt* itself, this does not mean that it is able to steal outside the text in which it appears, to some metarepresentational vantage point. Like the title, it is both inside and outside the text. Watt is forced to recognize that the picture, and his readings of it, are caught up in the combinative mobility which characterizes the occupants of Mr Knott's house, 'a matter of paradigm, here today and gone tomorrow, a term in a series, like the series of Mr Knott's dogs, or the series of Mr Knott's men, or like the centuries that fall, from the pod of eternity' (p. 129).

Thus our continually renewed belief in the singleness of a text like *Watt,* our belief that it has a centre, is questioned by the various kinds of repetition which are essential to it. *Watt* seems neither to be original, the centre of its own circle, or secondary, the reproduction of some other, earlier text (Sam's, or Watt's, 'actual words'), the circle produced from some other centre. What is original, as Derrida has argued, seems to be the fact of repetition itself, and the sense of lack which comes from it. In a way, writing is always already repetition:

> This repetition is writing because what disappears in it is the self-identity of the origin, the self-presence of so-called living speech. That is the center. The first book, the mythic book, the eve prior to all repetition, has lived on the deception that the center was sheltered from play: irreplaceable, withdrawn from metaphor and metonymy, a kind of *invariable first name* that could be invoked, but not repeated. The center of the first book should not have been repeatable in its own representation. Once it lends itself a single time to such a representation — that is to say, once it is written — when one can read a book in the book, an origin in the origin, a center in the center, it is the abyss, is the bottomlessness of infinite redoubling.
>
> (*WD*, 296)

Our belief in the self-containment of literary texts is liable to encounter difficulties with Beckett's work, anyway. For, in a real sense, his books are items in a series, rather than single, self-enclosed elements, so that the metonymic relationship of part to whole which is that of the title to the text is duplicated by the metonymic relationships of the novels to each other in the series which runs from *More Pricks than Kicks* through to the Trilogy and beyond. This sequentiality is attested to in the names of the characters, as no reader can fail to notice. The fact that most of the main characters have names beginning with 'M' has led some writers to try to conceive an 'ur-M', a character who runs together or sublates all the characteristics of Murphy,

Mercier, Molloy, Moran, Malone, Macmann and Mahood; for some writers the narrator of *The Unnamable* is this quintessential being.[15]

But the principle established by Watt's reversals of language (as many have noted, characters whose names begin with 'W' seem to represent inversion or negation for Beckett) seems to hold good for the sequence of novels as a whole.[16] That is to say, its ever-renewed movement of sequentiality prevents the sequence ever actually becoming a whole. Although the individual names of books mark resting points, the hold that they have over the books they designate is as tenuous as that maintained by *Watt*. *Molloy* names a novel in which two narratives are actually stitched together in a way that makes it difficult to decide which has priority. *Malone Dies* names a part of the text that is literally absent from it (Malone's dying) — indeed, Beckett thought for a time of calling the novel *L'Absent* (Admussen, 66). The relationship of title to text in *The Unnamable* is even more complex. For one thing, we are not sure what is supposed to be 'unnamable', the text, or the voice that speaks. We may presume that, in a sense, it is both, but then in both cases the name gives the lie to itself, for it does, if only by negation, name the text and, more dangerously, its character (a number of critics use the title to designate the voice, and therefore give it an inappropriate positivity). *The Unnamable* in fact names a difference, names the movement whereby names are conferred and abolished in sequence, 'I', 'Basil', 'Mahood' and 'Worm', each standing in a problematic and mixed relationship of identity and variation with what comes before. In doing so, *The Unnamable* also names a process of linguistic drift and dissolution that is apparent in earlier titles. As Frederick J. Hoffman points out, *Malone Meurt* incorporates the 'ur' sound in 'Murphy', the 'or' of Moran echoes the 'mort' to which 'meurt' is related, and the double-n of *The Unnamable* seems to recapitulate the sound of 'Knott'.[15] He might have added that 'Malone' blends 'Molloy' and 'Moran', and, if Malone's name encodes 'me alone', or, perhaps, 'man alone', then his surrogate 'Saposcat' seems to allude to 'homo sapiens' just as 'Macmann' means 'son of man'. Molloy's name undergoes this sort of associative disintegration in Moran's narrative. He cannot be sure whether he has heard 'Molloy', 'Mellose', or 'Mollose':

> Of these two names, Molloy and Mollose, the second seemed to me perhaps the more correct. But barely. What I heard, in my soul I suppose, where the acoustics are so bad, was a first syllable, Mol, very clear, followed almost at once by a second, very thick, as though gobbled by the first, and which might have been oy as it might have been ose, or one, or even oc.
>
> (*T*, 113)

Moran's remark about the self-consuming nature of Molloy's name resembles curiously Molloy's own remarks about the letter 'g', which abolishes the preceding syllables for him. Moran's declension of Molloy's names summons up a number of interesting verbal ghosts, including 'morose', 'mollusc' and even 'Malone'. It is interesting to note that Moran's intuition that Molloy is on the way to becoming Malone is not to be found in the first French version, in which Beckett had probably not devised the name of his next character. The French also has the variant 'Mollote', which may suggest 'mote', and remind us of Murphy, who aspires to be a mote in the 'absolute freedom' of will-lessness *(Murphy*, 66).[16] 'Mellose' may suggest mellowness, or mellifluousness and, in the French, 'mélange' or 'mêlée'.

The names of Molloy and Malone seem to resound through the language of the Trilogy in the same way as 'Watt' does in his novel; Molloy's name, for example, is replicated in the word 'mollify', which appears several times. Molloy's name is also associated with 'moly' — indeed, Molloy uses the word himself, speaking of the 'miserable molys of Lousse' (p. 54). The name of Malone, and its derivatives are similarly repeated, most notably at an important moment in *The Unnamable*: 'Me, utter me, in the same foul breath as my creatures? Say of me that I see this, feel that, fear, hope, know and do not know? Yes, I will say it, and of me alone. Impassive, still and mute, Malone revolves, a stranger forever to my infirmities' *(T*, 302). At this point, the voice is trying to declare his independence from his creatures, though he is aware that he has to do it in the same language that they use, and that brings them into being. His difficulty is confirmed for us a moment later, for, despite the fact that Malone is condemned as a stranger, his name is repeated subliminally in the vow to 'say it and of *me alone.*'

The problems and contradictions that we have been looking at stem from the dual status of the name, as both metaphorical substitute and metonymic association. After *The Unnamable*, Beckett's titles have tended to have a rather different relationship to the texts they name. Rather than attempting to name the whole text, and therefore to interpret it metaphorically *(Dream of Fair to Middling Women, More Pricks than Kicks, First Love, The Expelled)*, Beckett's titles have tended to be made up less grandiosely of words selected from the body of the text. Often the words or phrases are elements from repetitive sequences within them — *All That Fall, Ping, Eh Joe, Not I, ... but the clouds ... , That Time, Ill Seen Ill Said.* In some cases, Beckett has deliberately dropped a 'naming' title in favour of this kind of 'quoting' title, as when *Pim* became *How It Is* (Admussen, 32). In other cases, Beckett has preferred simple generic titles to titles which offer interpretations of the texts they name, as with *Film, Act Without Words* and *Rough for Radio.* Another example is *Play,* though of course, the title itself involves a 'play' on the different meanings of the word. Sometimes, the title is a repetition, not of some part of the text that follows, but of some other text or work of art, as with *Ghost Trio* (originally entitled *Tryst)* and *Nacht und Träume.* The words *Come and Go* do not feature in the play that they name, but the phrase is a favourite one for Beckett, so that the title constitutes a self-quotation of a rather different kind.

There are exceptions to this general rule regarding Beckett's later titles, the most notable being *Krapp's Last Tape, Happy Days* and *Worstward Ho;* these are all titles which stand firmly outside their texts and comment bitterly on them. But, in general, Beckett has come to distrust titles which pretend to this degree of metalinguistic authority over their texts. This represents a move from an authoritative kind of repetition to the more difficult sort of repetition that we have been looking at, in which the boundaries between text and context, original and copy, centre and margin are made problematic. As we shall see, this is no empty formalism, for such issues have a great deal to do with the intense exploration of the conditions of identity and power in Beckett's work.

One might see *Watt*'s attempts to undo language by repetition as a map or model for Beckett's project in his writing since the Trilogy. The plays and novels which followed this work often give the impression of being a tissue of quotations from earlier texts. More and more, his work has come to seem like the desperate attempt to say new things with the same old words and motifs, every new work an anxious return to old work in order to find a new direction in which — in both senses — to strike out.

Chapter 3

Repetition in Time: *Proust* and *Molloy*

For Beckett, the world is always already how it is. His characters inhabit worlds for which no narrative prehistory is provided, and no means of grounding that prehistory. Unlike other novelists, who might seek to separate out characters and their environments, in order slowly to explore the congruence between them, Beckett installs his characters in a world from the outset. Beckett's occasional remarks about his work stress this givenness ('Hamm as stated, and Clov as stated, together as stated, nec tecum nec sine te, in such a place, and in such a world, that's all I can manage, more than I could' [*Disjecta*, 109]). Being, for Beckett, is not something that lies behind or beyond the chaos of experience, not something essential, ultimate or other. Instead it is the place one starts from. Beckett seems to start from the Heideggerian condition of 'Geworfenheit', that 'being-thrown' into life, always under particular conditions. This is emphasized by the beginnings of Beckett's novels and plays, in their refusal to provide preludes of any kind: 'I am in my mother's room. It is I who live there now'; 'I shall soon be quite dead at last, in spite of all' *(T, 7, 179)*. One story and one play even begin with characters being literally thrown into the narrative space *(The Expelled* and *Act Without Words I)*. If being is impure, if there are irresolvable contradictions in human experience, then this, for Beckett, is not to be explained as a fall from grace, a disturbance or complication of original simplicity or unity. Rather, these impurities are congenital, or 'equiprimordial'.[1]

Beckett's work up to the end of the Trilogy is often said to have moved progressively away from the material world and its conditions, and to have withdrawn into the various different kinds of subjectivism and abstraction. But it's possible to see Beckett moving in another direction, too, towards an ever more intense awareness of the predicament of immanence. The narrators of the Trilogy and of *How It Is,* and the characters in the early plays, struggle to make sense of a world that they are always inextricably in:

It would help me, since to me too I must attribute a beginning, if I could relate it to that of my abode. Did I wait somewhere for this place to be ready to receive me? Or did it wait for me to come and people it? By far the better of these hypotheses, from the point of view of usefulness, is the former, and I shall often have occasion to fall back on it. But both are distasteful. I shall say therefore that our beginnings coincide, that this place was made for me, and I for it, at the same instant.

(T, 298)

The most important aspect of being-in-the-world, for Beckett, is being in time. We find it difficult to think of subjectivity except as living through time, and therefore somehow different from the flow of time that it inhabits. We regard the subject therefore as a solid, separable essence, which is plunged within time, or carried along by it, like a vessel in a stream. The most developed work of criticism which Beckett has produced, his essay on Proust, is given over largely to the rejection of that simple model, and the exploration of the complexities of living with 'that double-headed monster of damnation and salvation — Time' *(PTD, 11)*.

Beckett hits the central problem of definition right at the beginning of the essay. The temporal conditions under which the individual self exists, are in one sense, just this, conditions, or accidents, which therefore seem arbitrary and even provisional. But at the same time, being-in-time creates the condition of the individual self in the first place. In other words, it doesn't do to consider the self as something which exists somewhere else before its existence in time, in some Platonic antechamber. The self is brought into being by its existence in time, so that trying to decide which comes 'first', the self or time, is a vain exercise. But if time is what constitutes identity, it is also time that unsettles or 'deforms' it:

There is no escape from the hours and the days. Neither from tomorrow nor from yesterday. There is no escape from yesterday because yesterday has deformed us, or been deformed by us. The mood is of no importance. Deformation has taken place.... We are not merely more weary because of yesterday, we are other, no longer what we were before the calamity of yesterday.

(PTD, 13)

If we live always in time, then, Beckett insists, we live everywhere in time, not just in the (anyway ever-changing) present moment. Time is therefore both outside us and inside us; indeed, more than this, it is what makes it impossible to speak of outside and inside: 'Yesterday is not a milestone that has been passed, but a daystone on the beaten track of the years and irremediably part of us, within us, heavy and dangerous' (*PTD*, 13).

Later on, Beckett modifies the Proustian image of consciousness as an enclosing vessel within the stream of phenomena; for Beckett, the self is seen as 'the seat of a constant process of decantation, decantation from the vessel containing the fluid of future time, sluggish, pale and monochrome, to the vessel containing the fluid of past time, agitated and multicoloured by the phenomena of its hours (*PTD*, 15).

Of course, this is not the way that we think we live in time. 'Ordinary' experience or common sense make us want to believe that personality does persist, only slightly modified, through the erosions of time, and that there is therefore some meaning in speaking of our former selves as 'us', and claiming the experience of those former selves as our own — this is what the voice in *Company* wants the listener to do, to say 'Yes I remember. That was I. That was I then' (*Company*, 27). But the Beckett of *Proust* will have none of this. Such continuity of personality is an illusion, the result of a 'retrospective hypothesis' which is determined to edit out or forget everything that is disturbingly strange about the past, every sign of difference between our present and past selves. In a double confirmation of this hypothesis, the past self is reconstructed to accord with the present self, while the present self is imagined to be merely the repetition of this (misconstrued) past self. It is a process that Beckett calls 'that most necessary, wholesome and monotonous plagiarism — the plagiarism of oneself' (*PTD*, 33).

The contradiction between process and continuity is smoothed over for Beckett (and, he says, in the work of Proust) by the operations of habit, which is 'the generic term for all the countless treaties concluded between the countless subjects that constitute the individual and their countless correlative objects' (*PTD*, 19). Habit is what enables us to witness change in ourselves without *being* that change. This guarantees the continuity of the self, or, as Beckett puts it, its 'dull inviolability'. Its correlative is Proust's 'voluntary memory', which serves the utilitarian needs of a personality determined to sustain itself by an inviolable routine of repetition which blanks out every sign of difference within itself.

But the dominion of habit is not complete, either for Proust or for Beckett. Change necessarily takes place and there are, in any life, transitions between states of existence, or the temporary hypotheses of being. The stable and stabilizing ego tries its utmost to construe each different stage of being as merely a repetition of previous stages, but the transitions between these stages are periods of grave risk. Deprived of its anaesthetic unity, the ego is liable to become aware of the unstable world of multiplicity, disappointment and loss which it inhabits. Similarly, the voluntary memory can give way at odd moments to the action of involuntary memory, which can restore, in shocking intensity, everything that we once were, and now no longer can be.

It would be a mistake to see the arguments of the Proust essay as having a satisfactory unity, for there are in it important discontinuities. For all his sour self-assurance, Beckett seems to be not entirely certain of his attitude towards the state of affairs he describes. There is particular confusion as to what is the result of the collapse of the voluntary memory, the 'negligence or agony' of habit, as Beckett puts it. Sometimes the awareness of the nonrepeatability of personality is painful and nauseating, so much so that, for Marcel, it is not only life that is an illusion, but also the possibility of an afterlife: 'he thinks how absurd is our dream of a Paradise with retention of personality, since our life is a succession of Paradises successively denied, that the only true Paradise is the Paradise that has been lost, and that death will cure many of the desire for immortality' (*PTD*, 26). It is not just a matter of individuality and its self-division, for our habitual hypotheses about the singleness of other people are also unsettled:

> His gaze is no longer the necromancy that sees in each precious object a mirror of the past.... And he realises with horror that his grandmother is dead, long since and many times, that the cherished familiar of his mind, mercifully composed all along the years by the solicitude of habitual memory, exists no longer, that this mad old woman, drowsing over her book, overburdened with years, flushed and coarse and vulgar, is a stranger whom he has never seen.
>
> (*PTD*, 27–8)

But involuntary memory also seems to allow the possibility of repeating or retrieving the past self as it was. Thus an authentic repetition of the past momentarily replaces the bored multiplication of
empty facsimiles of the self:

> The identification of immediate with past experience, the recur-
> rence of past action or reaction in the present, amounts to a par-
> ticipation between the ideal and the real, imagination and direct
> apprehension, symbol and substance ... thanks to this redupla-
> tion, the experience is at once imaginative and empirical, at once an
> evocation and a direct perception, real without being merely actual,
> ideal without being merely abstract, the ideal real, the essential, the
> extra-temporal.
>
> (*PTD,* 74–5)

Beckett's language here is glamorized by philosophical superlative,
but there seems no doubt that there is a great pressure of desire behind his words, desire for a vision of the fullness of self, somehow mi-
raculously preserved in 'that ultimate and inaccessible dungeon of our
being to which Habit does not possess the key' (*PTD,* 31). But the language also betrays a crucial uncertainty. Here, available to involuntary
memory, is 'the essence of ourselves ... the firm essence of a smothered
divinity ... the pearl that may give the lie to our carapace of paste and
pewter' (*PTD,* 31). But how can the self be an 'essence' and the 'seat of
decantation' at the same time? If the condition of being is multiplicity
then how can one ever conceive of a single representative self derived
from that multiplicity, 'the essence of ourselves, the best of our many
selves, and their concretions' (*PTD,* 31)?

This contradiction involves two opposed notions of repetition.
There is, first of all, the repetition of habit, which protects the self
from the formlessness of being. In repetition alone is to be found the
consolation of an escape from the suffering that this formlessness can
induce. Winnie in *Happy Days,* for example, lives in a world of pure
repetition, in which there is hardly anything she says or does which
she has not said or done before. These repetitions enable her not to
recognize the terrifying approach of extinction, helping her to see every
day as just like every preceding day. Against this inauthentic repetition, Beckett sets the possibility of an authentic retrieval of the real,

underlying self which has been lost to consciousness by the obliterating operations of habit and voluntary memory.

This contradiction may come partly from Beckett's odd relationship to the object of his study in *Proust*. Though it is in some ways an excellent summary of Proust's ideas about the multiplicity of the self, Beckett's essay markedly overstates Proust's pessimism, and undervalues the possibility of rediscovering the selves lost to time that is presented in *A la Recherche du Temps Perdu*. The contradiction between the self as process and the self as essence is to some degree the manifestation of a struggle between the different positions of Beckett and Proust. Beckett is obliged to repeat Proust's claims for the possibility of authentic repetition, but seems to protest mutely against the idea by leaving his account of the unstable plurality of the self bitterly unmodified.

There is another way of reading this contradiction, however. Beckett's work hereafter will be committed to the struggle to isolate being, and to strip away everything that is extrinsic to the self in order to say what it really *is*—- to 'say I', in the opening words of *The Unnamable*. The self will be pursued as though it were a locatable essence, or a presence, even though that pursuit is to reveal the self as difference. As will become clear in the Trilogy, the two types of definition are inseparable, for the notion that the self exists singly and self-identically as a substance is entwined all the time with less comfortable possibilities.

It is this that accounts for the peculiar double movement in Beckett's fiction up to *How It Is*. As many readers have noticed, the works gradually move from the 'big world' of external materiality and other people to the 'little world' of individual consciousness. The abundance of narrative detail in *More Pricks Than Kicks* gives way in *Murphy* to a narrative centralized around one character, and in which all the other characters are acknowledged to be 'puppets'. In *Watt,* there is a move away from the wide-awake world within a few pages and, for the rest of the novel, we are at the mercy of Watt's obsessive consciousness. With the novellas, *The Calmative, The End* and *The Expelled,* Beckett begins in earnest his 'long battle of the soliloquy', in which he progressively flays away from the narrating 'I' everything material that surrounds and confirms it. Beckett seems to be re-enacting in narrative terms the regime of systematic doubt prescribed by Descartes, in which everything potentially deceptive, the external world, memory, the senses themselves, is ruled inadmissible for philosophical enquiry, until all the philosopher is left with is the flicker of doubt itself, the self-reflexive 'cogito' which is the ground and guarantee of being.

But Beckett does not follow Descartes exactly, all the way to this essential *cogito*. For Beckett, penetration into the little world of consciousness produces a proliferation of subsidiary characters. The series moves through Belacqua, Murphy, Watt, Mercier and Camier, Moran, Molloy, Malone, Macmann, Mahood, Worm, the narrator of *The Unnamable,* each successive character in the series being conceived of as a repetition and a reimagination at the same time. Although Beckett moves on after each character, replacing one character with another, so that each repetition is also a repudiation, the characters are strangely liable to recur. The voice in *The Unnamable* is therefore at the last extremity of solitude, and yet inhabits a space which is thronged with revenants: 'To tell the truth I believe they are all here, at least from Murphy on, I believe we are all here, but so far I have seen only Malone … we have all been here forever, we shall all be here forever, I know it' (*T,* 295). It seems as though the very drive to fix or position the self as an entity is what brings about the splitting of the self into simulacra.

These problems are dramatized most strikingly in *Molloy.* This is a story which is told twice, or, perhaps, two stories told in tandem. The yoking together of the two stories makes it difficult either to tell them apart from each other, or to unify them. This comes about in *Molloy* particularly because of difficulties in conceiving time; we find it difficult to establish whether the adventures described in the narrative take place at the same time, or one after the other, and, if so, in which order. Both narrators claim to have set out in high summer — Molloy speaks of the 'unreal journey … which I here declare without further ado to have begun in the second or third week of June' (*T,* 91) while Moran is quite specific that his journey began on a Sunday in August (*T,* 166) — and both journeys seem to come to an end in Spring. Both narratives seem to describe the passing of three seasons of the year, though there are inconsistencies within the narratives; Molloy is struck, for instance, by the appearance of a full moon apparently only two days after he has seen the new moon. Indeed, in both narratives, time seems to stretch and contract in alarming ways, with the suspension of time in such episodes as that of Molloy's sucking-stones alternating with the disposal of long periods of time in a few pages. But the reader's supposition that the two journeys are taking place at the same time is contradicted by certain hints. As Molloy nears the edge of the forest, he hears at intervals the sound of a gong, which it is difficult for the reader not to connect with the sound of the dinner-gong struck at 9 o'clock in Moran's home. But this would imply that Molloy is either arriving at the edge of the forest before Moran sets out, or after he has returned. The mysterious voice telling Molloy not to fret, that help is coming, might suggest the ministrations of Youdi, who is about to send Moran to Molloy's aid. But, on the other hand, there are also hints that Molloy is really a later version of Moran; his confusion, his reduced condition and the fact that he has in his possession a mysterious object very like Moran's silver knife-rest, seem to indicate that his journey succeeds rather than precedes Moran's.

The problem is intensified by the fact that the two narrators seem to inhabit time so differently. Molloy experiences time as massive, featureless and slow-moving. He tends to rely less on calculation than on instinct, and is therefore not unduly worried by such things as the inconsistency of the phases of the moon. In fact, he even suggests calmly that there may be two moons. During the period spent at Lousse's, his time seems to be suspended, or to slow down dramatically — 'the garden seemed hardly to change, from day to day, apart from the changes due to the customary cycle of birth, life and death' (*T*, 52) — or Homerically expanded, as when Lousse spends all night in the garden with Molloy trying to persuade him to stay with her. One way of interpreting this is to see Molloy as a figure of myth, who is more in touch with the slow rhythms of death and recurrence in the natural world.[2] But, actually, Molloy seems to have very little notion of time at all, and seems to be content to exist in that featureless mobility of 'decantation' which Beckett describes in *Proust*.

Moran, on the other hand, is obsessed by regularity and routine. He goes to Mass at the same time every Sunday, eats his meals at the same time every day and is anxious to keep a grip on time by measuring it — as, for example, by the diminishing stocks of his Wallenstein lager. As a special agent he takes a pride in bringing his subjects 'to a

certain place at a certain time' (*T,* 137). Moran solidifies and spatial-
izes time, making it part of the visible world rather than a formless
process, and his addiction to routine is an example of a self desperately
sandbagging itself with materiality in order to forestall the recognition
of emptiness. His desire to order and systematize seems to mark him as
a victim of the habit described in *Proust.* Clearly, however, his control is
threatened all the time by dissolution; he is horrified to reflect on how
ill-prepared he is for the journey:

> It was then the unheard of sight was to be seen of Moran making
> ready to go without knowing where he was going, having consulted
> neither map nor time-table, considered neither itinerary nor halt,
> heedless of the weather outlook, with only the vaguest notion of the
> outfit he would need, the time the expedition was likely to take, the
> money he would require and even the very nature of the work to be
> done and consequently the means to be employed.
>
> (*T,* 124)

Gradually, his grip on time loosens. Where, in the first part of the
narrative, he is still able to divide the days up, after the third day he
begins to lose all sense of temporal progression: 'I seemed to see myself
ageing as swiftly as a day-fly. But the idea of ageing was not exactly the
one which offered itself to me. And what I saw was more like a crum-
bling, a frenzied collapsing of all that had always protected me from all
I was condemned to be' (*T,* 149).

Like the subjects described in *Proust,* both Molloy and Moran
are impelled by desire, Molloy by the desire to get to his mother and
Moran by the desire to track down Molloy. But, as Beckett explains in
Proust, the mobility of the subject in time, its inability exactly to reconstitute itself from moment to moment, means that desire can never
be satisifed; it is always the desire of some other, for another still: 'The
subject has died — and perhaps many times — on the way. For subject
B to be disappointed by the banality of an object chosen by subject A is
as illogical as to expect one's own hunger to be dissipated by the spectacle of Uncle eating his dinner' (*PTD,* 14). In a curious way, Moran and
Molloy also desire themselves, as well as desiring some other. Narration
splits the subject into two, into a past self, the object of narration, and
the present self who is doing the narrating. One might see the problem

of narration as one of trying to enforce a bond of repeatability between these two selves. Here again, Moran and Molloy seem to have different attitudes to what they are doing. Moran is in the grip of voluntary memory, in that he wants to possess his past self, and affirm an absolute continuity between present and past; Molloy's desire for continuity is much less pressing.

Repetition is usually the means by which the self is stabilized for Moran, and by which the self maintains control over itself and the world. Moran is much given to repetition in his narrative, using it to pin down moments of doubt or uncertainty ('on this occasion, repeat, on this occasion' [*T,* 111]) and to enforce his authority over his son, when he makes him repeat his moral lessons. At times, repetition seems to take the narrative over involuntarily:

> Stop trying to understand, I said, just listen to what I am going to say, because I shall not say it twice. He came over to me and knelt down. You would have thought I was about to breathe my last. Do you know what a new bicycle is? I said. Yes papa, he said. Very well, I said, if you can't find a second-hand bicycle buy a new bicycle. I repeat. I repeated. I who had said I would not repeat. Now tell me what you are to do ... I repeated, Tell me what you are to do.
>
> (*T,* 143)

If repetition is the mark of control for Moran, then he is occasionally tormented by the sense that there may not be any real duplicates possible in the 'spray of phenomena': 'the noise of things bursting, merging, avoiding one another, assails me on all sides, my eyes search in vain for two things alike, each pinpoint of skin screams a different message' *(T,* 111). Though Moran can say with pleasure that 'to see yourself doing the same thing endlessly over and over again fills you with satisfaction' (*T,* 134), this delight in absolute repetition is founded on a sense that the observing or analytic self is somehow separate from this play of repetition. More disturbing for Moran is the lack of control which is brought with another kind of absolute repetition, the merging of the narrating and the narrated self. This kind of repeatability threatens the stability of the distinctions between now and then, present and past, narrator and narrated — even threatens the gap that establishes the very possibility of repetition:

For in describing this day I am once more he who suffered it, who crammed it full of futile anxious life, with no other purpose than his own stultification and the means of not doing what he had to do. And as then my thoughts would have none of Molloy, so tonight my pen. This confession has been preying on my mind for some time past. To have made it gives me no relief.

(T, 122)

Curiously, the sense of the 'negligence or agony of habit' also opens up for Moran the opposite sense, of the painful gap between present and past selves. Where he had been complacently lodged in his routine, the experiences of his journey have, by the time he begins to write his narrative, opened the sense of this gap; and his narrative is produced out of the tension between the continuous and the split self. His complacency in the early part of his narrative is regularly pierced by reminders of the discontinuity of the narrating and narrated selves. 'In such surroundings', he writes ominously on the second page of his narrative, 'slipped away my last moments of peace and happiness' (*T,* 9). Later on, he notes that 'the colour and weight of the world were changing already' and that 'I was losing my head already' (*T,* 97, 99).

By the end of his narrative, Moran may know more than he did early on, but this does not allow him really to escape the implications of time and the mobility of the self. For what he has learnt is that the self is truly multiple, that the present self can hardly be said to have any kind of priority over previous selves, since that present self is always in the process of passing away and being replaced. This mobility seems to be one guarantee of being able to suspend the present and inhabit the past completely, though Moran thinks of it as more a penance than an opportunity:

I shall say what little I knew, on leaving my home, about the Molloy country, so different from my own. For it is one of the features of this penance that I may not pass over what is over and straightway come to the heart of the matter. But that must again be unknown to me which is no longer so and that again fondly believed which then I fondly believed, at my setting out. And if I occasionally break this rule, it is only over details of little importance. And in the main I

observe it. And with such zeal that I am far more he who finds than
he who tells what he has found, now as then, most of the time, I do
not exaggerate.

(*T,* 133)

So Moran's life and narrative bring about a confrontation between
the two different kinds of repetition explored in *Proust*. There is the
comforting regularity of repetition-as-habit, or the 'plagiarism of oneself', in which repetition is a kind of control, and there is repetition
as the involuntary and unpredictable merging of past and present, a
merging which threatens the self's structures of control.

In some ways, Moran's experience of time repeats Molloy's. Molloy,
too, is a mobile subject, or, to be more accurate, a succession of mobile
subjects, but he is much less concerned than Moran at the disparity
and uneven overlapping of past and present selves. In recounting his
past, he is perfectly happy to tolerate contradictions and implausibili-
ties, as, for example, when he tells of waking in Lousse's house, going
to the door and windows, looking for his clothes, and finding a light
switch. Suddenly, he confronts us with an embarrassing inconsistency:
'I found my crutches, against an easy chair. It may seem strange that
I was able to go through the motions I have described without their
help. I find it strange. You don't remember immediately who you are,
when you wake' (*T,* 38). Molloy is serenely happy with this astonishing
and offhand explanation, content that narrative should not just repeat
or reconstitute past events, but should actually invent them as it goes
along. For a moment, just as one forgets who one is supposed to be on
waking, Molloy forgets that he is supposed to be a cripple. The passage
may be a conscious or unconscious repetition of a passage from *The
Guermantes Way,* in which Proust discusses the effects of sleep on the
continuity of the personality:

> How…searching for one's thoughts, one's personality, as one searches
> for a lost object, does one recover one's own self rather than any other?
> Why, when one begins again to think, is it not a personality other
> than the previous one that becomes incarnate in one? One fails to see
> what dictates the choice, or why, among the millions of human beings
> one might be, it is on the being one was the day before that unerringly
> one lays one's hand.[3]

Throughout his narrative, Molloy is prepared to grant his earlier selves an autonomy which Moran never can. The mobility of self brings about two different responses from Molloy. First of all, he is able to free himself utterly from the dominion of his present narrating self and identify completely with the past-tense self who is being narrated. This negative capability is often manifested in the form of repudiations of the present-tense narrating self: 'from time to time I shall recall my present existence compared to which this is a nursery tale. But only from time to time, so that it may be said, if necessary, whenever necessary, is it possible that thing is still alive?' (*T*, 61–2).

It is interesting that Molloy is as incapable of saturating himself in his past-tense narrative as Moran is of maintaining his position in the present tense. Molloy's ability to suspend the operations of habitual intelligence makes possible something like the full retrieval of past experience, but also, as with Moran, compels a sense of the split between past and present selves, the 'contradiction between presence and irremediable absence', as Beckett describes it in *Proust* (*PTD*, 41). However, unlike Moran, Molloy seems happy to multiply these discrepancies between past and present. He can, for example, disobey the principal rule of first person narration, which is that the life of the narrated character can be projected forward until it joins with the life of the narrator. On one occasion, Molloy describes himself putting to sea in a skiff but confesses his inability to remember ever coming back. Molloy seems to be incorporating into his own narrative the account given by the narrator of *The End* of his final moments (*CSP*, 68–70); this suggests that, in a curious way, to speak of oneself is always to speak of another. In a similar way, Molloy strands himself at the end of his narrative, declining to join up the end and beginning of his story by telling us how he escaped from the ditch or got to the room where he is. Breaking off from his own life, he sounds like a narrator breaking off from writing the life of a narrated character: 'Molloy could stay, where he happened to be' (*T*, 91). It is not surprising that Molloy cannot find a tense to accommodate his sense of multiple position in time: 'My life, my life, now I speak of it as of something over, now as of a joke which still goes on, and it is neither, for at the same time it is over and it goes on, and is there any tense for that? (*T*, 36).

For the reader, the real problems come from trying to understand the relationship between the two narratives, rather than the contradictions within each. Not surprisingly, this has been the issue that has exercised most commentators on the novel. For a large number of these, the novel presents a myth of reconciliation and unity, whether Molloy and Moran are seen as complementary halves, or the book is seen as a myth of progression, in which the materialistic Moran gradually attains the spiritual integrity of Molloy. Many of these readings focus on the strange and insistent similarities between Molloy and Moran, some stressing the parallelism of the two stories, with their accounts of gradual decline, others seeing Moran's adventures as primary and Molloy's as secondary.[4] However, the process of understanding the relationship between the two narratives is more fraught with difficulties and paradoxes than such smooth secondary revisions of the novel's material allow. For one thing, Moran's narrative doesn't actually precede Molloy's, as we perhaps feel it should. This means that the moments of *deja vu* that we encounter in Moran's narrative — the concern with bicycles, the wicket-gate, the confusion between green and blue, the murder of strangers, etc. — are both originals *and* repetitions. They are originals at the level of *sjuzet,* in the narrative that we may construct to relate Moran to Molloy, but are repetitions at the level of *fabula.* When we read the accounts of Moran meeting a stranger in the forest, or having his legs stiffen in the same way as Molloy's, it is hard not to have the sense that Moran is haunted or inhabited by some other, and that his life is a kind of shadowing of Molloy's. But if we do read the novel backwards, then, of course, what a first reading apprehended as primary may come to have the ghostly feel of a repetition. But it is not even possible to read the novel completely backwards, for this would lead to other problems with chronology; far from being in the future for Moran, Molloy clearly already exists for him, as for Youdi and Gaber. In fact, each possible reading of the novel, forwards and backwards, leaves important material unaccounted for. The problem is not so much that the novel doesn't give us enough material as that it gives us too much, allowing us to believe both that Moran becomes Molloy, and that Molloy's adventures precede Moran's.

This reversibility is underlined in a series of references throughout the book to family relationships. In one sense, Moran is Molloy's father — or at least, Molloy is his descendant. Moran, of course, has a son of his own, who bears his own name, and, by dint of bullying and blackmail, Moran seems to be trying to turn him into a replica of himself. Molloy is himself a son, though he is looking for his mother, not his father. But, at other times, Moran seems less like Molloy's father than his son. If he is an earlier version of Molloy, he is also younger than him: indeed at one point he hopes 'that Molloy, whose country this was, would come to me, who had not been able to go to him, and grow to be like a friend, and like a father to me' (*T,* 162). Molloy, too, is uncertain about his status as father or son, and in reminiscence the two are liable to invert, as when he remembers his mother calling him Dan, '1 don't know why, my name is not Dan. Dan was my father's name perhaps, yes, perhaps she took me for my father. I took her for my mother and she took me for my father' (*T,* 17). At the beginning of his narrative Molloy wonders whether he resembles his mother and thinks' All I need now is a son. Perhaps I have one somewhere' (*T,* 8). If one adopts the hypothesis that Molloy is an older Moran, then this son might be Jacques; but it might also be Moran, for 'he would be old now, nearly as old as myself' (*T, 8).*

This reversibility prevents any single identification of the two characters, even as complementaries or Jungian opposites. To postulate a relationship of similarity between Molloy and Moran is to imagine each as possessing some sort of identity, if only in a fixed and absolute difference from the other. But the extraordinary structure of repetitions or near-repetitions in the book prevents us from establishing firm points of reference for Molloy and Moran. Memory and recall of the book tend, like Proust's habit, to smooth out all the jagged inconsistencies in the narratives and to allow us to generalize about what sort of character Molloy or Moran is or isn't. But the ways in which the two characters differ from themselves are at least as striking and insistent as the ways in which they differ from each other. Rather than merely supervening on identities or divergences which are present in some extratextual space, it is repetition that itself produces the play of sameness and difference which is the text.

A close look at some of the repeated incidents in the two narratives can illustrate this raggedness of relationship between Molloy and Moran. The two, for instance, have similar difficulties with their stiff

legs, and both experience unwonted moments of joy, in riding their bicycles (though later on, both are deprived of their machines, [*T,* 16–7,
157–]). But the differences between the two bicycles are striking, too.
Molloy's is green, chainless and without cable-brakes, while Moran's
has no specified colour but has a carrier. Molloy rides his bike one-
legged (which Moran also thinks of doing) and Moran makes his son
do the pedalling. Molloy is interested by the horn of his bicycle, while
Moran's bicycle seems not even to have a bell.

It is difficult to be sure as readers whether the repetition here
serves to point out the similarity between the two men, or to point
up the contrast between them — between, say, Molloy's solitary as
opposed to Moran's cooperative riding. The differences are set against
a background of similarity, but then the similarities are perceived as
well against a background of divergence. We do not know which is
the more significant, sameness or difference, nor do we have access
to any principle in the text which would enable us to decide the question. Both characters refer in their narratives to the difficulty of telling
two nearly-identical things apart, Molloy remarking that he cannot
remember which leg he propped on the front of his bicycle, because
they are now both stiff, and Moran, in what seems to be an echo, saying that he cannot remember which wheel of the bicycle has a puncture
— 'as soon as two things are nearly identical I am lost' (*T,* 156). The
repetition of the remark is all the more disconcerting for seeming to
refer reflexively to the relationship between the two characters. It is the
problematic relationship of *near-identity* which makes the reader lose
the sense of priority and proportion between the two characters.

The most obvious and extended example of recurrence in *Molloy*
is the two meetings with the shepherd and his flock. Similarities between the two passages are both general and specific; both men meet
a shepherd, complete with sheepdog and flock, both ask a question of
the shepherd, both think about butchering, slaughter and black sheep,
and both fall into a reverie as they think about what will happen to
the flock. There are also resemblances in the language of the passages.
Molloy's 'Good God, what a land of breeders' seems to be paralleled by
Moran's 'What a pastoral land, my God' (*T,* 29, 159).

But the differences between the passages are striking, too. Molloy
is discovered by the shepherd in the morning, while Moran comes

across the shepherd at evening; Moran receives a reply to his questions, while Molloy receives no reply. And there are points of apparent resemblance which it is hard to account for: does the 'glittering dust' through which the sheep walk, as well as 'that mist too which rises in me every day and veils the world from me and veils me from myself' in Molloy's narrative (*T,* 29) have anything to do with the 'dim glow, the sum of countless points of light blurred by the distance' (*T,* 160) which is what Moran makes out of the town of Bally? Again, the repetition seems to insist on the parallel between the two without giving us any principle by which to measure its significance.

Another moment of repetition concerns the stiff legs suffered by the two narrators. We have already seen that Molloy experiences an unaccountable relief from his condition on waking up in Lousse's chamber; and something similar happens in Moran's narrative when he describes the mysterious return of his mobility when murdering the stranger who looks like him. After the murder, his stiffness returns — 'Already my knee was stiffening again. It no longer required to be supple' (*T,* 152). In both narratives there is a sense of arbitrariness, as though the whim of the narrator were affecting the solidity and reliability of the narrative. What is more, in both cases, there is a departure from the self — 'you don't remember immediately who you are when you wake.' This means that Molloy and Moran are being drawn together at the moment when they are unlike themselves, so that, again, the repetition includes a discrepancy. Things are made more complicated by another repetition in Moran's narrative, the fact that the stranger whom he has killed 'no longer resembled me' (*T,* 154). If Moran is repudiating repetition by killing his double, then the murder is precisely the means by which we come to identify him with his other double, Molloy; the rejection of repetition therefore reasserts it.

Similarity and difference are twisted together so indissolubly in *Molloy* because the repetitions in the novel complicate the model of original and copy that we customarily use to picture and understand repetition. One of the reasons for the acculturated disdain of repetition is that we think of the copy or facsimile as having merely a derived or secondary existence. Copies or repetitions are supplements to, and therefore somehow parasitic upon, what they reproduce, even though it is the secondariness of the copy which also confirms the primacy and unity of the original. To think of Moran and Molloy as repetitions of each other is simultaneously to rely upon and to learn to mistrust this original/copy dichotomy. If Moran is the 'original' of Molloy, with Molloy conceived of as a sequel or supplement to Moran, then Moran's story is also, in a chronological sense, the successor of Molloy's. In order to make sense of the novel one must at any time entertain one or the other hypothesis, even though that hypothesis is likely at any moment to be disproved.

Repetition seems to have an ontological dimension too. It seems to mark the place where the self divides itself from and confronts its 'other', in a structure which both guarantees and undermines the centrality of the self. For Moran, Molloy seems to represent that formlessness against which he defines his being: 'This was how he came to me, at long intervals. Then I was nothing but uproar, bulk, rage, suffocation, effort unceasing, frenzied and vain. Just the opposite of myself, in fact' (*T, 114*).

Moran's nightmare of what Molloy is like threatens his sense of self, even as it discloses and confirms it — there is some satisfaction in that 'just the opposite of myself, in fact'. Moran's conception of himself, as 'a man like me' depends on and is braced by the potential eruptions of Molloy into his life:

> That a man like me, so meticulous and calm in the main, so patiently turned towards the outer world as towards the lesser evil, creature of his house, his garden, of his few poor possessions, discharging faithfully and ably a revolting function, reining back his thoughts within the limits of the calculable so great is his horror of fancy, that a man so contrived, for I was a contrivance, should let himself be haunted and possessed by chimeras, this ought to have seemed strange to me and been a warning to me to have a care, in my own interest.
>
> (*T*, 114)

As the 'contrived' outside which gives Moran his fragile, jeopardized interiority, Molloy is produced by Moran, and in a sense belongs to him. He seems to be imagining and remembering at the same time when he speaks of Molloy and (astonishingly) Molloy's mother. His certainty about Molloy is based on a willed ignorance:

I shall force myself to say Molloy, like Gaber. That there may have been two different persons involved, one my own Mollose, the other the Molloy of the enquiry, was a thought which did not so much as cross my mind, and if it had I should have driven it away, as one drives away a fly, or a hornet. How little one is at one with oneself, good God.

(T, 113)

So Molloy is both inside and outside Moran, both self and other, alien and intimate. We should notice, nevertheless, that Moran's narrative prevents us from identifying the Molloy whose words we have read with Moran's Molloy. In appropriating, or anticipating, Molloy as other, Moran seems to acknowledge the possibility of difference. Merely thinking of or attempting to name Molloy produces new names, and maybe new characters: Mellose, Mollose, Molloc (*T,* 113).

Molloy, as we have seen, has less need to exclude; he is willing to embrace the polymorphous drift of personality. His is a self which is 'characterized' by the dissolution of the bar between self and other, even though he is given, like Moran, to varieties of self-designation — 'I was distraught, who am so seldom distraught … I managed somehow. Being ingenious' (*T,* 20). But his self-designations do not have the neurotic stability even of Moran's, as he drifts from feeling to feeling, characteristic to characteristic, in an unstoppable series of self-performances. Molloy represents himself with confidence, even though he, and we as readers, are deprived of the sense of who is doing the representing. Molloy's selfhood consists in his productivity of facsimiles.

So we can see how, in *Molloy,* repetition inverts and undermines the very model of opposition which brings it into being, the opposition between original and copy, self and other. In this text, the priority of original over copy is difficult to maintain; like the Möbius strip, one side of the opposition turns out, when followed to its logical extreme, to be its own reverse side. It is a process which is imaged or repeated in Molloy's involved disquisition about the relative degrees of stiffening in his two legs: when his 'good leg' begins to stiffen, it actually feels worse than his 'bad leg', because he is not yet used to it. Good and bad, worse and better change places erratically:

I no longer had one bad leg plus another more or less good, but now both were equally bad. And the worse, to my mind, was that which till now had been good, at least comparatively good, and whose change for the worse I had not yet got used to. So in a way, if you like, I still had one bad leg and one good, or rather less bad, with this difference however, that the less bad now was the less good of heretofore. It was therefore on the old bad leg that I often longed to lean, between one crutchstroke and the next. For while still extremely sensitive, it was less so than the other, or it was equally so, if you like, but it did not seem so, to me, because of its seniority.

(*T,* 77)

The vision of time which emerges from *Molloy* is more complex than the terms set up in Beckett's essay on Proust allow. In that essay, the opposition is between formless 'decantation' and retrievable 'essence'. But the mutually defining relationship between Molloy and Moran sets up a time scale which leaves no place for the idea of original or present time. Time, and the present moments or states of which it is made up, is endlessly reimagined, so that the present moment not only repeats another moment belonging to the past, but reconstitutes that moment. In this model, present and past coexist indissolubly at every instant, in a repeatedly renewed totality. Deleuze evokes this Bergsonian vision of time via the work of Proust:

Combray resurfaces not as it was in the present, nor as it ever could have been, but in a splendour which was never experienced, as a pure past which finally reveals its double irreducibility, not only to the present which it was, but also to the actual present which it might have been, in favour of a telescoping of the two.

(*DR,* 115)

Indeed, Deleuze goes further still, to imagine another kind of repetition. The totalizing synthesis offered in Bergson and Proust, he argues, comprehends differences 'but only as differences between levels or degrees' (*DR,* 374), that is to say, risks leaving intact a model in which states of being are conceived as simple and permanent. Deleuze moves towards a vision of a third kind of repetition in time, 'in which grounding dissolves into groundlessness, in which Ideas are detached from the forms of memory, and the displacement and disguise of repetition are joined with divergence and decentring as powers of difference' (ibid.). This perhaps provides a way of accounting for the resistance to totality and grounded difference which is offered by Beckett's temporal repetitions in *Molloy*. Because it is a model that resists totalization, it suggests that a single text, even a dual text, like *Molloy,* will never answer the purpose of the writer seeking to write (in) time, but will always require the supplementarity of further texts. The next chapter will consider the question of this supplementarity in the rest of the Trilogy.

Chapter 4

Centre, Line, Circumference:
Repetition in the Trilogy

Malone Dies

If *Molloy* shows us the paradoxical relationship of two subjects who are both subordinated to each other and yet possess autonomy, 'two separate and immanent dynamisms related by no system of synchronisation' (*PTD,* 17), then *Malone Dies* seems to turn away from the problems of duality. In this novel, one character appears to be in control of the narrative. We are lodged firmly in Malone's mind, just as firmly as he is lodged, dying, in his bed, and in his room. There are no alternative testimonies available. It is as though, after the problematic doublings of *Molloy,* Beckett were looking for some means of fixing and containing the disruptive play of repetition, to bring about, in the reduced conditions of *Malone Dies,* a narrative that will be single and identical with itself.

There is, in fact, an extraordinary note of optimism at the beginning of the novel about the possibility of bringing off such a perfect fusion of form and content, narrator and narrative. 'This time I know where I am going', Malone informs us (*T,* 180). This optimism seems to come from Malone's sense that he no longer has to tell stories about anything in particular, but can just tell stories. This objectless narrative is what he calls 'play', and he contrasts it with the more responsible activities of his former self, when he sought to play with real people, in the light:

> I turned on all the lights, I took a good look all round, I began to play with what I saw. People and things ask nothing better than to play, certain animals too. All went well at first, they all came to me, pleased that someone should want to play with them. If I said, Now I need a hunchback, immediately one came running, proud as punch of his fine hunch that was going to perform.

(*T,* 180)

This is a project that relies upon repetition. But Malone has clearly found this realistic project impossible to fulfill. He has ended up 'abandoned' and forced to struggle on in a world where no forms exist any longer, only 'shapelessness and speechlessness, incurious wandering, darkness, long stumbling with outstretched arms, hiding' (*T*, 181).

The escape from repetition on the one hand, and formlessness on the other, seems to be the activity of playing, the creation of a world of characters and forms which will be sufficient in themselves. Strikingly, Malone intends to finish, not with a story, but with that most inert of forms, an inventory of the material things in his possession. Malone's model of non-repetitive narration and his conception of the different stages of his writing seem to take us back to the three zones of Murphy's mind, the light, the half-light and the dark. The first zone seems to be the zone of Lockean ideas, mental forms deriving from and dependent on the sensuous experience of the objective world, though also, in a sense, able to supplement it; they are 'the forms with parallel, a radiant abstract of the dog's life, the elements of physical experience available for a new arrangement' (*Murphy*, 78). This is a world where repetition gives the pleasure of reversal and revenge: 'here the kick that the physical Murphy received, the mental Murphy gave. It was the same kick, but corrected as to the direction' (p. 78). In the second zone of the half-light, Murphy is able to conceive forms which are entirely abstract, or not dependent on repetition. These are the 'forms without parallel', images, conceptions and feelings which are not representations or compensations. The absolute self-sufficiency of this world means that it is not dependent in any sense on 'originals' elsewhere: 'this system had no other mode in which to be out of joint and therefore did not need to be put right in this' (p. 79).

These two conditions seem to be repeated in Malone's opening commentary. When he used to 'play', Malone inhabited a world of parallels, similar to Murphy's first zone, in which imagination was dependent upon the objective forms that could be summoned into the light. Malone seems to be proposing to commit himself to the 'Belacqua bliss' of the second zone of Murphy's mind, to a narrative in which the forms, if not strictly 'without parallel' (they are a man, a woman and a stone), are abstract, and not dependent upon the imperative of plausible representation.

For Malone and for Murphy there exists a third zone, a zone in which there are no longer either representations or pure forms. In this zone it is impossible even to conceive of self-identical forms, since it consists of pure becoming, a chaos of unstable difference, 'nothing but commotion, and the pure forms of commotion' (*Murphy,* 79). Where this is the acme of blissful impersonality for Murphy, it is something to be feared for Malone, as 'earnestness' that is liable to lead him back to the predicament of existence. For the time being, he prefers the non-repetitive autonomy of narrative as play, art without an object. Malone's project recalls not only *Murphy* but also some of the views about abstraction, which Beckett projects in the *Dialogues with Georges Duthuit,* and especially in the discussion of Bram van Velde. There Beckett argues that the most advanced modern art has turned away from all 'occasions', not only in the external world, but also the 'occasion' of self-reflection, in which the work takes itself or the artistic process as object (*PTD,* 121–2). The eschewal of the object is an eschewal of the repetitive function of art, and it may be that this parallels Malone's desire for narrative play.[1]

But the reasons for Malone's rejection of an art of reference, or occasion, are more than merely theoretical. He is, after all, about to die. As such, he has to find a way of living with the awareness of imminent nothingness, a way of comprehending non-being. Beckett attempts to show this non-being in writing, in a way that crosses the barrier separating language from death, the barrier insisting that, though death may be spoken *of* in language, it can never be spoken. Malone has to find a way to inhabit and to speak his own death; and he does this by using language, not to embody himself, but to repudiate himself. Though it is only at the end of his narrative that he resolves no longer to say 'I', in one sense the whole of his narrative enacts this abstention.[2] He decides that he will be inside his stories but separate from them, and that they will be unlike him in every possible respect. In this way, Malone can be present and absent at the same time; as the deviser of everything that we read, he will remain in control, but the narrative will form no part of him.

However, though he congratulates himself repeatedly on having devised narratives that do not resemble him ('nothing is less like me than this patient, reasonable child' [*T,* 193]), Malone is frequently disconcerted by leakages of self-consciousness into his narrative, fretting for example about the 'gull's eyes' he has given Saposcat, which remind him of 'an old shipwreck' (obviously Murphy, who has eyes of a gull's grey-blue), and, on another occasion, wondering anxiously 'if I am not talking yet again about myself. Shall I be incapable, to the end, of lying on any other subject?' (*T*, 189). Malone's very refusal to inhabit his stories is echoed within them, for Saposcat, like Malone himself, spends much of his time 'with his mind elsewhere, or blank' (*T*, 187). At times, Malone seems to try out his own death in his stories. The calm dignity of his description of the mule's burial by Lambert seem to embody some of Malone's own longing for the composure of death, and even the details of the slaughter-yard altercation seem to recapitulate the terms of relationship, or non-relationship, that Malone posits between his stories and their author: 'There they sat, the table between them, in the gloom, one speaking, the other listening, and far removed, the one from what he said, the other from what he heard, and far from each other' (*T*, 213).

These unconscious repetitions multiply. In musing about Mrs Lambert's discouragement from the task of sorting her pile of lentils, Malone might be considering his own narrative, and the difficulty of keeping it pure from the contamination of self:

> She could have gone on sorting her lentils all night and never achieved her purpose, which was to free them from all admixture. But in the end she would have stopped, saying, I have done all I can do. But she would not have done all she could have done. But the moment comes when one desists, because it is the wisest thing to do, discouraged, but not to the extent of undoing all that has been done. But what if her purpose, in sorting the lentils, were not to rid them of all that was not lentil, but only of the greater part, what then? I don't know. Whereas there are other tasks, other days, of which one may fairly safely say that they are finished, though I do not see which.
>
> (*T*, 214–15)

Something like the image of the pile of lentils recurs a few pages later in Malone's narrative, but with some significant changes: he now imagines the gradual dissolution of himself and the mysterious 'other' who inhabits him as 'two little heaps of finest sand, or dust, or ashes, of unequal size, but diminishing together as it were in ratio, if that means anything' (*T,* 223). A little later, the image recurs, again with a modification; instead of being an image of a chaos which is gradually sorted and separated, the pile suggests the inevitable adulteration of the self: 'I see us again as we are, namely to be removed grain by grain until the hand, wearied, begins to play, scooping us up and letting us trickle back into the same place, dreamily as the saying is' (*T,* 225). Now Malone is no longer in the position of Mrs Lambert, sorting the heap, but is himself the object of the hand's 'play', feeling the sensation 'of a blind and tired hand delving feebly in my particles and letting them trickle between its fingers' (*T,* 225).

The relationship of priority between these repeated images is difficult to assign. Though, in one sense, the image of Mrs Lambert sorting and sweeping together the lentils is a derivation from Malone's own predicament, and visualization of it, it could be said that, in another sense, his sensation derives from the image in his story. This reversibility is a recurrence of that kind of repetition that we saw at work in *Molloy,* in which two mutually-resembling elements remind us irresistibly one of the other, but it is difficult to say which of them is the original and which is the copy. This insistent repetition seems to come about because of the necessity of representing even the activity of non-representation: in order to hold back from or obliterate repetition it is necessary in some way to image or repeat that imaginative activity.

The most salient fact about Malone's life, or the end of his life, is that he spends it writing. Malone worries about whether his pencil is going to last out, wonders where he has got his exercise book from, and at one point actually does lose both pencil and exercise book. Despite the feeling of spoken immediacy which the text gives, it is in reality very far from an interior monologue, for we are reminded repeatedly of what, in *The Unnamable,* is called 'the manual aspect of that bitter folly' (*T,* 303), the uncomfortable and difficult materiality of writing. Writing, for Malone, is a means of retrieving and objectifying evanescent words. It is in order 'to know where I have got to' (*T,* 208) that Malone writes, and he comforts himself with the reassuring exteriority of writing — 'I really know practically nothing about his family any more. But that does not worry me, there is a record of it somewhere. It is the only way to keep an eye on him' (*T,* 208). Clearly, writing, as well as being an expressive medium, allows a partition or abnegation of self, which accords well with Malone's desire not to be in his narration. This seems to anticipate Derrida's diagnosis of the difference between speech and writing, in which speech is the sign of 'full' and present selfhood, while writing is the means and the symptom of self-division and plurality in the self. These qualities of writing come from its repeatability, its constitutive capacity to yield itself up unchanged for scrutiny, or rememoration; this repeatability seems to double itself, for it depends upon the fact that writing is, in the first place, the repetition of speech.[3]

Writing would seem therefore to occupy the position of voluntary memory, for Beckett, guaranteeing a kind of continuity through repeatability; if words and feelings are not retrievable, then the graphical repetitions or representations of those words and feelings surely are. But Malone does not seem to be able to rely quite so implicitly on writing. He seems only rarely to reread what he has written, and therefore is not able to take advantage of the retrievability that writing offers. This is dramatized in the physical difficulties that he experiences in writing: 'I have a short memory. My little finger glides before my pencil across the page and gives warning, falling over the edge, that the end of the line is near. But in the other direction, I mean of course vertically, I have nothing to guide me' (*T, 207*).

In fact, writing does not have the fixed, material self-sufficiency on which Malone pins his hopes. His narrative always seems in some way insufficient, always seems to point back to him as its originator or agent. Just as we have got used to the fact that everything we read is in Malone's exercise-book, he tells us that he has lost it: 'I fear I must have fallen asleep again. In vain I grope, I cannot find my exercise-book. But I still have the pencil in my hand. I shall have to wait for day to break. God knows what I am going to do till then' (*T*, 209).

Where are these words being written, if not in the exercise book? All of the hypotheses which we may generate to explain this fact rely on some sort of problematic doubling. Perhaps Malone has another exercise-book in which he can write about the loss of the first? Perhaps these words are not being written at the moment of their utterance, but later, after the recovery of the exercise-book, in a bogus present tense (in which case, how can we tell which present tenses are literal and which figurative)? Perhaps these words are actually being written by another, a witness, or stenographer, or someone else who is adopting Malone's voice and character? Of course, if the title page of the novel is to be believed this last is exactly the case. And if 'Samuel Beckett' is the other which these words seem to require to exist, then where are the words being written? It is disconcerting to discover that, as with many of Beckett's works, the words were in fact originally written *in an exercise book* rather like the one that Malone describes:

> It is ruled in squares. The first pages are covered with ciphers and other symbols and diagrams, with here and there a brief phrase. Calculations, I reckon. They seem to stop suddenly, prematurely at all events. As though discouraged. Perhaps it is astronomy, or astrology. I did not look closely. I drew a line, no, I did not even draw a line, and I wrote, Soon I shall be quite dead at last, and so on, without even going on to the next page, which was blank.
>
> $(T, 209–10)^4$

What Malone does not reveal, is that the exercise-book contains the last pages of *Watt;* Beckett did indeed begin *L'Absent,* as the novel was originally called, at the end of the manuscript of *Watt.* We should be cautious, however, of seeing this as a grounding of the fiction in the solidity of fact. The description is not an 'exact' one, and even if it were, would still be a fictionalization. In fact, to see the exercise-book in the Humanities Research Center at Austin as identical with the exercise-book in *Malone Dies* is, in a curious way, to project the 'actual' exercise book as a repetition of the 'original' described in the novel.

The paragraph in which Malone describes the loss of his exercise-book could of course be a lie. Malone seems to admit this possibility a little later: 'I have just written, I fear I must have fallen, etc. I hope this is not too great a distortion of the truth' (p. 209). This is one of the rare moments when Malone seems to have reread or at least to have recapitulated something that he has written, but the repetition leads to other difficulties. It is not clear what element of what he has written may be a 'distortion of the truth', whether it is the claim that he has fallen asleep again, that he has lost his exercise book, or that he has, in fact, even *written* 'I fear I must have fallen, etc.'. Malone proposes to add 'a few lines' to what he has written, even though he has nothing to write on and his position thus resembles, in a comically literal way, the plight of the artist as Beckett describes it in his second Dialogue with Georges Duthuit, having 'nothing with which to express, nothing from which to express, no power to express, no desire to express, together with the obligation to express' (*PTD,* 103).

Like the paradox of the Cretan liar, this passage of the text sets up a restless alternation between the linguistic and metalinguistic levels. Malone is using his words not only to represent himself and his meanings, but also to represent his own words. If Malone's problem is, in one sense, that he cannot sufficiently abolish himself *into* his text, it is, in another sense, that he cannot sufficiently escape from it. His editorial commentary on his text fails to maintain the gap between it and the text: 'I write about myself with the same pencil and in the same exercise-book as about him' (p. 208).

Not surprisingly, Malone's narrative turns out to repeat many of his own preoccupations with the physical activity of writing. The passages about his exercise book and pencil are followed almost immediately by a passage describing the Saposcats' anxieties about the pen they are planning to give their son before his examination. The whole passage has an extraordinary deadpan solemnity, as the two parents painfully elaborate all the possible arrangements for making sure that Saposcat appreciates the gift and is also stimulated by it to perform well in the examination. Malone shows himself to be a better narrator than he knows in rendering this conversation. If there is disdain for the absurd petit-bourgeois frettings of the Saposcats ('One day Mr Saposcat sold himself a fountain pen at a discount') there is also a wry sympathy, as in the account of Mr Saposcat's tight-lipped irritation at his wife's persistence about the size of the pen's nib (*T,* 211). The narrative begins in detachment, but, as often in Malone's narrative, detachment allows a kind of absorption and Malone proves to be speaking of himself obliquely all the way through it. Sapo's fountain pen is another version of Malone's dwindling pencil, with Sapo's impending examination corresponding to Malone's ordeal of narrative. The anxiety of the Saposcats about their son's familiarity with his nib seems to be a displacement of Malone's worry about his pencil lasting out, and, more particularly, about his capacity to bring his writing and his death into synchronization.

Malone's preoccupation with his writing implements results in other unconscious repetitions in his narrative. At the end of his narrative, in his dying delirium, Malone confuses Lemuel's hatchet with his pencil and his stick (*T,* 289). The logic behind the association between the pencil and the hatchet is obvious enough, for Malone is using his pencil to summon up and then to kill his fictional surrogates. Malone's pencil has already been associated with his stick, for, just as he uses his stick to bring his possessions towards him and, in fantasy, to make good his escape from the room, so he uses his pencil to call his possessions to mind and to escape in imagination from his death bed. His stick is also used at one point to retrieve his exercise-book (*T,* 209). Later on, the stick is lost, but seems to reappear shortly afterwards in the tightly rolled umbrella with which his mysterious visitor strikes him; this umbrella, like the stick and the pencil, is potentially a lethal instrument, though, unlike the pencil, it has 'a long sharp point' (*T,* 272). The pencil therefore seems to follow Malone in splitting itself off into a series of surrogates and simulacra.[5]

At the end of the narrative, it looks as though Malone is going to have just enough time to collapse narrative and narration together, killing off his creatures at the exact moment of his own dissolution. But the narrative refuses the triumphant merging of frame with interior and artist with work that is to be found at the end of *To the Lighthouse,* with the synchrony of Lily Briscoe's final brush stroke and the fulfillment of the long-deferred trip to the lighthouse, and instead presents the reader with an extended stammer, in which the various repetitive elements of the series refuse to join into absolute identity:

> Lemuel is in charge, he raises his hatchet on which the blood will never dry, but not to hit anyone, he will not hit anyone, he will not hit anyone any more, he will not touch anyone any more, either with it or with it or with it or with or
>
> or with it or with his hammer or with his stick or with his fist or in thought in dream I mean never he will never
>
> or with his pencil or with his stick or
>
> (*T,* 289)

If Malone has turned aside from the first of Murphy's zones in favour of a narrative based on the second, based, that is, on a narrative of self-sufficient, non-repetitive forms, he ends up with a narrative in which the hesitation between original and copy, world and mind, narrative and narration is fundamental and irreducible. There is no consummation to be hoped for in this literary death, since it is a dying into multiplicity and uncertainty, rather than an achievement of the 'blessedness of absence'. All Malone's attempts to partition and seclude the self from his narrative prove to be fruitless, as, despite all precautions, his narrative insistently repeats his own life and death.

The Unnamable

Despite all the typographical histrionics, there is no end for Malone, for his voice, or a voice like his, resumes, almost immediately for the reader turning the page of the Trilogy, in *The Unnamable*. Where there is continuity, there is also gap. *Malone Dies* ends with near-hysteria but *The Unnamable* begins with a series of slow, grudging questions: 'Where now? Who now? When now?', which answer themselves in the prescription of a new task for the narrator: 'I, say I' (*T,* 293). The injunction here is in distinct contradiction to Malone's declaration in his final moments, 'That is the end of me. I shall say I no more' (*T,* 285). The narrator of *The Unnamable* returns repeatedly in the first half of the book to this determination to articulate the self, and, unlike Malone, to have nothing to do with substitutes, claiming that 'it is now I shall speak of me, for the first time. I thought I was right in enlisting these sufferers of my pains. I was wrong ... There, now there is no one here but me ... these creatures have never been, only I and this black void have ever been' (*T,* 305–6). In one sense, the voice shares Malone's ambition, for, like him, it tries to eschew repetition. But, whereas Malone tries to create a narrative world which will not be a repetition of his own, and therefore will be empty of him, the voice, recognizing that fictional surrogates are always false repetitions, is trying to separate itself from these repetitions and establish itself as autonomous and original. Malone's gaze is fixed on the simulacrum, the voice's on itself as original.

The problem is that the voice cannot seem to find a way to proceed that does not lead it back into repetition. As so often, the very denials which the voice utters in the first pages of *The Unnamable* have the structure of repetition, for they seem to shadow the opening of *Malone Dies*. In both texts there is a deceptive, if rather cautious straightforwardness: 'I shall pay less heed to myself, I shall be neither hot nor cold any more … I shall not be alone, in the beginning. I am of course alone. Alone. That is soon said' (*T,* 180, 294). But where Malone has been systematic, promising himself that he will tell three stories and dividing them according to their subject matter, people, animals and things, the voice in *The Unnamable* rejects system from the very beginning: 'People with things, people without things, things without people, what does it matter, I flatter myself it will not take me long to scatter them' (*T,* 294). The beginning of *The Unnamable* is therefore tense with the repudiated presence of Malone, the one that the speaker is and yet is no longer. As though to complete this repudiation, Malone is summoned up, reduced, and yet with a ghostly persistence, into the vault where the voice imagines itself sitting (*T,* 294).[6]

The voice begins by refusing to believe in its narrations and by negating every position, in 'affirmations and negations invalidated as uttered, or sooner or later' (*T,* 293). But it is not long before the voice discovers that it cannot do without the narrative fabrications which it despises, for it is necessary repeatedly to invoke these inauthentic simulacra in order to exorcise them. The voice is therefore soon left, like Malone, to multiply stories of characters who repeat and displace its own experience. Simply to think is to slip 'towards the resorts of fable' (*T,* 310). Within a few pages of its beginning, the voice has invented the name 'Basil', to designate all those words, ideas, feelings and concepts which seem to come from outside its real, authentic self. Basil quickly becomes Mahood, just as Sapo becomes Macmann in Malone's narrative, and, even as the voice congratulates itself on 'expunging' Mahood's voice from its own, it finds itself contemplating the possibility of Mahood's insidious return, in the very necessity of speaking, with the encrusting falsifications that language brings with it: 'still today, as he would say, though he plagues me no more his voice is there, in mine, but less, less. And being no longer renewed it will disappear one day, I hope, from mine completely. But in order for that to happen I must speak, speak' (*T,* 311). Speaking is precisely what lets Mahood back in, for language is the place where all the artificial stories of time and identity are endlessly recirculated. Speaking is the only means available for knowing the self, but, at the same time it only ever allows the articulation of a borrowed self, since one can never speak with one's own voice: 'It is not mine, I have none, I have no voice and I must speak, that is all I know, it's round that I must revolve, of that I must speak, with this voice that is not mine, but can only be mine, since there is no one but me, or if there are others, to whom it might belong, they have never come near me' (*T*, 309). The voice moves, therefore, from affirmation to negation-by-repetition, seeking the terms of a 'pensum' which it can repeat and thereby free itself from the ordeal of repetition. However, this pensum can only be a preliminary, it seems, to the 'lesson' that must subsequently be repeated, 'before I have the right to stay quiet in my corner' (*T*, 213-13). The voice can only hope to find its origin and identity by an act of non-orientation.

Presence and repetition, the new and the familiar, are therefore hard to distinguish in *The Unnamable,* since every new thing is likely to seem like a repetition, though without the sense of security or continuity that might be hoped for from this:

> If only I knew what I had been saying. Bah, no need to worry, it can only have been one thing, the same as ever. I have my faults, but changing my tune is not one of them ... if I could remember what I have said I could repeat it, if I could learn something by heart I'd be saved, I have to keep on saying the same thing and each time it's an effort, the seconds must be alike and each one is infernal.
>
> (*T*, 337, 399)

The voice seeks to multiply its positions, admitting the necessity of generating another narrative, in order to find the self through negation: 'There's no getting rid of them without naming them and their contraptions, that's the thing to keep in mind. I might as well tell another of Mahood's stories and no more about it.... That's an idea. To heighten my disgust' (*T*, 328–9). This enables the voice to be and not to be at once, to reject its narratives as it recites them, by reminding us and itself that the voice is not its own, but that of another ('Mahood dixit'). This kind of multiplication of position is dangerous, too; for the denial brings into being the possibility of another personality, who is doing the denying, a personality which may be as inauthentically *en-soi* as Mahood. The process of regression becomes more and more apparent as the voice continues speaking of and denying the relationship between itself and Basil, Mahood and subsequent impersonations, with every affirmation a denial, and every denial an unwilling affirmation:

> But Worm cannot note. There at least is a first affirmation, I mean negation, on which to build. Worm cannot note. Can Mahood note? That's it, weave, weave. Yes, it is the characteristic, among others, of Mahood to note, even if he does not always succeed in doing so, certain things, perhaps I should say all things, so as to turn them to account, for his governance. And indeed we have seen him do so, in the yard, in his jar, in a sense. I knew I had only to try and talk of Worm to begin talking of Mahood, with more felicity and understanding than ever.
>
> (*T,* 342)

Worrying that it too may come to consist merely in the weaving movement between surrogate characters, the voice begins to fall back into the idea that it might achieve full selfhood, not by denying its surrogates, but by embracing or incorporating them; in an exact repetition of their words and substance, it hopes, full being may be found. But this possibility is not a serious one, either, for the fact that the voice *is* repeating an earlier voice means that there is a tiny but irreducible difference in the 'naked' repetition that it desires, a delay between the voice it quotes and its quotation of it: 'I shall submit, more corpse-obliging than ever. I shall transmit the words as received, by the ear, or roared through a trumpet into the arsehole, in all their purity, and in the same order, as far as possible. This infinitesimal lag, between arrival and departure, this trifling delay in evacuation, is all I have to worry about' (*T,* 352).

A similar kind of difficulty attends the voice's attempts to repeat itself by being another, the mysterious, impalpable Worm. Worm is a kind of replica of the voice; he occupies a vault of indeterminate size, surrounded by grey light, weeps ceaselessly and is watched patiently by his masters, who wait for him to come to life. Worm comes out of an attempt to find a new sort of character. The voice reasons to itself that, if all the other adopted surrogates are false and unsatisfactory in being too positive, then it will attempt to be itself by identifying itself with a surrogate who is almost entirely negative, in being formless and place-less. But the very action of imagining Worm, even as negation, makes him (Worm) a kind of positive, as he comes to occupy a physical space, and to possess a rudimentary kind of physical being. At this point Worm ceases to match the voice, which denies that it has a voice, or body, or place, and so the voice refuses to see him as an authentic rep-etition. As such, Worm comes to seem merely a repetition of the other characters whom the voice sees as temptations: 'Mahood won't get me out, nor Worm either, they set great store on Worm, to coax me out, he was something new, different from all the others, meant to be, perhaps he was, to me they're all the same' (*T,* 381). In order to be able to proj-ect itself as Worm, to want to recognize itself in Worm, the voice has to repeat itself, and it is this necessity of repetition which opens up the invalidating distance between it and its image: 'I'm Worm, no, if I were Worm I wouldn't know it, I wouldn't say it, I wouldn't say anything, I'd be Worm' (*T,* 350). The complexity of repetition here runs together affirmation and negation, making them difficult to distinguish, and confirming Beckett's own judgement that 'la négation n'est pas pos-sible. Pas plus que l'affirmation'.[7]

The voice seems to arrive at the same paradox in whatever direction it turns. If it attempts to live apart from repetitions, to discover its sin-gular selfhood, then, like Malone, it discovers itself to be constituted in the midst of a shadowy dance of repetitions, its very words the repeti-tions of others', its selfhood only imaginable and expressible as simula-tion. If, on the other hand, it attempts to use the principle of repetition to constitute and sustain itself, then it is similarly disappointed, be-cause it inhabits a world in which exact repetition is impossible; every attempt to identify itself utterly in repetition leaves some infinitesimal residue of difference unaccounted for, a residue that points back to the originating self. Neither abstention from or identification with repeti-tion can enable the self to 'say I.'

Under these circumstances, it is very difficult to speak of the voice as existing anywhere but in the movement of play between the differ-ent versions of itself — or in the action of repetition itself rather than in what is being repeated. This sense of being-between is itself dramatised by the voice, and, as always, it has to resort to the approximations of metaphor to speak of it:

> In at one ear and incontinent out through the mouth, or the other ear, that's possible too. No sense in multiplying the occasions of error. Two holes and me in the middle, slightly choked. Or a single one, entrance and exit, where the words swarm and jostle like ants, hasty, indifferent, bringing nothing, taking nothing away, too light to leave a mark.
>
> (*T,* 357–8)

Later on the voice imagines itself as the partition separating two areas of being, 'two surfaces and no thickness, perhaps that's what I feel, myself vibrating, I'm the tympanum, on the one hand the mind, on the other the world, I don't belong to either' (*T,* 386). It is this congenital transitionality which prevents the voice in *The Unnamable* from ever being satisfied with where it is in consciousness, language or story. It must always inhabit a 'space' which is a 'space between', always inside and outside its stories, signifier and signified, gazer and spectacle, original and copy, between the terms of all the other metaphorical polarities which are used to represent representation.[8] One might be tempted to identify the voice with language itself. Certainly, in the last thirty-five pages or so of *The Unnamable,* the voice seems progressively to lose its hold on the sense of what it is saying, and to allow language to speak through it, so that its *parole* comes increasingly to be possessed by its *langue* — 'I'm in words, made of words, others' words...' (*T,* 390). But even this comfortable identification is only partial. The voice's real position again appears to be in some space *between* being and language: 'I'm all these words, all these strangers, this dust of words, with no ground for their settling ... and nothing else, yes, something else ... something quite different, a quite different thing, a wordless thing in an empty place, a hard shut dry cold black place, where nothing stirs, nothing speaks' (*T,* 390).

At the end of the narrative, the speaker comes to a kind of conclusion, but does not close off this alternation of 'I' and 'not-I'. The narrative closes with repeated images of transition, those of a threshold and door; these images again function like Derrida's hymen, for although they suggest penetration and arrival, the approach to some long-deferred, long-concealed truth, they also suggest a persistent interstitiality. This difference is maintained in a poem which Beckett wrote at about the same time as he was writing *L'Innommable,* 'Je suis le cours du sable qui glisse/My way is in the sand flowing', in which the speaker looks for some escape from the 'long shifting thresholds' of his life, but can only produce the image of a door, which suggests both closure and the continuing fluctuation between extremes. The final image of the poem, like the last words of *The Unnamable*, creates a hymeneal suture between cessation and continuance:

> my peace is there in the receding mist
> when I may cease from treading these long shifting thresholds
> and live the space of a door
> that opens and shuts
>
> (*CPEF*, 57)

Centre, Line, Circumference: The Novellas

If *Murphy* was a novel that could proclaim that it had 'nothing new' to offer, then the tension between novelty and repetition is much greater in *The Unnamable*, with its desperate, unprecedented reiterativeness. This is a novel that depends from the outset on an awareness of the novels that have preceded it, which it tries to forget and supersede, but seems in the end only able to repeat.

The Unnamable is linked to the novels which come before it as what Derrida calls a 'supplement', an addition to or repetition of an original which confirms and completes it and yet also opens up in it areas of uncertainty and deficiency.[9] That *The Unnamable* didn't originally form part of Beckett's plans for the connected sequence is indicated by the 'premonition' that Molloy has in beginning to write his account. In the English version of *Molloy*, he promises himself 'this time, then once more I think, then perhaps a last time' (p. 8). The French version does not have the last phrase. This can be explained by the fact that, when writing the French version, Beckett apparently did not envisage a third novel in the sequence, but that, when translating *Molloy* into English, he knew that there already *had been* a third time through for his transforming narrator.[10]

If *The Unnamable* is a supplement to *Malone Dies, Malone Dies* is itself a supplement to *Molloy*. The movement that is suggested is a recession away from originality into more and more degraded or in-ferior versions. What contradicts this is the fact that the narrator of *The Unnamable* sees itself as original, claiming that the others who have preceded it in the series are crude, inaccurate facsimiles, who have 'made me waste my time, suffer for nothing, speak of them, when, in order to stop speaking, I should have spoken of me and of me alone' (*T,* 305). In one sense, then, *The Unnamable* could be considered as the master-text of the Trilogy, the centre from which all the other nar-ratives radiate; this would put the elusive 'I' of the novel in the middle of a network of surrogates that would include Molloy, Moran, Malone, Saposcat, Macmann, Basil, Mahood and Worm. Such a conception proves difficult to maintain in any absolute sense.

The image that is used often in the Trilogy, as it is in *Watt,* to explore the relationship of ontological supremacy and subordination is that of a circle, with its centre and circumference. The voice in *The Unnamable* imagines itself as occupying the centre of its vault, with other characters wheeling round it like heavenly bodies round the fixed earth of the medieval cosmos. But, though the voice concludes that 'the best is to think of myself as fixed and at the centre of this place' (*T,* 297), it also concedes that 'nothing is less certain than this fact', recognizing that being circled by Malone need not imply its own fixity, but could indicate that both are in motion. The image of the centre of the circle is a suggestive one. A centre forms part of the circle that it occupies even as it represents its inner, originating principle. But, as the latter, the centre is also, in a sense, outside the circle, as the still point where all is at rest, with no extension in either of the circle's two dimensions.[11]

The voice in *The Unnamable* is not able to conceive itself securely either as centre or circumference. For one thing, the centre is in some ways a disadvantageous position, for it does not allow its occupant to face all ways at once. For this reason, the voice wonders whether it wouldn't in fact be better off at the circumference. At the same time, in its claim that it is 'absent' from the actual place which it occupies, and which exists for and around it, the voice does seem to occupy the paradigmatic position of the centre.

But the centre/circumference opposition is not a stable one, as Watt has discovered. The opposition designates a fluid and continuously renewed relationship rather than a fixed pair of positions. The voice wonders whether its 'real' position is not somewhere in between the centre and the circumference, but in fact it is in both positions and neither at once, for every 'centre' may also be part of some other circumference, called into being from another centre. This is dramatized later on in the narrative when the voice imagines Worm, seated on a mound in a vault, the object of perception by others who are gathered in a ring around him (pp. 358–60). The voice is surprised that automatically, as it were, Worm has been centred by being the object of perception. And this alternative centre places the voice at the periphery, among the watchers.

The problem with the centre/circle metaphor is precisely that it is a metaphor, which attempts to account for the processes of duplication by duplication; the metaphor is an attempt on the voice's part to describe its own position *in* its story, while being, at the same time, an imaging of the speaker's relationship *to* its story. The metaphor does not allow a satisfactory distance to be established between it and the story, whose terms it repeats, does not offer any vantage point outside the spatial metaphors of the story from which to understand the story. The continual attempts to recoil or withdraw from the story, to set up a line or division between story and reflection upon it, never succeed, because the line of division and the attempt at recoil are drawn back into the story. Metatextual repetition reverses each time into textual repetition.

This abolition of the sense of centre has similar consequences for *The Unnamable's* relationship to the other books in the Trilogy. Despite its claims to be different and apart from the narrators and texts that precede it, *The Unnamable* is continuous with them in two distinct senses. Firstly, for all its self-consciousness, the voice repeats all the errors of identification and false identification that are to be found in *Molloy* and *Malone Dies*. Secondly, its very attempt to repudiate these errors is also a repetition of earlier repudiations, and its fraught relationship with these earlier texts is a repetition of the fraught relationships between different levels of narrative within those texts, not to mention the attempts in these earlier texts to repudiate other, earlier texts. Thus, the famous rejection of 'all these Murphys, Molloys and Malones' in *The Unnamable* is a repetition of a similar moment of repudiation in *Malone Dies:* 'But let us leave these morbid matters and get on with that of my demise, in two or three days if I remember rightly. Then it will be all over with the Murphys, Merciers, Molloys, Morans and Malones, unless it goes on beyond the grave' (*T,* 236–7). The first time that Malone names himself in his narrative is to reject himself. Reading this passage after reading *The Unnamable,* or with it in mind, gives an uncanny sense of a quotation-in-advance of the later voice, which seems to pierce through the membrane separating it from Malone.

Though there are clear differences between *Malone Dies* and *The Unnamable,* not least in the contradictory desires with which they begin, Malone wanting to be absent from his narrative and the voice wanting to find a way of being present in its, these differences are also what draw the two texts together; for each narrator contradicts himself in similar ways, each text shows absence and presence as necessary parts of each other. Under these circumstances, it is hard to know what metaphors to use to express the relationship and difference between the two narratives. Each of the voices in the Trilogy, though it may have its distinctive characteristics, has to define itself against the interruption of other voices at various times. One of the most striking of these occurs at the beginning of Molloy's narrative, where Molloy is discussing the difficulties of beginning:

> I began at the beginning, like an old ballocks, can you imagine that? Here's my beginning. Because they're keeping it apparently. I took a lot of trouble with it. Here it is. It gave me a lot of trouble. It was the beginning, do you understand? Whereas now it's nearly the end. Is what I do now any better? I don't know. That's beside the point. Here's my beginning. It must mean something, or they wouldn't keep it. Here it is.
>
> (*T,* 8)

The reader's problem here is to decide what 'the beginning' is. The obvious answer is that it is the next paragraph, which begins 'This time, then once more I think'. These words, Molloy is telling us, were written at the beginning of his narrative, but are now prefaced by a paragraph added on after the rest of the narrative has been written, the paragraph we are now reading.

As it happens, there is some manuscript evidence that Beckett did in fact compose the first paragraph of the French version of *Molloy* last of all, or at a late stage, in any event, and added it to the inside cover of the exercise-book containing the text.[12] But this does not really resolve the problem, of course, which is one of structures and relationships within the fictional text. Here, it is difficult to be positive that Molloy means the second paragraph when he refers to his 'beginning'. The slightly anxious repetition of 'Here it is … Here's my beginning … here it is' seems to indicate that the beginning referred to may be the actual words that are being written and read at this moment — which are, of course, the 'real' beginning of the narrative. This would provide one explanation of the puzzling remark that the words are his 'beginning. Because they're keeping it apparently': this might mean, 'if you can read these words, it means they have kept them.'

Even more difficult to decide is what Molloy means by 'the end', or 'nearly the end'. The end of what? Molloy's narrative? Or the novel as a whole? (If it is this, then perhaps it is actually Moran speaking, as it were, contributing a preface to Molloy's narrative just as he is on the point of becoming Molloy.) But perhaps it is Malone speaking? (For him, it is, much more literally, 'nearly the end'.) Or perhaps 'the end' is the end of the Trilogy, with this as an early appearance of the voice of *The Unnamable?* It is not impossible that these opening remarks, in which we 'hear' the voice of Molloy most distinctively, actually are an adulteration or interference of voices, in which Molloy quotes or is quoted by a later voice. When the French version was written, of course, this could not have been meant, though, as we have seen, Beckett drew upon his subsequent knowledge of what lay in store for the reader and narrator in the English translation. Of course, once the English translation exists, with the possibility of 'overwriting' that it activates, this possibility is extended to the French version, too. In the light of the English translation, it becomes possible for the French version to incorporate the voice of the 'end' of the whole Trilogy at its beginning.

What makes these difficulties of relationship worse is that the narrators of the Trilogy constantly refer outside themselves to the other texts that precede it. As far as Malone and the voice in *The Unnamable* are concerned, the series of narrative impostures does not begin with

Molloy, but extends back at least as far as Murphy, and possibly even Belacqua. On a couple of occasions, Watt is mentioned (particularly odd, this, given that *Watt* was not published until some years after the Trilogy). There are also a number of references to the texts which were being written closest in time to the Trilogy, *Mercier and Camier* and the novellas, *The Expelled, The End, The Calmative* and *First Love*. These texts were Beckett's first forays into French in prose, and have generally been regarded as preliminary sketches for the Trilogy, as moons obediently orbiting its dominating mass.

However, the narrators of the Trilogy seem less sure of the distinction between them and the novellas. Molloy, as we have seen, 'remembers' setting forth in an oarless skiff, like the narrator of *The End;* but, since this narrator is presumably dead, it seems unlikely that Molloy and he are the same. There are other moments when the novellas are recalled in the Trilogy. The hat that Moran ties to his button seems to be inherited from the narrator of *The End,* who adopts a similar arrangement (Macmann, too, has his hat tied to his greatcoat). The narrator of *The Expelled* remembers being given a hat, which may be the same one that is mentioned in *First Love*. The greatcoat worn by nearly every male Beckett character makes an early appearance in *The Calmative* (*CSP,* 38).

Similarly, many of the events described in the novellas seem to foreshadow incidents in the Trilogy. The narrator of *The Calmative* hears the sound of a great owl hooting 'like a tocsin' in the woods (*CSP,* 38), which may be recalled by the gong that Molloy hears; the same narrator's entry into the city through the 'Shepherd's Gate', seems to be repeated in Molloy's entry into the city shortly after his encounter with the shepherd (*T,* 29–31); Molloy's reckless careering through the city causes the death of Lousse's dog (*T,* 32), which may remind us of the dangerous motion of the narrator of *The Expelled,* who brings down 'an old lady covered with spangles and lace who must have weighed about sixteen stone' (*CSP,* 41–2). The modes of motion of the narrators form a chain of repetitions and resemblances, with the 'reeling' of the narrator of *The Expelled* and the glimpse that the narrator of *The Calmative* catches of himself in a shop-window as 'a great cylinder sweeping past as though on rollers', along with his spiral ascent of the tower (*CSP,* 41–2), recalled in the Trilogy by Molloy's fear of going in a circle through the forest (*T,* 90), Malone's account of Macmann rolling through the rain (*T,* 246–7), Malone wheeling past in front of the speaker in *The Unnamable* and Mahood's spiral progress on his one leg. Molloy seems to undergo some of the same experiences as the characters in the novellas, for he is taken into a house, and subjected to compulsory welfare; Macmann, too, is taken in, like the narrators of *The Expelled* and *The End.*

All this might seem to indicate that these are earlier versions of the narrators in the Trilogy, or successive versions of a single self. This is re-inforced by Malone's memory of the possession of a little phial, which seems almost certainly to be the calmative given to the narrator of the earlier story (*CSP,* 256), the contents of which the narrator of *The End* seems to swallow. The speaker in *The Unnamable* seems to remember being one of these narrators, or at least writing one of the novellas, for it quotes the first few words of *The End,* as an example of 'the light touch' in writing (*T,* 314). The accumulation of these repetitions gives the sense, as Eric Levy puts it, that the stories 'are better considered as an indefinite series than as wholly independent narrations'.[13]

However, there are things to contradict the sense of indefinite se-ries. What is haunting about these stories is the way that they refuse to be definitely assigned to any fixed relationship with the Trilogy. If we see the stories as forming a group preliminary to the Trilogy — with the gradual erosion in them of narrative detail, and intensification of focus on the narrating 'I' — they also seem to form a triad which shad-ows or anticipates in itself the three stages of the Trilogy. The events described in the stories seem to mark the stages of a life, or, rather, a death, just as the Trilogy takes us from Moran, through the dying Molloy and Malone to the posthumous voice of *The Unnamable.* The events described in *First Love* have taken place in youth, or middle age, after the death of the narrator's father. In *The Expelled* and *The Calmative,* the narrator seems to tell stories from later in his life, when he has become stranger and more withdrawn from the world. In the last story, *The End,* the narrator takes us to the last moments before his death, as Malone does. It might be, therefore, that the stories should not be gathered together as a group and placed before the Trilogy, but rather interleaved with the Trilogy. So *First Love* and *The Expelled* might come between Moran's and Molloy's narratives (though another

place for *First Love* might be in the absent portion in Malone's narrative between Sapo's disappearance and Macmann's appearance), *The
Calmative* might be laid alongside Molloy's narration (or perhaps after
it), while *The End* would run parallel with *Malone Dies*. Certainly, the
last scenes in *The End* and *Malone Dies* seem to plait together very interestingly: the narrator of *The End* drifts out in a boat towards death,
surrounded by a vision of the mountains, while Malone, remembering
the hills of his childhood, imagines Lemuel and the others drifting out
into the bay.[14]

There are, of course, inconsistencies. The narrator of *The Calmative*
is, like Malone, 'alone' in his bed, telling himself stories to keep calm,
to keep from talking of his imminent death, 'for I'm too frightened this
evening to listen to myself rot' (*CSP*, 35); but, at the same time, he is
already dead, and therefore more like the narrator of *The Unnamable*,
both dead and alive, leading a facsimile life in his stories: 'is it possible that in this story I have come back to life, after my death? No,
it's not like me to come back to life, after my death' (*CSP*, 35). *The
Calmative* might, then, represent not so much a preface as an epilogue
to *Molloy* and *Malone Dies*. An additional complication comes from
the fact that Beckett suggested to John Fletcher alternative titles for
the stories which suggest a different order: *L'Expulsé* might be called
Prime, La Fin, Limbo and *Le Calmant, Death*'.[15] *La Fin* here seems to
precede *Le Calmant* (odd idea that it is, limbo certainly does seem to
precede death in the Trilogy). At least one writer has taken this to be
the order of the stories.[16]

Many critics have fallen back on biography in an attempt to stabilize the chronology of the series, even though what is at issue is the
relationship that the texts imply between themselves as fictions. Even
here, there are uncertainties. Beckett suggests, for example, that *Mercier
et Camier*, as his first attempt at a novel in French, 'could not have
preceded *Nouvelles*'. But there are no manuscripts for the stories before
October 1946, whereas *Mercier et Camier* had been largely completed
by September 1946. It is clear that *Premier Amour*, which, after its publication, Beckett made the first of the stories, was written after *Mercier
et Camier* and *L'Expulsé* (and perhaps also *Le Calmant;* see Admussen,
9). So in at least one case, the order of composition does not map on to
the narrative order in which the texts appear to be ranged.[17]

All this is complicated further by other factors. We are accustomed to think of Beckett's writing for the theatre as a sudden swerve away from the writing of fiction, as a 'relief' from it. But it is still something of a shock to remind oneself that *En Attendant Godot* was actually written between *Malone Meurt* and *L'Innommable,* and therefore represents another kind of enclosure within the Trilogy. Another play has to be stapled into a somewhat incongruous place, for manuscript evidence indicates that *Eleutheria* was written before *Molloy.*[18] Attempts to range Beckett's work in an orderly chronological sequence seem to indicate curious intersections and doublings-over, which match the discontinuities established between the works at the level of allusion and fictional parallel.

As if this weren't enough, the issue is complicated still further by the introduction of another sequence, the sequence of translations. In one sense a translation is just a repetition of the work that has already been done. But it is clear that, for Beckett, translation involves an intense and self-conscious act of reworking that it is hard to reduce to mere self-quotation. The English versions of the texts we are considering here were written in a rather different order from the French. *Molloy* was translated first, alongside some collaborative translations of *La Fin* and *L'Expulsé* with Richard Seaver (1953). Then followed *Malone Meurt* and *L'Innommable* (1954-8). It seems that the next text to be translated was *Le Calmant,* in order to make up the set for the English text in *No's Knife,* in 1967. *Mercier et Camier* was not translated until 1974, two years after *Premier Amour.* One result of this is that some works were being translated into English at the same time as very different works were being written in French. Since every text now has a double existence, in two languages and in two different places in Beckett's authorial chronology, it is even harder to assign an order of composition and priority. Although the chronological and fictional series are theoretically separate, sometimes the external factors of chronology combine with internal factors at the narrative level in the texts, to disturb this relationship; the English translation of *Molloy* both is and isn't aware of what is to follow it, and stands before and after *The Unnamable.*

It is surprising to find how uniformly critics of the Trilogy and its associated texts have pressed its play of repetition into the service of the

Same. Time and again, the distinctions between narrative levels and narrators are collapsed, to yield the image of a single, primal, underlying voice, and to make of the Trilogy 'a compendious abstract of all the novels that have ever been written, reduced to the most general terms'.[19] And regularly, the primal narrator is then identified with a universal human subject:

> each of the characters is interchangeable basically with any other and…each is consequently representative of man as such.
> Beneath the apparent complexity, is the archetypal storyteller. Beneath irrelevant associations is the human condition at its most elemental level.
> Their [Becketts characters'] condition transcends the boundaries of a single life, of a particular society, of a specific moment in history, to become the expression of man's universal fears, hopes, anxieties, desires and doubts.[20]

But Beckett's multiplication of repetitive inter(re)ference between the texts of the Trilogy and the novellas escapes any attempt to perform what, in an unfavourable review of a study of Proust, he called the 'creditable act of integration'. In this review, Beckett sneers at a literary critic's attempt to 'cook into unity' the complexity of Proust's *A la Recherche du Temps Perdu* and to restore to it a 'narrational trajectory that is more like a respectable parabola and less like the chart of an ague'. For Beckett, Proust's work consists in its involuted incompleteness, and his description of it anticipates suggestively his own work: 'The book is the search, stated in the full complexity of all its clues and blind alleys, for that resolution, and not the *compte rendu* after the event, of a round trip. His material, pulverized by time, obliterated by habit, mutilated in the clockwork of memory, he communicates as he can, in dribs and drabs' (*Disjecta*, 64, 65).

In the constellation of texts surrounding and including the Trilogy, there is no verifiable centre, to which every other portion of the sequence can be subordinated or related, nor any consistent, universal 'self'; all that we have are relationships, and especially relationships of repetition, resemblance and recall. What they have in common is not some essentially Beckettian quality, conceived as a continuous, informing essence, but a continuing inter-iterability, which divides them internally in the same ways in which they are divided from each other. Each text is merely a point of incision into a body of fiction which, once penetrated, will prove never to have been imaginable as a self-contained volume, but always to have been split and dispersed.

Chapter 5

Repetition and Self-Translation:
Mercier and Camier, First Love, The Lost Ones

Most of the writers who have turned their attention to the strange phenomenon of Beckett's self-translation have concentrated upon the extraordinary facility he displays in this, by all accounts, unenjoyable task. There has been some disagreement about such matters as the relative proportions of obscenity or humour in the French and English versions of his work, but most critics have stressed Beckett's uncanny ability to replicate the effects of the originals in his translations, reinventing puns, and compensating with new material for anything which resists translation. Most critics therefore feel that is safe to assume for Beckett an oeuvre consisting of a number of pairs of near-identical twins.[1]

It may be that there is more at stake in this than at first sight appears. The question of translation is intimately at one with the structures of repetition that guarantee the unity and integrity of texts. Indeed, for literary texts, translation, or translatability, is the promise and projection of identity, because to translate a text is to confirm that text as an original, with solidity, definition and presence (if only by demonstrating the ways in which translation must always fall short of it). In the case of Beckett, it is possible to see the translation of a work as something more than a disreputable shadowing of it. Instead, given their shared status as definitively authorized works, translation and original can be seen as organically continuous with one another, in a relationship that may in turn underwrite the identity of Beckett's entire oeuvre; as Tom Bishop puts it, 'the act of self-translation has given us the full texture of Beckett's oeuvre; each translation is not a superfluous addition, but an expansion of the work itself.[2] But what seems to underlie the metaphors of supplement and expansion alike is a sense of a unifying force or essence, which runs through and is repeatedly revealed in Beckett's works in French and English, but is not identical with them. For Derrida, the concept of translation is above all what maintains the possibility of the strict separation between form and content, and the metaphysical doctrine of the immunity of the signified from the signifier. 'In effect', he writes, 'the theme of a transcendental signified took shape within the horizon of an absolutely pure, transparent and unequivocal translatability. In the limits to which it is possible, or at least *appears* possible, translation practices the difference between signifier and signified.'[3]

All this depends upon translation considered as replication rather than as reproduction, 'naked' repetition rather than clothed repetition, or repetition with difference. Certainly, there is very close (though rarely complete) correspondence between the French and English versions of Beckett's texts where he has set about his translation immediately upon — or even, in some cases, before completion of the original.[4] But in cases where there is a time lag between the two versions there is considerable evidence in the translations of changes in outlook, stylistic priorities and attitude towards the originals, with a corresponding increase in disparity between original and translation.

The amount of variation is particularly great in the French versions of *Murphy* and *Watt* (the latter produced in collaboration with Ludovic and Agnes Janvier) and the English versions of *Mercier et Camier* and *Premier Amour;* and the translations of the novels of the Trilogy, which were also subject to some delay in being translated, show more variants than such texts as *Company* or *Ill Seen Ill Said*. A.R. Jones has shown how the alterations in the French *Murphy* seem to register Beckett's dissatisfaction with the first of his fictional self-embodiments,[5] and the English *Mercier and Camier* has a large number of revisions of the same kind. Many of these are due, no doubt, not only to the long gap between writing and translation, but also to the delay in publication of the original version. (*Mercier et Camier* was written in 1946 but not published until 1970. The English translation occupied Beckett from 1970 to 1974 and appeared in 1974. *Premier Amour* was written in October-November, 1946 and translated April-May, 1972. See Admussen, 66–8, 81, 52–3.) Examination of the revisions introduced in the translations of these texts in particular reveals more than just Beckett's barely-curbed irritation with his earlier work, however; for his exploitation of the implications of self-translation connects this exercise with the more general question of the successive reconstruction of the self in language and narrative. This means that the work Beckett performs upon his texts from the outside uncannily repeats the textual work of displacement which occurs on the inside of them. Such an interference of levels throws into doubt the idea of translation as a simple transfer of preformed significance, and requires instead a sense of what Derrida has described as 'a regulated transformation of one language by another, of one text by another' (*Positions*, 20).

The most obvious difference between the two texts of *Mercier and Camier* results from the amount of material that Beckett omits in the English. The omitted material varies from the odd line or phrase to two or three pages at a time, and amounts at a conservative estimate to a loss of about 12 per cent of the material in the French version. These losses are compensated for only by the addition of a few phrases here and there. A large proportion of the omissions seems to result from Beckett's impatience with passages which he considered simply ineffective. Thus, two pages of dialogue are lost early in the first chapter in which Mercier and Camier try to make sense of the commands of the park ranger;[6] and Beckett shows a tendency throughout to compress or drop altogether the more laborious passages of bewildered wrangling between the two. (See, for example, Minuit, 95–7, 121–4, 125–7; omitted, Calder, 60, 75.)

Beckett's excisions seem to have a thematic as well as a cosmetic purpose. Already, in the French version, Mercier and Camier are strangely cut off from the world of ordinary people and objects, hardly communicating and finding it easier to discard than to retain possessions. Beckett intensifies this divorce in his translation by the frequent omission of details which might link Mercier and Camier to any realistic world. At the beginning of the book, we are told that 'Things were getting ponderously under way' (Calder, 12), but the specification 'et notamment les véhicules lourds, tels camions, charrettes et transports en commun' (Minuit, 15) is lost. Similarly, the omission of passages in which Mercier and Camier plan the retrieval of their luggage, or plot their course forward (Minuit, 151–2, 173–4; omitted, Calder, 90, 101) serves to focus attention upon the couple's poverty of purpose no less than of equipment. And at one point, Beckett omits a reference to Camier paying for his drink (Minuit, 104; Calder, 63), a change which seems wanton and incomprehensible unless seen in the context of other moves made in the translation to detach Mercier and Camier from ordinary physical affairs.

There are two other ways in which Beckett tries, if not exactly to spiritualize, then to 'discarnate' his two heroes. The French version of the book has a number of references to food and drink and episodes of comic byplay involving them, and Beckett takes care when he can to remove these. The conversation in chapter 2, for example, about what the two have eaten, and the altercation following Mercier's request for a 'massepain', are completely left out (Minuit, 46–7; Calder, 30). The relish with which the barman in the pair's first port of call describes the food he has available is much diminished — we are told that he 'rattled off a list' (Calder, 44), but not that he has 'beaucoup de bonnes choses' (Minuit, 68). Camier's request for a 'petit collation' is omitted (Minuit, 71; Calder, 46), as is Mercier's demand 'Donnez nous a manger' (Minuit, 67, Calder, 44) and throughout the book Beckett makes similar changes. Some of these involve only shifts of emphasis, but are the more convincing because of this — as when, in the French, Camier reassures the vomiting Mercier 'Ça te fera du bien' (Minuit, 105), but reinforces the prejudice against food in the English by saying 'You'll feel better without it' (Calder, 65).

In a series of related revisions, Beckett also seeks to diminish the prominence of sexuality in the book. Though enough survives to make it clear what kind of services are available in Helen's hotel, a couple of substantial omissions reduce Camier's involvement with them. In the French chapter 7 (chapter 5 in the English), Camier disappears a second time up the stairs and keeps his comrade waiting around even longer than he has done previously, before reappearing with the sheepish apology 'C'est toujours un peu plus long la deuxième fois' (Minuit, 125; omitted, Calder, 75) and, towards the end of their journey in chapter 7 (chapter 10 in the French), an interchange is left out in which Mercier upbraids Camier for his lasciviousness (Minuit 171–2; Calder, 100).

Ruby Cohn has observed that Camier seems to be the slave of his senses much more than the intellectual Mercier, and has suggested that, like Vladimir and Estragon in *Waiting for Godot*, they dramatize the relationship of body and soul.[7] But, in fact, this distinction between the two is deliberately much less apparent in the English version, which, of course, did not exist at the time that Ruby Cohn was writing. There are signs, too, of Beckett's attempts to make the friendship of Mercier and Camier more fragile in the English version. The two seem less solicitous for each other's health after the omission of passages where Camier asks how Mercier is feeling (Minuit, 42, 92; Calder, 28, 58), or where Mercier shows a kindly interest in the state of Camier's cyst (Minuit, 172; Calder, 100). No doubt, the same motive impels another omission when, in the English, we are told that Mercier and Camier 'raised their glasses and drank', but not, as in the French, that it was 'à la santé l'un de l'autre' (Minuit 140; Calder, 83). It is probably in order to make the relationship of the two colder and more remote that Beckett also omits the following passage from the final English version; in it, we see the rapport which remains in some of the exchanges between Vladimir and Estragon in *Godot,* but which the grimmer vision of the older Beckett seems not to be able to accommodate:

> I personally to be quite frank see nothing whatever any more, neither the road, nor my feet, nor my legs, nor my chest (admittedly hollow). A wisp of beard, perhaps, to be quite honest, a snow-white wisp. We might have passed before the Scala, a night of gala, and I none the wiser. It's a wreck you are towing, my dear Camier, with your customary loving-kindness.
>
> And I went a wool gathering, said Camier. It's unpardonable.
>
> You have every excuse, said Mercier, every excuse, with no exception. Don't let go my hand whatever you do. The gymnastics of despair, by all means, to your heart's content, they help, while they last, but don't let go my hand.
>
> For Camier had been suddenly seized by a sort of convulsions.
>
> Poor Camier, said Mercier, you're done in, don't deny it. I'll show you if I'm done in, said Camier.
>
> Your little arse is hurting you, said Mercier, and your little penis.
>
> No turning back from now on, said Camier, come what may.
>
> (translation of Minuit, 177–8; omitted, Calder, 102)[8]

Beckett even seeks to diminish the bonds of memory between the two; when they discuss their pasts, the narrator remarks in the French version that 'Ils ne se connaissaient pas alors, mais depuis qu'ils se connaissaient, ils en avaient parlé, de cette époque, trop parlé, par bribes, suivant leur coutume' (Minuit, 13). Beckett translated this in his second draft as 'They had not known each other then, but ever since they knew each other they had spoken of those days, immoderately, sporadically, after their fashion'; but even the habit of shared recall is denied them in the final version, where Beckett omits all but the bald comment that, in those days, they 'did not know each other' (Calder, 11).

There are many other kinds of change made in the translation of *Mercier et Camier,* and, as we might expect, most of these are the symptoms of Beckett's deepening pessimism and bitterness; the Beckett who set to work in 1970 on the translation of what John Fletcher describes as a 'warm and funny book,[9] had escaped the celebrated impasse reached after *L'Innommable* and had begun to produce the calm, scrupulous, but uncompromisingly bleak texts which characterized the 1960s and 1970s — *Le Dépeupleur, Bing, Imagination Morte Imaginez.* Thus, the voices which speak to Mercier and Camier in the English version of the book have become as unreliable as they are in *The Unnamable;* 'la petite voix implorante ... qui nous parle parfois de vies antérieures' of which Camier speaks (Minuit, 94) becomes 'the faint imploring voice ... that drivels to us on and off of former lives' (Calder 59); and the voice 'qui veut me faire croire que je ne suis pas encore mort' (Minuit, 94) is, for Mercier, 'the one that tries to cod me I'm not yet dead' (Calder, 59). Christopher Ricks pointed in an early review of *Mercier and Camier* to some other comic intensifications and diminishments; Camier 'had felt even worse', for 'Il ne sentait pas trop mal' (Calder, 110; Minuit, 191), and Mercier's cry of 'Speak up ... I'm not deaf' for 'Je n'entends rien' (Calder, 85; Minuit, 143).[10] In a similar way, it is the 'plus fort' of the two who gives the 'plus faible' to drink in chapter 2 of the French, but the 'less weak of the two' who gives 'the weaker' in the English (Minuit, 33; Calder, 23), and it is not of 'leurs déboires ... leurs espoirs' that the couple speak to Helen, but of 'their hopes both shattered and forlorn' (Minuit, 114; Calder, 70).

Similar intensifications are to be found in the translation of *Premier Amour.*[11] 'Cette situation' (Minuit, 31) becomes 'this plight' (*CSP,* 10), 'un sujet plus gai' (Minuit, 17) becomes 'less melancholy matters' (*CSP,* 5), and 'plus mort que vif' (Minuit, 36) becomes 'even more dead than alive than usual' (*CSP,* 12). The play between excess and deficiency is carried on in other places in the translation, where, for example, a barren landscape 'qui exhibitait à sa surface plus d'orties que d'herbe' (Minuit, 26) becomes 'richer on the surface in nettles than in grass' (*CSP*, 8).

Like *Mercier and Camier, First Love* shows evidence of a desire to shrink down and impoverish, as can be seen from this passage, which Beckett dropped from the English version, presumably in order to diminish the narrator's confident and expansive cultural range: 'J'ai beaucoup aimé, enfin assez aimé, pendant assez longtemps, les mots vase de nuit, ils me faisaient penser à Racine, ou à Baudelaire, je ne sais plus lequel, les deux peut-être, oui, je regrette, j'avais de la lecture, et par eux j'arrivais là où le verbe s'arrête, on dirait du Dante' (Minuit, 44; omitted, *CSP*, 25).

Unlike *Mercier and Camier, First Love* also incorporates some significant additions. The effect of these additions, however, is usually to intensify pain and bitterness, or, as in the following expanded list of foot complaints, to provide a surplus of physical deficiency (items added in the English are in italics): 'the feet beloved of the corn, the cramp, *the kibe,* the bunion, *the hammer toe,* the nail ingrown, *the fallen arch,* the common blain, *the club foot, duck foot, goose foot, pigeon foot, flat foot,* trench foot and other curiosities' (Minuit, 25; *CSP*, 8).

The dwindling of energy, purpose and certainty which Beckett emphasizes in his translation of *Mercier et Camier* and *Premier Amour* recapitulates (anticipates, too, in a sense) the concentrated studies of decay and renunciation to be undertaken in later work, and resembles in particular the entropic running down which is represented in those two-act plays like *Waiting for Godot, Happy Days, Play* and *Quad,* in which the second act is a repetition and a contraction of the first act. There are interesting resemblances between the self-repetition involved in these plays, especially *Play,* where the actual words of the first act are repeated, and the self-repetition involved in translation. In both cases, the repetition is the same as and yet different from the original utterance, an addition to and yet also a diminution of it.

It is interesting to find this principle confirmed even in a text like *The Lost Ones,* in which, although there was some delay between the original and its translation, there does seem to be a very close equivalence between them.[12] As with *Mercier et Camier,* translation provides

Beckett with the means of intensifying the plight of his characters in the narrative. Life seems to be running down in the cylinder in the French, but the English gives examples of conditions becoming even more restrictive and unpleasant. Where in the French the niches are large enough 'pour que par le jeu normal des articulations le corps puisse y pénétrer et de même tant bien que mal s'y étendre', the English allows room only 'to crouch down a fashion'.[13] At times, cliche is interrupted or distorted to assist this sense of entropic decline: 'tant pis', for example, becomes 'so much the worst' (Minuit, 21; *CSP*, 164), in a joke that recalls similar inversions in *First Love* and *Mercier and Camier* and looks forward to the play of comparative and superlative in *Worstward Ho*. The most telling intensification of gloom is to be found in the removal in the English version of a passage from the last section alluding to the imagined way out of the cylinder: 'Dans les feux sombres du plafond le zénith garde encore sa légendé' (Minuit, 54).[14] Here the omission sets up a self-reflexive overlap between the original text and the activity of translating it. If the French version remains faithful to the 'notion' that the 'fatuous little light' of the imagined escape will linger to the end of existence in the cylinder, the English version is faithful to another, earlier notion, that 'the way out transfers from the tunnel to the ceiling prior to never having been' (*CSP*, 163). In the English text the way out is indeed forgotten as though it had never been, though the very absence of the phrase in the English is, like the disappearance of the light itself, not a 'pure' absence, since it is only visible against the ground of the lingering light in the French version. Once again, translation seems to be providing the means for a dissolution that is merely referred to in the first text but acted out in the second.

Entropic revisions like these emphasize the intrinsic complexity of a translation, the fact that it always has two levels of signification; its signified is both the story that it tells, with its actual characters and events — in other words, the signified of the original signifier — and also the previous version itself, the signifier which now becomes the second signified of the translation. The translated text alludes all the time to its dependence upon the signifiers of the earlier text, even as it tries to reject or curtail that dependence. In *The Lost Ones* this takes the form of a determined shrinking down of the minimal vitality which is still available in the French version. In *Mercier and Camier,* there are other, more visible forms of interference set up between the two levels, as the second text does not just tamely replicate the original but comments upon it and upon the act of translation. Much of this commentary is given to the narrator of the book, who seems in the English version a great deal more intolerant and even disdainful of the characters of the book and the book itself than in the French (though the French narrator is also prone to fits of exasperation with them). At one point in *Mercier et Camier* the narrator, true to his opening promise that he was with his heroes 'all the time', reflects on the necessity for reader and narrator to cleave closely to them: 'Suivons-les attentivement, Mercier et Camier, ne nous en éloignons jamais plus que de la hauteur d'un escalier, ou de l'épaisseur d'un mur. Qu'aucun souci d'ordonnance, ou d'harmonie, ne nous en détourne jamais, pour l'instant' (Minuit, 96). The English narrator has no such scruples about this, apparently, for, taking permission from the uncertainty of 'jamais, pour l'instant', the whole passage is omitted (Calder, 60). Beckett's translation of the passage was actually retained until his final typed draft, but already reflects the narrator's growing distance from his characters, with the sly hint in its penultimate phrase of the unworthiness of his subjects: 'Let us now follow them closely, Mercier and Camier, never lose them by more than the height of a stairs, or a wall's breadth, never again let our love of ordinance, or of harmony, divert us *to worthier objects,* for the time being' (my emphasis).

The attitude of the narrator to his characters and the narrative itself becomes more problematic in the English version of *Mercier and Camier.* In fact, the narrator does not merely come to despise his characters, and the revisions of the English version give evidence of a complex mingling of sympathy and criticism. At the end of the French version there is a passage in which the taste and culture of the two heroes are admired:

> Dommage que Dumas Père ne puisse nous voir, dit Watt.
> Ou l'un des évangélistes, dit Camier.
> Mercier et Camier, c'était tout de même une autre qualité.
>
> (Minuit, 195)

Of course, the final comment is sourly ironic, but there is a kind of affectionate admiration there too, which is magnified by its context in the elegiac last section of the book. In the English version this admiration is more mixed, however, for the oblique and conceding 'tout de même' becomes, more explicitly, 'for all their faults' (Calder, 112).

At times, the friction between the new, more critical narrator and his French predecessor is brought out into the open. The new narrator has the advantage of being able to see the book whole from start to finish, and so can hint at oddities and mistakes in the design, as when, reporting the plans which Mercier and Camier are making for their journey, the narrator remarks 'No mention of the sack' (Calder, 19). This is an addition made in the translation, and a comment upon the French version, which, indeed, makes no mention of a sack (Minuit, 27), until later, when there is an agitated discussion as to the value and purpose of the sack and its contents — though Beckett subsequently omits this discussion in the English version. The comment the English narrator makes is directed at the French narrative, and the translation makes sure that it can have no meaning except by reference to this other, absent version of the text. This is a small but telling example of the logical paradoxes which the act of self-translation is liable to generate, paradoxes which reflect Beckett's sense of the 'issueless predicament' that is experience and narration.

We can find the English narrator commenting elsewhere in the book on the shortcomings of his French predecessor; at one point the English narrator seems to draw attention to the failure of the French narrator to provide enough circumstantial detail, when Camier says to Mercier, 'I was on the point of not keeping our appointment' and the English narrator sniffs 'So they had an appointment' (Calder, 91; Minuit, 153). At other times excessive fussiness of diction is mocked; Mr Gall informs Mercier and Camier that his inn is *gemütlich,* 'in a tone of tentative complicity, whatever that sounds like' (Calder, 43). There is a double joke here, however, because, though this looks like a rebuke to a previous version of the text, the French in fact reads, unexceptionably, 'd'une voix basse et comme tâtonnante' (Minuit, 66). The over-elaborate 'tentative complicity' is only added in the second draft of the English translation, with the sneering aside only appearing in the third draft. The comment refers us to a previous but absent text (the manuscript draft) in the same way as the comment about the sack, and, in doing so, seems to open up the prospect of even more, hitherto undetected, previous 'versions' or translations of a text, each of which may add a layer of self-reflection to it. So the 'final' text comes to seem less like an end point than just a stage in a continuing process of self-division and self-modification.

Where the English narrator of *Mercier and Camier* makes the most striking interventions, however, is in the ordering and editing of his material. Ways have frequently to be found, in the translation, of knitting together passages where substantial amounts of material (often dialogue) have been omitted, and ways of shortening passages which have come to seem tediously long. An example of how this is done is an extended passage in the French in which Mercier and Camier give detailed accounts of their states of health, which is shrunk down in the English to the dry comment that 'Before going any further they asked and told each other how they felt' (Minuit, 92; Calder, 58). There are a number of ellipses like this in the English, and it is interesting that they are rarely neutral; rather they convey the narrator's disapproval of or impatience with the original, and therefore provide, not an elegant concealment of the ellipsis, but an elaborate allusion to it. At one point, for example, a passage of conversation about Mercier's desire for a 'massepain' is omitted, but the translation alludes to the absence by telling us wearily that 'an altercation ensued, too foolish to be recorded, so foolish was it' (Minuit, 46; Calder, 30). Other examples of the translator alluding to his own revisions can be found in passages where the direct speech of the French is rendered in indirect speech in the English:

Quand ils eurent fini de courir, Camier [sic] dit:
     Nous allons arriver chez Hélène dans un bel état, mouillés jusqu'aux os.
     Nous nous déshabillerons aussitôt, dit Camier. Nous mettrons nos vêtements à sécher, devant le feu, ou dans l'armoire à linge où passent les tuyaux d'eau chaude.

(Minuit, 37)

When they had done running Mercier deplored the nice state, soaked to the buff, in which they would arrive at Helen's, to which in reply

Camier described how they would immediately strip and put their things to dry, before the fire, or in the hot-cupboard with the boiler and hot water pipes.

(Calder, 25–6)

Here, the indirect construction clearly results in no economy at all. In fact, the construction seems to exhibit its own redundancy, and the devices of *style indirecte libre* ('the nice state, soaked to the buff') to clash with the bureaucratic formality of 'described' and 'deplored', and the specifications 'in which', and 'to which in reply', so that the editor's presence is not obscured but made fussily obtrusive. And again we are given the impression that what is being described for us here is not an event from the narrator's memory, or anything that has ever happened in the real world, but a passage from a previous text, with which the present text is in conflict, even as it colludes with it. Something similar happens in the English version of *Premier Amour,* though here the translation not only highlights the narrator's sarcastic comments at his own expense ('précisons, précisons' is sharpened to 'that's the idea, every particular', [Minuit, 45; *CSP*, 15]), but also increases the friction between the narrator and his readership ('cunts like you', *CSP*, 8); 'si ce n' est pas tout dire, c'est assez dire', for example, becomes the irritable 'if that doesn't give you some idea nothing will' (Minuit, 29; *CSP*, 9).

Of course, this sort of thing is by no means a new departure in Beckett's writing. From the very beginning he had been fond of representing the vexed relationship between an author, or editor, his readers and his texts, and in a novel like *Watt* seems deliberately to create a narrator who has only imperfect control of his material. Similarly, there are plenty of indications in the French *Mercier et Camier* that the narrator's testimony is unreliable. The poker faced 'résumés' that are placed after every pair of chapters do not succeed in hiding beneath their blandness the caprice that governs the choice and emphasis of material. In the résumé of chapter 7, for example (chapter 5 in the English), nothing is said of one of the most interesting episodes in the book, Mercier's encounter with an old man who looks like the narrator of *The Calmative,* while the extraordinary passage of meditation following this encounter is shrunk ruthlessly down to the designation 'Cerveau de Mercier' (Minuit, 163; Calder, 95). In the résumé of the next chapter, there is an outright distortion, when the murder of the police constable becomes the prim 'Mort de l'agent' (Minuit, 164; the English goes further in omitting this item altogether, Calder, 96).

Hugh Kenner has rightly seen these summaries as anticipations of Krapp's entries in his ledger of tapes; 15 like the non-committal entry 'Farewell to Love', the dry résumés seem like attempts to control and neutralize the unruliness of the preceding material. Indeed, we might also see these as anticipations of Beckett's own attempts to shrink down his fiction in the search for a hardness and abstraction to replace the molten intensity of the earlier 'battle of the soliloquy'. And since the résumés are repetitions that are at the same time revisions, they are themselves a kind of intermittent self-translation within the original French text. So the French is again shown to be different from itself in something of the same way that it is different from the English text which follows and revises it.

As we have seen, repetition often serves in Beckett's work as a drive towards an ending, often in the attempt to 'unsay' what has already been said. But if the compulsion to repeat has the need to close off at its basis, then it also has, as an unlooked-for consequence, the need to carry on repeating as long as the tiniest anxiety remains that the original may not have been satisfactorily unsaid. Already, in the French *Mercier et Camier,* Beckett seems to be demonstrating, by the imperfect correspondence between narration and summary, that the desire for consummation through repetition is always liable to be balked. As we might expect, the summaries provided in the English version continue to differ from the text they summarize; Beckett omits more material from the summaries, sometimes, it is true, because material has vanished from the main chapters, but also, apparently, as the result of changes of mind as to the relative importance of various incidents. Thus, the reference to the 'Colère d'un barman' (Minuit, 54), is changed to 'The bicycle' (Calder, 35) and the reference to the 'départ des fermiers' (Minuit, 112) is removed (Calder, 68), as are references to Mercier's arrival in the bar, the wind, and the death of the policeman (Minuit, 163–4; Calder, 95–6).

The issue of Beckett's self-translation is closely related to his actual style and language in his work. One of the most interesting things about Beckett's turn to French is the way that it connects with the decided shift in his style, after 1946, from the baroque elaboration of the earlier work to the conversational directness which characterizes the Trilogy. However, by 1970, when Beckett began to translate *Mercier et Camier,* his style had moved into a third phase, one of calm, exact austerity; in *Bing, Le Dépeupleur, Imagination Morte Imaginez* and *All Strange Away* Beckett's energies have been devoted to the stylistic control of the resonances of language, rather than the multiplication of associations and implications. With the simultaneous shriveling of narrative content, style became more and more important as the bearer of meaning in Beckett's work, and he became ever more scrupulous and exacting in his translations, seeking to exert the same rigorous control over both versions of a text. This view of Beckett's stylistic development is often articulated within a conventional narrative in which reduction and concentration are associated with growth towards, or even retrieval of final, essential form. According to this narrative, Beckett seems to be moving closer and closer to the heart of what he has to say, by doing away with stylistic extravagance, in a hygiene or *ascesis* of the signifer.

Translation plays its part in this process, since translation is conventionally supposed to necessitate an increased focus upon the meaning of a text, rather than upon the textuality of its original. As Philip E. Lewis observes, translation is usually thought of primarily as a metaphorical rather than a metonymic activity:

> the translating text works principally and principially by substitution and gives priority to re-presentational processes — to the identification of substitute signifiers, to metaphoricity — whereas it tends to subordinate or lose sight of the order of syntax or metonymy, in which the signifiers of the original are linked to one another and in which that more or less poetic activity that we might term 'textual work' is carried on.[16]

In many ways, Beckett's self-translation seems to accord well with this model. The reduction of the range of evocation and connotation in his translations (and his instructions to translators of his work to do the same in other languages), for example, seems to embody the increased concentration upon fundamental content, the work of the translation being to efface the metonymic 'textual work' of the earlier version.[17] Indeed, Beckett represented his own turn to French and subsequent return to English in something like these terms, claiming, famously, that it was easier for him to write 'without style' in French, and that he returned to English when it had become a foreign language to him again — in other words, perhaps, when the effort of translating his thoughts into English could allow the disciplining of the stylistic impulse towards accretion.[18]

One might expect to find this model of progressive intensification confirmed in some new stylistic austerity in the translations of *Mercier et Camier* and *Premier Amour,* but this does not seem in general to be the case. Apart from the obvious excision of material which he finds to be flabby or unnecessary, the general tendency in Beckett's translation of these works is to emphasize their similarities with his earlier works, like *More Pricks Than Kicks, Murphy,* and *Watt,* rather than to try to draw them into line with his later stylistic practice. Time and again, in *Mercier and Camier,* Beckett takes the opportunity of increasing the range of obscure allusions, introducing archaism, compressing, polishing and even distorting the language of the original. Where the French version is pitched more or less in the solid middle ground of ordinary colloquial language (though with a few quirky departures from it), the idioms of the English are drawn from much more widespread and often incompatible sources, ranging from philosophical jargon to the fierce obscenity of the street. Beckett often shows a preference in the English for inkhorn Latinisms, which can seem very awkward when compared to their French equivalents:

> Il tenait du dédale, le petit square, on y circulait avec gêne, et il fallait bien le connaître pour en pouvoir sortir à la première tentative.
>
> (Minuit, 11)

> It had something of the maze, irksome to perambulate, difficult of egress, for one not in its secrets.
>
> (Calder, 9)

The early drafts show Beckett working towards the ironic and self-defeating elevation of this sentence. His first translation of the end of its last phrase was 'difficult to leave, for one not knowing it well' which is closer to the original, but also flatter and less effective. A similar comic elevation of language is brought about by the translation of the description of Mercier's and Camier's frequent collapses on the road; 'ils s' effondraient tous les deux en même temps, comme un seul homme, sans s'être concertés et dans une parfaite indépendance l'un de l'autre' (Minuit, 179–80); in the English, Mercier and Camier collapse 'simultaneously, as one man, without preconcertation and in perfect interindependency' (Calder, 102).

Although the French version of *Mercier and Camier* is sometimes itself very elaborate and very funny, it seems nowhere to match the range of comic discontinuity between registers and idioms to be found in the English. The piece of description which begins chapter 7 (chapter 10 in the French) shows this clearly: throwaway asides ('a thousand feet above sea-level, two thousand if you prefer', Calder, 97) alternate with self-conscious poeticisms like 'the sea … pale plinth as pale as the pale wall of the sky' (Calder, 97), the alliterative density of which contrasts with the more conventional and explicit syntax of the French — 'elle n'a guère plus de couleur que le ciel qui n'en a guère, elle est comme une cimaise' (Minuit, 165). At times, Beckett approaches lampoon: 'des deux ports, ils avancent bras minuscules dans la mer vitreuse, on les sait à plat mais on les voit levés' (Minuit, 166) becomes 'tiny arms in the glassy sea outflung, known flat, seen raised' (Calder, 98). It is difficult to decide whether Beckett has adopted this compression in order to charge up the sublimity of his description or actually to dissipate it. The latter seems to be suggested by the draft versions of this passage which show a working towards parodic intensification, with 'the tiny arms stretched out in the glassy sea', and 'two tiny arms stretched out in the glassy sea' as first attempts. The ugly grinding of gears in the cadence of 'known flat, seen raised' seems deliberate, too, with the substitution in Beckett's second draft of 'known flat' for the smoother 'known level'.

Similarly, the (sometimes rather stiff) colloquialism of *Premier Amour* is often rendered in a specialized or elevated diction in the English version. Speaking of his father's arrangements for his occupancy of the apartment, the French narrator says 'c'était peut-être même la condition dont il faisait dépendre tout le reste', but the English says, more legalistically, 'he may even have given it the force of condition precedent' (Minuit, 12; *CSP*, 31); elsewhere, 'ces longues, ces atroces séances aux cabinets, aux water' are similarly heightened to 'those long, those cruel sessions in the necessary house' (Minuit, 14; *CSP,* 41), which recalls darkly Shakespeare's 'sessions of sweet silent thought', as well as Beckett's own allusion to Chesterfield's 'necessary house' in Murphy's will (*Murphy,* 183). The first French draft of the story shows that Beckett thought first of 'stations', which, though effectively suggesting the excruciation of constipation, might have seemed like overdoing it alongside the references to the picture of Christ on the lavatory wall).[19] Later, when the narrator of *First Love* says that he thought of Anna in 'long long sessions' (*CSP,* 10), where the French has the more innocuous 'beaucoup, beaucoup' (Minuit, 30), the repetition confirms the story's unpleasant association between love and the difficulties of evacuation.

The translation of *Premier Amour* often introduces ironic and bathetic poeticism, as well, as with the translation of 'craquant de gel' as 'tinkling with rime' (Minuit, 32; *CSP,* 10) and of 'qui me faisait pleurer' as 'that so unmanned me' (Minuit, 33; *CSP,* 11). Not all the revisions are in this stylistic direction, however, for sometimes the English is deliberately blunter than the French, as with the rendering of Lulu's polite 'faites moi une place' as 'shove up' (Minuit, 19; *CSP,* 5). In fact, as with *Mercier and Camier,* Beckett seems concerned in this translation to emphasize the clash and friction of registers. Sometimes he achieves this within one sentence, as when the chatty diminuendo of 'Elle était triste, du moins je le suppose, car au fond je ne sais rien' becomes the odder, terser 'She watched, in sorrow I suppose, though not necessarily' (Minuit, 41; *CSP,* 14), or with the translation of 'ni de la merde ni du ciel' as 'the shitball and heaven's high halls' (Minuit, 23; *CSP,* 7).

It is often as though Beckett were trying deliberately to hamstring his language in the translation, or to induce by stylistic incongruity the sense that the language is reformulating, retranslating itself before our eyes. And where there is awkwardness in the original, Beckett will often highlight rather than emend this in the translation; the description of Mr Graves's voice has a certain jingling oddity in the French — 'sa voix basse et grasse de patriarche pastoral débutant' (Minuit, 73) — but the clotted English version — 'his incipient pastoral patriarch's thick bass' (Calder, 47) — is deliberately and desperately strange. Beckett also shows in translation a fondness for mixed and self-defeating metaphors, which reveal and undermine metaphorical translation within language as such, as when Mercier is left 'on fuming tenterhooks' (Calder, 31), where the French has the less concrete 'guet raguer' (Minuit, 48). Such undermined metaphors are found throughout *First Love:* 'd'attaque presque pour les descentes lentes' becomes 'soon I'd be up to the slow descents again' (Minuit, 45; *CSP,* 15), for instance. Usually, these metaphorical doublings involve a grotesque insistence on the physical, as when' A sa place, je serais parti sur la pointe des pieds' becomes, queerly, 'I in her shoes would have tiptoed away' (Minuit, *45; CSP,* 15) or the unremarkable 'personellement je n'ai rien contre les cimetières' yields the charnel-joke 'personally I have no bone to pick with graveyards' (Minuit, 8; *CSP,* 1), or when the extreme state of the narrator's constipation is emphasized by replacing 'à cette epoche' with the suggestive 'at that juncture' (Minuit, 14; *CSP,* 4).

Nor is this effect confined to *Mercier and Camier* and *First Love.* There is evidence that Beckett tried in his translation of *Le Dépeupleur* as well to find new ways of pitting language against itself, often by his favourite devices of tautology and incapacitated metaphor. There are already plenty of examples of this kind of thing in the French, which relishes, for example, the situation in which a climber is forced to come down a ladder 'précédé par son successeur', or a searcher's eagerness to climb can be described as 'precipitation' (Minuit, 23). In a darker inversion, young children in the cylinder are said to be 'à croupetons par terre dans des poses précoces' (Minuit, 26). Here, Beckett screws a further turn out of the logic that says that a baby who does things early is impressively beforehand, even if what it does is to anticipate the reversion of the aged to their helpless beginnings.

There are signs that Beckett has sought to multiply these effects in the language of the English version. The sprawling old-young babies are recalled in the remark that only the ladders can 'wean' the sedentary from their fixity (*CSP,* 174), where the French is much plainer, saying that it is the temptation of the ladders which 'peut rompre la fixité des sédentaires' (Minuit, 46). The drafts for the translation show Beckett trying to generate other kinds of redundancy. Discussing the number of missing rungs on the ladders, he thought of writing in ts1 that 'the want of three running calls for acrobatics'. Running connects in an obvious way with acrobatics, though, of course, it is also a wonderfully inappropriate word, given the decrepit state of the ladders. (In the end, 'running' became 'in a row', [*CSP*, 160.]) On the other hand, Beckett does not feel able to reproduce the cruel joke in the French description of the dessicating effect of the air on human flesh: the sentence 'les muqueuses elles-mêmes sont touchées ce qui serait sans gravité n'était la gêne qui en découle pour l'amour' suggests 'the discomfort flowing thence' in ms and ts1, but becomes, more obviously, 'its hampering effect on the work of love' in the final version (Minuit, 47; *CSP*, 174–5).

But there are other instances in the English of entropic tautology. The opportunity is taken, for example, to reinforce physicality in the description of the searchers' deteriorating eyesight, 'which, with the best will in the world it is difficult not to consign at the close of all its efforts to nothing short of blindness' (*CSP*, 174). Another writer might have tried to avoid the sad congruity between the metaphorical 'close' of the eye's efforts and its literal blindness, which is not to be found in the French 'au terme de son effort' (Minuit, 46; the reference to blindness also resonates in the English with the earlier description of 'a long tunnel abandoned blind' [*CSP*, 161], translating 'un long tunnel abandonné en cul-de-sac' [Minuit, 11]). There is a striking and similar tautology in the phrase 'in accordance with the notion requiring as long as it holds' (*CSP*, 163), for 'conformément à la notion qui veut tant qu'elle dure' [Minuit, 16]). A notion may 'hold' in the sense of 'persist', or 'be maintained', but it may also 'hold' in the sense of logically requiring — which yields the internal translation of this phrase 'the notion which holds as long as it holds' .

In another example, Beckett thickens a tautology that is already to be found in the French. The narrator is discussing various forms of conversion and reversion among the various categories of searcher in the cylinder. The non-searchers are, in fact, ex-searchers, he says, whose desire to search may one day rekindle. But the narrator consoles himself with the thought that there will always be some continuing languor in some of the ex-searchers:

Mais il en restera toujours assez pour abolir chez ce petit peuple à plus ou moins longue échéance jusqu'au dernier vestige de ses ressorts.

(Minuit, 14)

> But enough will always subsist to spell for this little people the extinction soon or late of its last remaining fires.
>
> > (*CSP*, 162)

The irony that what there will be enough left of is the capacity for diminishment is well brought out in the eventual choice of the word 'subsist' ('remain' in ms); for 'subsist' summons the ghosts of 'submit' and 'desist' alongside 'exist'.

However, as with *Mercier et Camier* and *Premier Amour,* the most striking thing in the translation of *Le Dépeupleur* is the increased variation of register. This takes place within limits, of course, for both versions of the text use a language markedly drained of feeling, a bureaucratic language of icy, uninvolved discrimination; it is, as A. Alvarez disapprovingly puts it, like a report by a Civil Service commission into the conditions in Purgatory.[20] It is a language longwinded in qualification and miserly in affect, which seems oddly to suggest that the fearful locale of the cylinder may be some vast copyright library, in which readers shuffle incessantly about, climbing the ladders to the upper shelves in endless pursuit of lost volumes. This world also, however, involves frenzy, violence and desperation, even if these are damped down by the force of convention, and something of the same effect is to be found in the language, in the sense which it gives of the momentary, intermittent flickerings of feeling. The increased use of tautology and oxymoron is one of the ways in which this is achieved, as we have just seen; but it is also apparent at those moments where the language seems to speak in tiny but telling excess of the monotonous reality it describes. As a result, new and dissonant voices are added to the text, and opportunities are seized to underline the resultant jarring of register.

This may consist simply of the substitution for a neutral seeming expression in the French of an expression in the English which suggests a more elevated, or specialized, or poetic register. In the following sentence, for instance:

> Et enfin beaucoup plus tard que de loin en loin et pour très peu de temps celle-ci se calme.
>
> > (Minuit, 32)

And finally much later that ever and anon there comes a momentary
lull.

(*CSP,* 169)

'Ever and anon' is a literary cliche that seems to sneer in its place
in the English, even as it testifies to an impulse to dignify its subject. A
similar effect occurs a page or so later. With the momentary lull in the
pulsation of the light, the lovers in the cylinder freeze and then, on the
resumption of the light, the French tells us, 'les accouplés reprennent
le colliée' (Minuit, 33) — a phrase which might have been translated
as 'the lovers get back to the grind.' But the English gives 'the lovers
buckle to anew' (*CSP,* 169). In one way, this is less immediate than
the French, but the phrase also adds a momentary dignity to the action, prompting admiration for the persistence of the lovers (Beckett
originally had the crude 'copulating lovers', but subsequently dropped
the adjective) even as we become aware of the horrible futility of their
efforts.

Beckett often produces such inappropriate excess in the language
of his translation. The fists which halt in mid-swing are 'en voie de
cogner' in the French (Minuit, 33), but 'on their way to smite' in the
English (*CSP,* 169), transforming a squalid brawl into a scene of righ-
teous, Biblical anger. A similar increase in decorum comes with some
terms used for parts of the body in the English: the pupils of the eyes
are imagined in the French to dilate until they consume the entire
'cornéé' (Minuit, 35), but the medical precision of this word gives way
to the mock-grandeur of 'the orb' in English (*CSP,* 170). Perhaps a
similar effect comes from the rendering of the eyes condemned to stare
at each other with 'regards faits pour se fuir' (Minuit, 48) as 'fain to
look away' (*CSP,* 175), in which the hint of medievalism again both
mocks and heightens. A little later, a hand is allowed the modesty of
descending to cover 'some private part' (Calder, 40), as opposed to the
baldy explicit 'sexe' in the French (Minuit, 36). The two versions set
up different relationships to the action being described, so that, where
the French word brutally uncovers what the hand tries to conceal, the
English participates in the modest screening of the private part.

Consistently, in the English version of *Le Dépeupleur,* Beckett
employs a language which heightens or poeticizes: 'air qui y circule'

(Minuit, 34) becomes 'ambient air' (*CSP*, 170), 'les coups de tête et de poing contre le mur' (Minuit, 49) becomes 'skulls and fists dashed against the wall' (*CSP*, 175), and 'bref étonnement' (Minuit, 48) becomes 'a brief amaze' (*CSP*, 175). Usually these heightenings work by sheer incongruity. Sometimes, however, they allow extra jokes to be worked in, as in the translation of the passage describing how, in the beginning of life in the cylinder, everyone was a searcher, including 'les nourrissons dans la mesure où ils se faisaient porter' (Minuit, 31), translated as 'the nurselings insofar as they were borne' (*CSP*, 168). The word 'borne' allows the peripheral meanings 'insofar as they were born', i.e. insofar as they were fully alive (so many Beckett characters seem not to be) and simply by dint of having been born. And the strangeness of much of the language in the English often comes from the intensified awareness of the etymological roots of a word. The use of the word 'vacation' for the French 'absence' in the following sentence makes us hear the words 'vacuum' and 'vacancy', so that their meanings overpower the acquired sense of holiday or respite: 'unable to endure it any longer and fortified by the long vacation he renounces the ladder and resumes his search in the arena' (Minuit, 45; *CSP*, 174).

The effect of translation for Beckett is therefore to thicken the density of the signifier, while at the same time suggesting its fragility, or unreliability. This fragility is suggested in another obvious way by the hair-raising jokes that Beckett plays in the translation of *Mercier et Camier* by allowing the leakage of one language into another. Just as some critics have seen the evidence of Anglicism in Beckett's early French writing,[21] so *Mercier and Camier* is studded with imperfectly-digested Gallicisms — Mercier tells Camier that he has looked for the umbrella 'longly' ('longuement' Calder, 89; Minuit, 149), and later says to the manager of a bar, 'Your whisky likes us' (this looks like a bungled translation of 'il nous plaît' but the French has the — equally odd — 'Votre whisky est succulent' [Minuit, 201], which Beckett translated literally in his second draft). *First Love* seems similarly to introduce Gallicisms self-consciously into English, as when 'sous peine de se montrer désobligeante' becomes 'out of common savoir-faire' (Minuit, 41; *CSP*, 14). These may, of course, represent Beckett's grim revenge on himself for the embarrassing Anglicisms to be found in his early French work. But, at the same time, such intentional slips form part of an elaborate network of allusions to the absent French text, allusions which remind us of the dependence of the two texts one upon another.

Similar effects can be found in *The Lost Ones,* where the strangeness of the English often derives in part from what seems like an incomplete or over-literal translation. Beckett's insistence on re-embodying the French 'commutateur' as the strange and obsolete 'commutator' forces us to think of commutation of a life- or death-sentence: 'the two storms have this in common that when one is cut off as though by magic then in the same breath the other also as though again the two were connected somewhere to a single commutator' (*CSP,* 171).

Something more complicated happens with the translation of the sentence which describes the difficulties of making love in the cylinder:

> Le spectacle est curieux alors des ébats qui se prolongent douloureux et sans espoir bien au-delà de ce que peuvent en chambre les amants les plus habiles.
>
> (Minuit, 47)

> The spectacle then is one to be remembered of frenzies prolonged in pain and hopelessness long beyond what even the most gifted lovers can achieve in camera.
>
> (*CSP,* 175)

There are a number of shifts in the translation. The spectacle is more than merely 'curieux' in English, it is 'one to be remembered'; the playful 'ébats', which might have been translated more directly with the ironic 'revels' becomes the highly-coloured 'frenzies'; and, if the French offers the irony that it takes skill and experience in lovemaking to prolong it in pain and hopelessness to this degree, then that irony is increased in the English, where to be able to sustain that pain and hopelessness is now called a 'gift'. But the most conspicuous shift is in the adoption of the abstruse 'in camera' for 'en chambre'. As usual, Beckett began in the ms draft with the straight translation 'in private'. The joke would then have consisted in the English as in the French simply in the contrast between private and public performance of this act. But by adopting the legal phrase 'in camera', Beckett suggests that the difference between public and private love-making is merely the difference between an open and a closed trial — witnessed or unwitnessed it is still an ordeal. The incongruity is the more delicious for the fact that 'in camera' seems like the most literal translation of 'en chambre', but is, in fact, at the opposite pole from it.

The English version of *Le Dépeupleur* often seems to bend back towards the French via Latinate forms in this way. The use of 'the quest' and 'the vanquished' translates the French 'quête' and 'vaincu' in a way that is both literal and very indirect, for it highlights the exotic foreignness of the chivalric terms in English. Sometimes such effects are produced in conspicuous excess of the literal translation, as. in what happens to the word 'place' in the following phrase:

> ceux qui...ne quitte jamais la place qu'ils ont conquise.
>
> (Minuit, 12)

> those who...never stir from the coign they have won.
>
> (*CSP*, 161)

It may be that 'coign' supplies some of the martial associations of 'conquise' which are missing from the paler 'won', but the substitution of so French a term to translate the shared word 'place' is striking. As often, this denaturalizing of the English concentrates a sense of the etymological relationships of the word — and here, 'coign' suggests the French 'coin', though in an oblique way only, since the point is precisely that there are no accommodating comers of privacy in the relentless smoothness of the cylinder wall.

When Beckett translates the phrase 'amateurs de mythe' as 'amateurs of myth' (Minuit, 19; *CSP*, 164), the effect is similar: the scornful specificity of the word 'amateur' needles an awareness of its amorous roots, an association which is again activated in order almost immediately to be cancelled. (This repeats the move made by the text itself, which specifically denies the suggestion that, as in the Lamartine poem from which the French text takes its name, the quest for the lost one is an amorous quest: 'Whatever it is they are searching for it is not that' [*CSP*, 169].) When the narrator speaks of a certain interval of time which is 'unerringly timed by all' (*CSP*, 164), translating 'que chacun sait mesurer à une seconde près' (Minuit, 20–1), the English gains

by awakening the metaphor of wandering in 'unerringly', and by the
ironic dissonance of ideas which this stirs up — how can these restless
searchers (for whose movement the French indeed uses the word 'errer'
[Minuit, 27]) possibly be called 'unerring' in anything?

Occasionally, a similar effect is achieved from what seems like gra-
tuitously inexpert Gallicism:

> Le transport non plus ne se fait pas n'importe comment.
>
> (Minuit, 24)

> Similarly the transport of the ladders is not left to the good pleasure
> of the carriers.
>
> (*CSP*, 166)

Here, the English seems like an inadequate translation of the French
expression 'à (votre) bon plaisir', 'at (your) convenience', but, since it
translates 'n'importe comment', it is really as though the English were
beginning to retranslate itself back into French. The gain is in the
wincing absurdity of speaking of any kind of pleasure in the cylinder.

The imperfectly concealed traces of French and Latin words in
Beckett's English translation often induce awareness in this way of the
metaphors at work within the most seemingly abstract terms, and this in
turn gives a sense of a translation that itself requires further translation or
reinterpetation. Sometimes, the English text seems to begin to do this:

> It is therefore on those at the head of their lines as being the most
> likely to create the vacancy so ardently desired that the eyes of the
> second-zone watchers are fixed as they burn to enter the first.
>
> (*CSP*, 172)

> C'est par conséquent les premiers de file en tant que les plus suscep-
> tibles de créer le vide si ardemment désiré que guettent ceux de la
> seconde zone travaillés par le besoin de passer dans la première.
>
> (Minuit, 41)

The English not only translates the French, but begins to translate
itself, as 'ardent desire' summons up 'burning to enter'. In fact, Beckett
often translates the French via the intermediary of Latin, even where
this is not alluded to in the original, for example, where the 'petite

lumière inutile' of the belief in a way out becomes, via *ignis fatuus,* a 'fatuous little light' (*CSP,* 163). And Beckett not only allows French words to pass over apparently untranslated into his English version (the English word 'aperçu' may overlap to a large degree with the French 'aperçu', but it also has a layer of ironic nicety added to it), but also introduces French terms into the English where they do not exist in the original. The 'guetteur à l'affût d'un départ' (Minuit, 45) becomes 'the searcher on the qui vive for a departure' (*CSP,* 174), in which the grim question '(long) live who?' hidden within the cliché is activated.

It seems as though, far from confirming the difference between English and French, Beckett's translation is concerned to bleed the two languages together into a mixed or mongrel condition. Indeed, at extravagant moments, Beckett's translation can drift into near-opacity, as with the extraordinary translation of 'à arracher à pleines mains les orties' with 'to divellicate urtica *plenis manibus'* in *First Love* (Minuit, 31; *CSP,* 10), where the Latinate translation is actually so impenetrably foreign that we have to return to the original for a gloss. The merging of languages which can take place in translation has suggested to more than one commentator a troubled limit to our conception of translation. Walter Benjamin, for example, sees it as the duty of the translator to disconfirm the natural separateness and autonomy of languages, stretching the limits of the translator's own language to bring it closer to the language of the original.[22] This offends markedly against the dictum of reduction through translation. Beckett's translations of *Mercier et Camier* and *Premier Amour* stand in a relation of unruly excess to their originals, their stylistic elaboration refusing the customary parsimony of the signifier in translation. But Benjamin suggests that this disproportion may actually be a principle of all translation:

> while content and language form a certain unity in the original, like a fruit and its skin, the language of the translation envelops its content like a royal robe with ample folds. For it signifies a more exalted language than its own and thus remains unsuited to its content, overpowering and alien. This disjunction prevents translation and at the same time makes it superfluous. ('Task of the Translator', 75)

Despite Benjamin's confidence in the cooperation of languages in their shared aspiration to a post-Babelian 'pure language', translation for Beckett would seem always to be at one and the same time an act of confederacy, and of secession, which always distinguishes two languages in the act of uniting them. Though the act of translation reacquaints Beckett with his *Mercier et Camier* and *Premier Amour*, translation is simultaneously a means for distancing himself from these works. Beckett reaches into his own past but finds there no confirmation of the singleness and continuity of his identity but rather evidence of otherness, of the divided nature of experience and memory. The act of translation, like the act of memory, repeats the past in order that it may be rejected; Beckett, in translating *Mercier et Camier* and *Premier Amour*, deliberately makes the texts different from himself, translating them into a caricatured version of the idiom of his earlier works, like *More Pricks Than Kicks, Murphy*, and *Watt*, rather than in the manner of any of the works that he was composing in the late 1960s and early 1970s. It is perhaps significant that Beckett had spent some considerable time revising the translation made by Ludovic and Agnes Janvier of *Watt* before embarking on *Mercier and Camier;* this may be a further indication of Beckett's sense that to have done with or unsay the past it is necessary somehow to repeat it. It may account, too, for the peculiar intensity of the style of *Mercier and Camier*, compounded as it is of equal parts of fascination and loathing, which seems the result of a curiously double impulse to repudiate the earlier work, even as it is being repossessed.[23]

What results from this is the loss of a single definitive work which can orientate and control the play of derived or secondary versions; with Beckett as both originator and translator, the two versions of his text have an equal claim to be 'definitive'. Oddly, the effect is to reduce the autonomy of each version of the text. Each becomes merely a version of the other, and is apprehensible as itself only by virtue of its difference from its partner, which in turn has identity only in *its* differences from the other text. This also necessarily abolishes the precedence of original over copy, since the English text is not only a 'mutilation' of the original, but also, in some senses, an improvement upon it, so that the French might be considered as in some respects as an inferior, derived version of the English. As with the texts in the Trilogy discussed earlier, translation is a 'supplement' or sequel to the original text which, while appearing to guarantee the integrity of that original, actually subverts that integrity by opening up areas of absence or 'lack' in it.[24] As we have seen, this lack of priority is instanced within each text itself, with the unreliable résumés within *Mercier et Camier,* for instance, which give us translations into a different idiom of events that have already been narrated, but do not give us the means of deciding which version to prefer.

This may be seen as a structure of mutual debt between original and translation. We are accustomed to the idea that a translation owes a duty of fidelity to its original, indeed owes its being to it, but perhaps less accustomed to the idea that the original also owes a debt to its translation. As Derrida argues, following Walter Benjamin, every original calls out to be translated, requires translation as its guarantee of being: 'if the structure of the original is marked by the requirement to be translated, it is that in laying down the law the original begins by indebting itself *as well* with regard to the translator. The original is the first debtor, the first petitioner; it begins by lacking and by pleading for translation'.[25]

The labour of translation under these circumstances of mutual insolvency is therefore never to be understood as replication, or repetition in the service of originality. Beckett's translations resist the condition of derivation from or shadowing of autonomously individual works and, instead, reach back into those works to interrupt and complicate their autonomy. As Barbara Johnson says, it is 'precisely the way in which the original is already an impossible translation that renders translation impossible'.[26] Translation can never be something that is merely 'done to' a preexisting, fully formed text, for the act of translation repeats the successive reconstitution of the self which forms the subject of many of the texts; the relationships between Molloy, Moran, Malone and the characters in *The Unnamable* are oddly like those between the successive translations of a text — so that it seems no accident, for example, that Molloy has an Irish name, while Moran's Christian name is French, or that Malone has a spare pencil somewhere in the bed 'made in France, a long cylinder hardly broached' (*T,* 223) — just as the relationships between Beckett's 'pseudocouples' remind us of the strange similarity-in-difference obtaining between his originals and translations.[27] If translation-as-repetition depends upon or summons up the integrity of the original text, then it can also disclose the inherent self-division of an original text which is itself a process of internal repetition and self-translation.

Nor do the problems end with the French and English versions of the text. As Derrida points out, the structure of repetition is tripartite rather than double, since once the integrity of an original has been broken into by repetition, there is always the possibility of another repetition still, followed by further repetitions (*WD*, 299). We should remember that Beckett does not confine himself to two languages, for he took an interest in the German and Italian translations of his work, and directed plays in German as well as in French and English. Beckett's direction of his own plays presents itself too as an interesting example of self-repetition or self-translation, for each new production is in a sense different from the text which it repeats, even as Beckett strives to make it definitive. The two activities of translation and direction sometimes overlap, as when Beckett prepared himself for directing *Endspiel* by scrupulously overhauling the German text with his translator, Elmar Tophoven.[28] But, in the echo chamber of Beckett's oeuvre, nothing can be unsaid, except by being perpetually reiterated, and therefore no character, no story can ever be brought to conclusion, as Henry seems to acknowledge in *Embers:* 'stories … I never finished any of them, I never finished anything, everything always went on for ever' (*CDW*, 94). Beckett's translations dramatize the gnawing sense that 'le langage n'est qu'une fiction, une traduction sans original.'[29]

Chapter 6

Presence and Repetition in Beckett's Theatre

Beckett's turn to the theatre has often been represented as the expression of a longing for an art of visibility and tangibility as a relief from the epistemological disintegrations of the Trilogy which Beckett described in his interview with Israel Schenker in 1956 — 'no "I", no "have", no "being", no nominative, no accusative, no verb. There's no way to go on.'[1] Michael Robinson, for example, sees the theatre as 'the only direction in which a development was possible', since the theatre 'promises a firmer reality than a subjective monologue written and read in isolation; perhaps on the stage the reality behind the words may be revealed by the action which often contradicts that literal meaning'.[2] Beckett himself testified to the sense of relief that he got from working in drama: 'Theater ist für mich zunächst eine Erholung von der Arbeit am Roman. Man hat es mit einem bestimmten Raum zu tun und mit Menschen in diesem Raum.'[3]

Perhaps the most emphatic statement of this view of Beckett's turn to the theatre is that offered by Alain Robbe-Grillet. Writing early in Beckett's dramatic career, he stressed the sense of sheer *presence* that is given by Vladimir and Estragon, deprived as they apparently are of all the conventional dramatic supports of script, plot or properties. We see them, he says, 'alone on stage, standing up, futile, with no future or past, irremediably present'.[4] For Robbe-Grillet, Beckett's theatre embodies the Heideggerean apprehension of *Dasein,* of primordial being-there: 'The human condition, Heidegger says, is to be there. Probably it is the theatre, more than any other mode of representing reality, which reproduces this situation most naturally. The dramatic character is on stage, that is his primary quality: he is there' (*TNN,* 119). As Bruce Morrissette observes, Robbe-Grillet also finds in *Waiting for Godot* an assertion of Sartrean freedom *en situation.* The very absence of programme or a priori principles is what guarantees this freedom. Vladimir and Estragon have nothing to repeat; everything is happening for the first and last time: 'They are *there;* they must explain themselves. But they do not seem to have a text prepared beforehand and scrupulously learned by heart, to support them. They must invent. They are free' (*TNN*, 126)[5].

Other writers have elaborated or modified this theme by stressing the reflexiveness of the plays which, instead of undermining the audience's sense of presence, seems to intensify it, by focusing attention on the actual forms of the performance. William Worthen argues that Beckett 'literalizes' the plight of his characters in the visibly straitened conditions in which his actors are required to work, so that a piece like *Play* 'dramatizes the essential dynamics of stage performance'.[6] Sidney Homan argues in a similar way for self-reflection as a guarantee of presence. They turn in on themselves, he argues, to join playwright, play and audience in a mutually mirroring autonomy. The plays therefore no longer require reference to a preexisting world, or the addition of any commentary to elucidate meanings which are hidden or allegorically elsewhere; the plays are simply what they are, in an elementary performing present, without before or after, the action 'complete, pure, itself and immediately experienced by the audience'.[7] Beckett's occasional remarks about his plays have encouraged this view of their 'extreme simplicity of dramatic situation' (*Disjecta*, 109), and his intense jurisdiction over his plays embodies this sense of their almost physical simplicity of form. In his direction, Beckett is concerned not so much to control the meaning or interpretation of his plays as to control this physical form, in the details of light, sound, decor and pacing.

In many ways, this view of Beckett's turn to the theatre reproduces conventional views about theatre itself and its relation to the other arts. It is conventional, for instance, to oppose the living art of the theatre to the dead or abstract experience of private reading. If we merely imagine characters and events in written texts, it is often said, then in the theatre, and in other visual media, we 'actually see' those characters and events, 'actually hear' their voices. Of course, the dramatic text usually exists in a written as well as in a physical form, but this double existence often focuses claims about the drama's difference from other arts. While it is usual to see the dramatic performance as subsidiary or secondary to the written text — in that it must be 'faithful' to it, must repeat it accurately and efficiently — it is also quite common to find the hierarchy reversed with the performance of the play claimed as its real or primary condition. Here, it is the written text that is considered to be empty or incomplete, while the essence of the play is embodied in that perfect production which fuses text and performance, idea and utterance. This need not be imagined as a single or particular performance: in one of the subtlest formulations of this principle, Hans-Georg Gadamer suggests that the essential nature of a play is developed in its slow organic evolution through different forms. In Gadamer's formulation, the model of the text as absolute origin and the performance as variable and imperfect repetition is abandoned, for now reproducibility — in Deleuze's 'clothed' repetition — guarantees the permanence of the being of the play through multiple embodiments.[8]

Another influential formulation of the belief in the priority of the performed play is that of Antonin Artaud. What makes Artaud's writings particularly useful for examining Beckett's work and the critical constitution of it is not only the widely diffused influence of Artaud's ideas, but his particular stress upon and opposition to repetition as a model for theatre. Throughout his essays of the 1930s, Artaud argues for a non-repetitive theatre, one no longer slavishly obedient to the written texts which precede and control it. The Theatre of Cruelty projected by Artaud escapes the tyranny of the verbal altogether and speaks its own, intrinsically theatrical language of mime, gesture, dance, music, light, space and scene. Throughout the essays in *The Theatre and its Double,* Artaud insists on the physicality of the theatre, maintaining that 'the stage is a tangible, physical place that needs to be filled and ought to be allowed to speak its own concrete language'.[9] Once the drama rediscovers its own language, Artaud argues, 'we can repudiate theatre's superstition concerning the script and the author's autocracy. In this way also we will link up with popular, primal theatre sensed and experienced directly by the mind, without language's distortions and the pitfalls in speech and words' (The Theatre of Cruelty: Second Manifesto', *TD,* 82–3). This escape from the script is an escape from the compulsion to repeat. The spectator of the drama will no longer be forced to try to read the performance back into its original script, since what he or she beholds will be both performance and text. Closing the gap between text and performance will also eradicate the hiatus between meaning and interpretation for the spectator: 'This involved gesticulation we see has a goal, an immediate goal, towards which it aims by effective means, and we are able to experience its direct effectiveness. The thought it aims at, the states of mind it attempts to create, the mystical discoveries it offers are motivated and reached without delay or periphrasis' ('On the Balinese Theatre', *TD*, 42).

Of course, there is much in Artaud's formulation that is very unlike Beckett's theatre. Where the self-sufficiency of means in Beckett's work is a function of restriction and indigence, the self-proclaiming autonomy of Artaud's Theatre of Cruelty is an enactment of its 'blind zest for life'. Nevertheless, there are times when Artaud's arguments suggest very strongly the features of Beckett's theatre — or those features which criticism of Beckett has found most congenial: 'We might say the subjects presented begin on stage. They have reached such a point of objective materialisation we could not imagine them, however much one might try, outside this compact panorama, the enclosed, confined world of the stage' (*TD*, 43).

If, in one sense, Beckett's theatre is aptly described as a theatre of presence, or, in Artaud's terms, a theatre freed from repetition, then there are also important ways in which his work seems to undermine not only the particular claims of individual critics, but the more general cultural claims upon which they often rest and from which they derive their credibility. It is no accident that Beckett's international fame came first of all as a playwright and not as a novelist, for it has been the prevailing critical and cultural consensus about the theatre and its strengths and capacities which has allowed his work to be absorbed and rewritten as a humanist theatre of presence, a theatre which directly and powerfully embodies real and universal human predicaments. In various ways, and particularly in the intricate play of its different repetitions, Beckett's theatre makes this critical representation seem inadequate, and asks questions of common conceptions about the theatre as a whole.

The Doubling of Presence: *Waiting for Godot, Endgame*

One can understand why Robbe-Grillet should have found his views about the theatre so amply demonstrated in *Waiting for Godot*. It is undeniable that the restriction of the play's plot, setting and dialogue focus attention on the sheer fact of being on stage in a way that had never before been experienced so unrelievedly in the theatre. But what Robbe-Grillet doesn't explore are the implications of the fact that, as Vivian Mercier puts it, this is a play in which nothing happens, twice over, in which Vladimir and Estragon undergo the ordeal of their sheer presence on stage, *twice*.[10] It is a repetition that makes all the difference, for it demonstrates to us that the sense of absolute presence is itself dependent upon memory and anticipation. We may see Vladimir and Estragon with our own eyes, and see them nowhere else but on the stage, which is their only home, but this seeing has to contend with the knowledge that they have actually left the stage, have been or imagine themselves to have been elsewhere. At the beginning of Act 2, we only recognise their being-back-again, or even their still-being-there, because of our awareness of the break that has taken place between the acts. Indeed, the appearance and meeting is established for us at the beginning of both acts as a repetition: — 'Is that you again?', 'You again' (*CDW*, 10, 53). This, combined with the fact that Vladmir and Estragon do not leave the stage at the end of each act, but seem mysteriously to have left it at some point between Acts 1 and 2, makes their continuing 'presence' on the stage something other than simple or unbroken.

To reappear, to be on stage again, is in itself to allow the shadow of absence or non-being to fall across the fullness and simplicity of *Dasein*. It opens up the forked anxiety of living in time, an anxiety expressing itself in the two questions 'am I the same as I was yesterday' and 'will I be the same as I am today?'. When Vladimir and Estragon meet, they have painfully to reconstruct the events of the previous day. As an audience we are in the same position as Vladimir and Estragon, certain or almost certain of what we can remember about the events of the previous act, though we cannot be certain that this is indeed the previous 'day' that Vladimir refers to. To reconstitute the day in memory and representation is to open up that gap between the original and its repetition which can never entirely be closed, either for the characters or for their audience; we can never be sure again of the simple factuality of the day and its events. What is more, the present moment will come to seem more and more dependent upon recapitulation in the future. So, when Vladimir sees the boy for the second time, he is concerned to make sure that he will indeed tell Godot that he has seen them. Despite the uncertainties of memory and recapitulation, it is not enough simply for Vladimir to be there: he must confirm this simple present tense by reference to an anticipated retrospect.

Once repetition has been set up in the play, it proves to be congenital. Once the second act is revealed to be a repetition or near-repetition of the first, then the first itself loses its self-sufficient repletion. If the second act encounter with the boy sends us back to the similar encounter in the first act, then we may remember that this has already struck Vladimir as a repetition:

> Vladimir: I've seen you before haven't I?
> Boy: I don't know, sir.
> Vladimir: You don't know me?
> Boy: No, sir.
> Vladimir: It wasn't you came yesterday?
> Boy: No, sir.
> Vladimir: This is your first time?
> Boy: Yes, sir.
> *Silence.*
>
> (*CDW*, 47-8)

In a similar way, every presence in *Waiting for Godot* seems likely to turn out to be a ghostly repetition, or even an anticipation. (In the curious *deja vu* structure of *Waiting for Godot*, it might even be possible to read the boy in the first act as a repetition-in-advance of the boy who appears at the end.) Stranded as they are in their agonizing space of waiting, Vladimir and Estragon seem to encounter the paradox of all time; that is, that the only tense we feel has real verifiable existence, the present, the here-and-now, is in fact never here-and-now. The present tense can never simply 'be', because the 'now' of the present tense can only be apprehended the split-second before it happens, or the split-second after. It is never itself, but always the representation of itself, anticipated or remembered, which is to say, non-present. Vladimir and Estragon, stranded in the not-yet or intermission of waiting, poised between the past that they no longer inhabit and the future which cannot commence until the arrival of Godot, can never *be* fully in their present either. The longer they spend on the stage, the more, for them and for the audience, the simple immediacy of the present becomes drawn into the complex web of relationship and repetition that is all experience of time.

In fact, there seem to be two main versions of the repetitive enacted in *Waiting for Godot*. The first is circular, and suggests the impossibility of any stable present because past and future are ranged about it so ambiguously. The circular song that Vladimir sings at the beginning of Act 2 provides the model for this kind of repetition. In this, priority and progression seem to be disallowed, since every element in the song is both before and after every other element. The other model of repetition is linear. Some of the repetitions in *Waiting for Godot* seem to indicate not endless reduplication, but entropic decline. Chief among these is the reappearance of Pozzo in Act 2, blind and without his watch, with a servant who is now unable to think because dumb. In later plays, Beckett insists more and more on this kind of repetition-with-decrease, to give us, for example, the gradual burying of Winnie in the earth, the slowing down of the speakers in *Play,* the weakening of the auditor's gesture in *Not I* and the enfeebling of the woman's voice in *Rockaby.*

All these suggest repetitive series rather than repetitive circles. It is hard to say whether this kind of repetition is more or less corrosive of the audience's sense of presence. It would seem to be true that the idea of a repetitive series at least retains the direction of time, and therefore stabilizes the repetition, for in a repetitive series it is possible to distinguish and rank different stages of decline, and consequently possible to mark the passage of time by them. This kind of repetitive series also seems to promise an end point which circular repetition does not.

But even in a repetitive series there is a decentring effect which makes the sense of immediate presence difficult to sustain. For how do we begin to consider the two 'halves' of a Beckett da capo play? As with all such repetitions the first time through will strike us as new, and primary, and the second is likely to seem a derivation from the first, its ghost, or shadow. But the ubiquity of repetition and the insistence of series in Beckett's work prevents us from seeing the first time through as necessarily primary, or the second time through as terminal. Both are equally repetitions, and we are therefore deprived of the sense of priority or finality; each is doubled on the inside, as it were, by what it repeats, and what will repeat it. This is surely the reason why Beckett's repetitive structures rarely go into a third phase (though the Trilogy might seem to be an important exception). To pass into a third phase is to suggest transcendence, or commit oneself at least to the triangular shape of transcendence as it has been conceived in many philosophical models; it is to rank the previous two possibilities as opposites and perhaps to suggest their dialectic subsuming or resolution in the third repetition. Here, repetition is the sign of redemption, the guarantee of memory and destiny. It might also be to remind one, in a less exalted way, of the superstitious values attached to the third repetition in myth and fairy tale, which always marks the moment of return, or the resolution into pattern of endless open process. The fixity conventionally established by the triad is most plainly stated by Lewis Carroll's Bellman, in *The Hunting of the Snark,* when he declares 'what I tell you three times is true'.[11] Beckett's theatre, on the other hand, leaves repetitive possibilities to extend arbitrarily and uncontrollably into the future beyond the play — and therefore in a sense to infiltrate the performance too.

One exception to this prevailing double-structure might seem to be *Endgame* — and this is also the most uncompromising representation in Beckett's work of repetition allied to entropic running down. Certainly, Hamm and Clov may be on the point of leaving at the end. But it might still be argued that withholding the repetition of the day from the audience has the effect of highlighting the self-sufficiency, the unique presence of this particular passage of time in a way that distinguishes it from other plays. We know that these players will return to the stage night after night — but, in the theatre, we see them once and for all.

Another way of putting this might be to say that *Endgame* impresses us with its unity. It is a unity that is foregrounded by repetitive devices. Beckett said of the play that it 'ist voller Echos, alle antworten einander',[12] and there does indeed seem to be a thickening of internal repetition in the play. The various parallels in the action, Clov watching Hamm at the beginning and the end of the play, Hamm taking off and putting on his old handkerchief, and the verbal echoes in Hamm's first and last soliloquies, as well as the repetitions of words and phrases shared by Hamm and Clov, all seem to give a sense of closure, completeness and self-identity to *Endgame*.[13]

But against all this are the various factors which resist this apprehension of unity. Near the beginning of the play, Hamm asks Clov 'What's happening, what's happening?', only to receive the reply 'Something is taking its course' (*CDW,* 98). These words suggest the non-identity of experience and meaning. If all that is happening is precisely what we see, consists simply in the two characters being there, then, for Hamm and Clov, this being there is agonizingly insufficient. For Hamm especially, meaning or significance cannot inhere in experience, but must be imposed from the outside, as the supervention of an imagined outsider, a 'rational being' who, as he surmises, might happen to visit them and 'get ideas into his head' (*CDW,* 108). Because of this dependence on meanings ascribed from the outside, the endless process of Hamm's and Clov's lives never comes of itself to any point of significance or understanding; the best that can be managed is the asymptotic approach to meaning or identity which is imaged in the allusions to the millet-heap of the philosopher Sextus Empiricus. Clov looks forward to the coming of being as one looks for the moment when a succession of millet grains added one to another can suddenly be recognized as a heap: 'Grain upon grain, one by one, and one day, suddenly, there's a heap, a little heap, the impossible heap' (*CDW,* 93). When the metaphor recurs in Hamm's words, it seems clear that the moment when the grain becomes a heap will recede infinitely: 'Moment upon moment, pattering down, like the millet grains of ... *(he hesitates)* ... that old Greek, and all life long you wait for that to mount up to a life' (*CDW,* 126).[14] In this hell, as in Sartre's *Huis Clos,* it proves impossible to imagine a life brought to completeness. When death comes it will not confer a meaning, but will simply, arbitrarily, bring the process of living to a halt.

So we can see that *Endgame* refuses the consummation of the ending that its form and title suggest. Time and again in Beckett's work, we encounter the anxiety that it will not be possible to come to an end because there will have been no full existence prior to that ending; and, for all its powerful theatrical presence, *Endgame* shows us characters who fear that they will never have been enough in the present to vanish. Hamm shares with characters in the Trilogy, especially the voice in *The Unnamable,* that repetitive structure of consciousness, in which it is impossible to be fully oneself, because fullness of being is always one step further on, always deferred to the future. Hamm's life, as he says, was always 'the life to come' (*CDW,* 116). As Robbe-Grillet recognizes, a present contaminated in this way by lack ceases to exist: 'under these conditions, the present becomes nothing, it disappears, it too has been conjured away, and lost in the general bankruptcy' (*TNN,* 129).

If Hamm's life is always deferred, then it is also true that it is a life lived in repetition and retrospect. It is as though every unfinished moment requires repetition to bring it to completeness, or significance. So, as we listen to his endless attempts to retrieve the past in his portentous narrative we sense what may happen to the present moment. As in *Waiting for Godot,* the present fades into its reconstitution in future repetition. Indeed, for all the locked closure of this play, there is an insistent self-doubling that takes place at every moment. This, surely, is the effect of all the moments of theatrical self-reflection in the play, Hamm's posturing grandiloquence, mimicked by Nagg's story, Clov's sarcasm at the audience's expense and the references to 'playing' of all kinds, from Hamm's opening words to the explicit references to asides, exits and soliloquies. All these features induce consciousness not of the stage as simply itself, but of the stage as a space of representation — even if it is the minimal representation of itself. No matter what is stripped away of character, plot and setting on the stage, there always persists, within the most reduced performance, a residual self-doubling — the stage owning itself *as* stage, *as* performance. If we see *Endgame* initially as a play which acts out the coming to an end of one kind of repetitive series, then in another clear sense it is a play which demonstrates the necessary and inescapable continuation of repetition. This necessity is described well by Derrida in his critique of Artaud's prescriptions for the Theatre of Cruelty:

> There is no theater in the world today which fulfills Artaud's desire. And there would be no exception to be made for the attempts made by Artaud himself. He knew this better than any other: the 'grammar' of the theater of cruelty, of which he said that it is 'to be found', will always remain the inaccessible limit of a representation which is not repetition, of a re-presentation which is full presence, which does not carry its double within itself as its death, of a present which does not repeat itself, that is, of a present outside time, a nonpresent. The present offers itself as such, appears, presents itself, opens the stage

of time or the time of the stage only by harboring its own intestine difference, and only in the interior fold of its original repetition, in representation.

('The Theater of Cruelty or the Closure of Representation',
WD, 248)

The moment of pure theatre that Beckett seems to show us, Hamm declaiming as an actor in the dying moments of the play, with no pretence that he is anything else, is in reality not the limit of full self-identity. The actor who plays the part of Hamm cannot — by definition — be the same actor whose part Hamm represents himself as playing. There is certainly close resemblance between the two, but if we recognize the collusion between the actor who speaks the words of the text and the character who repeats the words of his oft-rehearsed story, then that is because we also recognize the sustaining difference between them. In other words, we recognize the resemblance as one of repetition rather than identity. And the closer the performance comes to an identity with its text, the more Derrida's obstinate 'interior fold of its original repetition' reasserts itself.

There is another way of thinking about this. For the theatre to be theatre, it must be observed, must be staged in a particular place for a particular audience. Traditionally, the playwright and actor have depended upon, and sometimes regretted, this necessity. Billie Whitelaw has recently said that Beckett himself thinks of his plays as ideally a drama without an audience.[15] But, though it is certainly possible to imagine a performance without an audience, it is doubtful whether such a thing could count for anyone as a performance unless the element of spectacle were retained. This residual doubling asserts itself at the moment of Hamm's withdrawal from the theatre at the end of the play. After he has discarded all his petty theatrical paraphernalia, he is left merely with words and, when they cease, with darkness and silence. His final words seem to show him embracing this final retreat. His story has concerned his rebuff to the man he has hired (Clov?), whose son he would not permit to live with them. But if Clov is a kind of son to Hamm, then the closure of possibility in Hamm's story is contradicted by Clov's continuing presence on stage. Hamm's words may seem like an embracing of solitude, but they show in their hesitations and gaps the awareness of a potential audience — for example in the phrase 'there we are, there I am, that's enough,' in which the second phrase sounds like a retraction or correction of the first. However, the first person plural recurs a little later when, having whistled and sniffed to see if Clov is still alive and then having cautiously called his name, he settles back, saying 'Good ... Since that's the way we're playing it ... let's play it that way ... and speak no more about it' (*CDW*, 133). The conventional 'we' here includes the possibility that Clov may still be there, as indeed he is, and may help to confirm the audience's suspicion that this little scene has been played out between them before. The last lines of the play have Hamm withdrawing into solitude, after he has pierced the barrier between audience and spectacle with the whistle that he throws into the auditorium. But Hamm's solitude remains an enacted solitude, enacted for us and for the still-visible Clov. Hamm has discarded all but his 'old stancher', and closes his soliloquy with an affectionate address to it — 'You ... remain' (*CDW*, 134). The irresistible affect of his words is to suggest the presence of the audience who do indeed remain, for the time being anyway, watching him. Hamm's words seem to acknowledge the necessity of the Other, even as he repudiates it. Only as long as they 'remain' to watch can he 'remain' in enacted solitude.

Voice and Mechanical Reproduction:
Krapp's Last Tape, Ohio Impromptu, Rockaby, That Time

The drama's claim to embody a 'metaphysics of presence' rests largely upon two claims: that it represents human beings with the actual bodies of other human beings, and that it represents spoken words with words spoken by those actual human beings. The relationship between these claims is an intimate and necessary one. Thus it is a commonplace to argue that the theatre's reliance on speech rather than on 'dead' writing gives it an immediacy which the novel, or any other written narrative, can never match. In the case of Beckett's theatre, there is a particular potency invested in the idea of the voice, given the point which seems to have been reached in *The Unnamable*. Although the speaker is surrounded and penetrated by voices, murmuring and babbling, it cannot be sure if any of those voices are its own, cannot even be sure that its own voice is its own: 'I must speak, with this voice that is not mine, but can only be mine ... it is I who speak, all alone, since I can't do otherwise. No, I am speechless' (*T*, 309). For Beckett, the opportunity that theatre offers for full and unambiguous speech was clearly not to be resisted. But this opportunity is also a drawback. For if one of the drives behind Beckett's work is to speak the self, to 'say I', then his work is also the victim of the desire to retract, efface, or otherwise cancel out speech. This must provoke the question of how an art of effacement can work with the dominating palpability of 'living' speech in the theatre.

One of the important ways in which this is attempted is by a return to the repetitive and auto-citational devices of the fiction. The refrains which echo through *Waiting for Godot* and *Endgame* work against the sense of immediate utterance. As we hear the formulaic interchanges being repeated, we become aware that, faced with the giddy nothingness of being on stage and having nothing to say, Vladimir and Estragon have to fall back on what they have said before. They quote themselves, or, it might perhaps be felt, their language begins to quote them.

In the conventional opposition between the living voice of theatre and the dead letter of written literature, criticism reproduces that phonocentric prejudice which is fundamental to Western thought. As we have seen, repetition and iterability form a central part of Derrida's critique of phonocentrism. Where writing is considered to be abstract and dead because it can be removed from its intentional or performative context — can, in other words, be subjected to repetition (and possibily alteration) — speech is commonly thought to be immune from this danger, since speech and the social contexts which define and allow speech are, by definition, immediate and apparent. One of the most influential proponents of this view is J. L. Austin, with his theory of performative language — that is, language which 'performs' rather than simply stating its meaning, and whose success or significance can be measured in terms of the receiving context in which the speech-act takes place.[16] Derrida points out that, in order to maintain his position, Austin has to exclude from consideration all so-called 'non-serious' uses of words and verbal formulations, such as the quotation of words in other contexts, or the use of language in the drama. But Derrida argues that the possibility of language being repeated in another context is not an accidental aberration, or special case, but is the enabling condition of all language, written and spoken. The meaning of an utterance is therefore more correctly to be found, not in the momentary environment of its production, but in the subsequent possibilities of its repetition and alteration in other contexts. This is conventionally agreed to be true of written language, but Derrida argues that it is just as much the condition of spoken language:

> This is the possibility on which I wish to insist: the possibility of extraction and of citational grafting which belongs to the structure of every mark, spoken or written, and which constitutes every mark as writing even before and outside every horizon of semiolinguistic communication.... Every sign, linguistic or non-linguistic, spoken or written (in the usual sense of this opposition), as a small or large unity, can be *cited,* put between quotation marks; thereby it can break with every given context, and engender infinitely new contexts in an absolutely nonsaturable fashion.[17]

In a sense, *Waiting for Godot* and *Endgame* demonstrate precisely this iterative principle, though in these cases repetition may not seem to engender the rich multiplicity of interpretative contexts that Derrida imagines here. In *Krapp's Last Tape,* his next extended play for the theatre, Beckett examines the iterative possibilities brought about by the tape recorder. Although writing can provide a repeatable version of nearly any utterance, it does so inevitably by translating that utterance into another medium, so that what is recorded is only a version of the words, and not the acoustic materiality of the words themselves. A tape recorder, on the other hand, makes possible the absolute retrieval of spoken words, in what seems to promise a fusion of the written and the spoken.

Krapp's Last Tape demonstrates how little is kept in such a 'faithful' recording. For Krapp to listen to the tape of himself as a man of thirty-nine is to reveal clearly his ironic non-coincidence with himself. Where the younger Krapp can talk brashly about his mother's 'viduity', the older Krapp no longer remembers what the word means, just as he cannot remember the details set down in the ledger about the 'black ball' or the 'memorable equinox'. In fact the ledger that Krapp consults forms an interesting counterpoint to the spoken voice that he hears on the tape. The effect of seeing Krapp as puzzled by the voice as by the written redaction of what the voice has to say, though able in both cases to stop and go over the material again, is to run together the two forms of language, making recorded speech like a kind of writing.

Something of the same conflation is suggested by other parallels. As in *Malone Dies,* Beckett insists on the material facts involved in the process of reading, stressing the weight and inaccessibility of the ledger, with its entries difficult for Krapp to read with his failing eyesight and, especially, the necessity of breaking off reading to turn the page — 'Farewell to — [*he turns page*] — love' (*CDW,* 217). The effect of bathos is intensified by the splitting of the word in the French version — 'Adieu a l'a ... (*il tourne la page*) ... mour' — with the obvious hint that it gives of love turning to death.[18] But Beckett exploits the simple physical fact of the turning of the page as well. Written language allows — one might almost say necessitates — gaps and interruptions, for its unchanging material form means that it can be broken off and resumed at the same point. The immediacy of speech, however, means that it cannot be suspended in this way without being lost forever. In this play, the ability to break off, the possibility of introducing gaps, is evident both in the written and the spoken text — the ledger and the tape; and this ability is coincidental with the fact of the written text's iterability. The awareness of the function of gaps gives a sense of other parallels between speech and writing. In particular, the hesitations in the younger Krapp's voice, which punctuate his confidently continuous dialogue with moments of indecisive silence, open up possibilities of alteration or difference. So Krapp's 'Farewell to — [*he turns page*] — love' is matched by the voice on the tape saying 'I love to get up and move about in it, then back here to — [*hesitates*] ... me' (*CDW,* 217). Such a hesitation functions at the same time, of course, as an indicator of authentic speech. The indicators of speech and writing seem to be mingled in a complex way, the hesitations allowing the possibility of revision and reformulation and undermining the authority of the spoken, or at least setting up a friction between the authority of the speaker and the density of his linguistic medium. The younger Krapp's hesitations are like the moments when the older Krapp winds back and pauses before resuming:

> ...intellectually I have now every reason to suspect at the [*hesitates*]...crest of the wave — or thereabouts.
> The grain, now what I wonder do I mean by that, I mean... [*hesitates*]...I suppose I mean those things worth having when all the dust has — when all *my* dust has settled.
> The face she had! The eyes! Like...[*hesitates*]...chrysolite!
> ...perhaps no place left in my memory, warm or cold, for the miracle that...[*hesitates*]...or the fire that set it alight.
> (CDW, 217, 220)

On a couple of occasions, the speaker's self-punctuation and the listener's interpolations of silence or commentary are run together, or counterpointed: 'Ah well...[*Pause*] These old P.M.s are gruesome, but I often find them — [*Krapp switches off, broods, switches on.*] — a help before embarking on a new...[*hesitates*]...retrospect (CDW, 218).

And sometimes the older and younger Krapp collude more closely in listening and responding to the words as they are being spoken: 'The voice! Jesus! And the aspirations! [*Brief laugh in which Krapp joins.*] And the resolutions! [*Brief laugh in which Krapp joins.*] To drink less in particular. [*Brief laugh of Krapp alone.*]' (CDW, 218). Here older and younger Krapp both break up the continuity of the utterance with derisive commentary upon it. The fact that the older Krapp adds a layer of disillusion only emphasizes the citational nature of the original utterance, in which the young Krapp is in turn appropriating the recorded words of *his* younger self in order to deride them.

Though Krapp's spoken journal into the tape recorder may sound spontaneous, it is not. The voice and style of the younger Krapp suggest speech under the particular stress that the awareness of a recording brings with it, speech darkened by the threatening shadow of repeatability. This may account for the nervous hesitations in his speech; it is as though the threat of repetition redoubles itself by forcing moments of self-critical review at the moment of vocal delivery. As a performance, the younger Krapp's report shows the influence of another more obvious kind of writing, as well, the notes that he has jotted down on an envelope from which he may be reading or improvising. The older Krapp seems to have retained this habit — so that, when we first hear about the envelope from the younger Krapp, we might wonder for a moment whether it isn't the same envelope that the older Krapp has produced at the beginning of the play. Certainly the older Krapp gets little assistance from his notes, for he soon crumples it up and resorts to improvised speech. Like Vladimir and Estragon, the older Krapp is now vulnerably scriptless and cannot keep up the flow of speech, without resorting to repetition, the repetition of the delicious word 'spool', the repetition of his song, the allusive repetitions in the memories of Christmas and Sunday mornings on Croghan, and, finally, the surrender of his own words to the repetition of the previous tape. But if Krapp resembles Vladimir, Estragon, Hamm and Clov in having to produce unscripted language for an audience, then his predicament differs from theirs, too. Unlike their free speech, his recorded words are destined to enter into the condition of iterability, marked in advance with the sign of writing.

The envelope is indeed a fit emblem for this kind of writing. Krapp's recordings are intended to provide a firm and unambiguous record of a moment of time, but instead show how every utterance can be taken up or enveloped by some other occasion, some other context of understanding. Krapp's recorded life then comes to seem less like a logically continuous series of discrete utterances, each located firmly in its intentional context, than a web of mutually enveloping, self-quoting moments, each endlessly displaced from its originating context, and regrafted elsewhere. In all these ways, *Krapp's Last Tape* moves to dissolve or undermine the dramatic qualities most commonly associated with speech — immediacy, originality and continuity. Crucial to this, as we have seen, are the physical materials necessary for the reproduction of language: the book, the envelope, the tape recorder. These articles are simultaneously the means for preserving language and the means by which meanings in language are decoyed into new contexts. The material forms of reproduction are there to remind us of the iterative possibility of all speech and the consequent death into writing of every living word.[19]

The paradox is that it is precisely the unalterability of repeatable texts that guarantees their instability of meaning. By ignoring the main part of the tape, the account of the moment of inspiration which the younger Krapp feels is the most significant part of his yearly report, and concentrating on the 'farewell to love', Krapp seems in an almost literal way to be rewriting the record — and, of course, in doing so, making it plain that the 'farewell to love' is one that will be infinitely repeated. That the audience catches only tantalizing snippets of what it may feel is at least as interesting as the farewell to love, the younger Krapp's aesthetic credo, is the demonstration of another context of response and understanding for the tape. This is emphasized by the final moments of the play, in which we finally hear the end of the recording. The simple dramatic irony of the words on the recording, 'I wouldn't want them back. Not with the fire in me now. No, I wouldn't want them back', coming so soon after Krapp's longing to 'be again, be again' (*CDW*, 223), is made the more powerful because we assume that by this time Krapp is no longer listening to himself. This highlights again the tension between speech and text which motivates the whole play. The final words both assert the primacy and durability of speech across the years and frame it in the dead and iterable condition of writing. The haunting power of the words comes from their incomplete jurisdiction over their listening context and from the overlayering, in the language, of urgent subjective presence and the merely mechanical fidelity with which those words are reproduced. By the end of this play, with the displacement of the breathing, visible Krapp by the voice of another absent Krapp, the theatre has been transformed from a place of being to a place of writing.

The possibilities opened up by the mixing and conflict of voice and text, or 'original' utterance and mechanically reproduced utterance, are explored in a number of other Beckett plays. In most of these plays — like *That Time*, *Rockaby* and *Ohio Impromptu* — the ratio of the recorded to the 'live' material that we see on stage is much greater. *Ohio Impromptu*, for instance, shows us little more than one character reading to another from a book (the only 'live' word being the reader's 'yes' [*CDW*, 446]), and might seem to have lost all the qualities of dangerous and free presence admired by Robbe-Grillet in *Waiting for Godot*. Far from abandoning its script, this play seems to flaunt its dependence upon the written word, and the characters to highlight the play's involuted disdain of action by the way that they shield their faces from the audience. The language of the narrative itself has a crystalline remoteness, and the repetition of crucial phrases identifies it as 'written': 'and here he named the dear name … then disappeared without a word … saw the dear face and heard the unspoken words … so the sad tale a last time told … little is left to tell … nothing is left to tell'. In Alan Schneider's production, at the Harold Clurman Theatre, New York, in 1983, David Warrilow's delivery intensified the sense of the mechanical impersonality of the text, with its slowness, depth and unvarying tone.

Nevertheless, the whole play depends upon the complications attending the reproduction of this piece of text. The six knocks which the listener delivers have the effect of halting the narrative just as surely as Krapp's tape recorder, and the control is so total that another knock is required to start the narrative up again. The very comprehensibility of the code of knocks depends upon frequent repetition, too, for it can only have been through repetition that the code has been established between reader and silent listener. In this it may resemble the code of raps on the skull used by Molloy to communicate with his mother (*T*, 18).

What makes these knocks and repetitions more interesting are the places in the narrative where they occur. There are five sentences which the listener asks to have repeated: 'Little is left to tell', 'Then turn and his slow steps retrace', 'Seen the dear face and heard the unspoken words, Stay where we were so long together, my shade will comfort you', 'Little is left to tell', 'Saw the dear face and heard the unspoken words, No need to go to him again even were it in your power', and 'Nothing is left to tell.' In every case but one the repetition seems to be there to allow the listener to relish the prospect of an imminent end — either of his life, or of the narration (not that the two are clearly separable). In each case a small but complex turbulence is set up by the suspension and repetition of the narrative; the listener pauses, perhaps to assure himself of the truth of what he has just heard, and to remind himself that the end is approaching, even though by delaying the narration he actually pushes the moment of ending further into the future. The irony of this is most apparent when the listener requires the repetition of the words 'Nothing is left to tell.' The most effective confirmation of the end of the narrative would obviously be silence — this is the response that the listener gets to his next knock — but, as with the ending of *Ill Seen Ill Said*, discussed in the first chapter, the listener seems to feel the need to reanimate the narrative just at the moment of its expiry, to be told once more that there is nothing left to tell.[20] If the ending of this play has been reached, the effect of these delays is to hint that it may not be as absolute an ending as it may appear. It is the end of *this* narrative, but since the narrative is written down and always available for repeated rereading, there is no reason why it shouldn't be resumed at a later date. This is true despite the hints given in the narrative that the speaker will not come again, for it will always be possible for the narrative to be read by someone else and/or to someone else, in some other place.

Problematic iterability seems to be built into the structure of the narrative, and its relationship with the spectacle presented on the stage. As most audiences quickly realize, there are very close parallels between the situation described in the narrative and what is seen before us: the two 'grow to be as one' in the audience's minds. But the very fact that this can be realized is the mark of its impossibility. Obviously, to be able to narrate something is to stand temporally outside it, in a way that this narrative logically cannot or not without a change of tense, anyway -if it tells of what happens after its narration has ceased. As the narrative progresses we feel awareness first of all of the coincidence of words and action and then progressively, of their non-coincidence; so that, at the end, it is hard to know whether the listener and hearer are sharing the narrative of themselves, or whether they are another couple, or another narration. If the second or third is the case, then it seems possible that the series will not end here, and that a further narrative may be being prepared about this narrative. The truth claims of the narrative seem to depend upon a writing whose iterability paradoxically disturbs the claims to authority.

There are certain resemblances between the use of the book in *Ohio Impromptu* and the use of recorded material in *Rockaby*. The woman in the chair calls out for the tape to resume, just as the listener knocks for a resumption of the reading. If the written text of *Ohio Impromptu* tells the story of the play itself, then the recorded voice in *Rockaby* seems to be telling the woman her own story. But there are differences between the two plays, as well. If the recorded voice of *Rockaby* is full of repetitions, they are automatic repetitions, which the woman cannot control in the way that the listener can, once she has actually set the sequence going. Ironically, the limit of her control over the flood of utterance is in joining in with the words 'time she stopped' — and she doesn't even do this towards the end of the play. The relationship between voice and text is therefore even more unbalanced than in *Ohio Impromptu,* for the 'real' voice of the actress on stage is almost entirely subordinated by the mechanical reproduction of her words.

As with *Ohio Impromptu,* the dramatic interest of the play comes from the emerging relationship between what is described in the recorded monologue and what the audience sees before it. And in this play something important does happen after the monologue ceases — the woman's head sinks slowly and comes to rest, in what Alan Schneider's production presumed was her death. But, even though this is something that simply happens, in front of us on the stage, it is given meaning only by the words that have preceded the action, and these words establish her dying in advance as a repetition. She has gone down into her mother's old rocking chair in the basement, to die, just as her mother has. Indeed, as throughout the text, the shifting pronouns bring about a merging of identity between the mother and the daughter who replicates her life and death.

In fact, the repetitive structure of the monologue does not allow the easy resolution with W's death at the end of the play, for, despite the emphatic and shocking non-repetitions at the end, 'rock her off/stop her eyes/fuck life/stop her eyes/rock her off/rock her off' (*CDW* 442), the tape seems to be caught in a series of self-recalling loops, each tending towards an end, but also stimulating an apparently infinite series of delays for recapitulation. In a sense, the play follows the familiar Beckettian pattern of 'leastening' or progressive diminishment, W's cries for 'more' being met each time with the less and less there is 'left to tell'. But it is also true that she does get more each time, for each passage of narrative is longer than the previous one, and the last passage, with seventy-seven phrases, is over half as long again as the first. The reason for this expansion-in-diminishment is that the less there remains to tell, and the further the voice is on in the narrative, the more there is to recapitulate. Once again, the necessity for repetition makes for a deferral of ending; and the repetitive structures of the written are given ascendancy over the alleged immediacy and truthfulness of the spoken.

There is another difference between *Rockaby* and *Ohio Impromptu.* As spectators, we may realize that the voice we hear is recorded, but this is not demonstrated for us on the stage, in the way that it is in

Krapp's Last Tape. Beckett experiments in other plays with prerecorded voices which are not identified openly as such. The effect of this is to complicate even further our sense of the relationship between the phonic and the textual. Probably the most complex version of this is to be found in *That Time,* which shows us an old man, listening to three voices (identified by the text as his own), speaking of different times in his life. It is as though the situation represented in *Krapp's Last Tape* had been logically extended; now the old man does not even begin to contribute to the voices, but loses himself in the repetitious evocations of past time. Where Krapp is still just about able to order and categorize the different periods of his life, his ledger separating out youth, middle age and age, distinguishing 'this time' from 'that time', the listener in *That Time* is suspended between the voices, and the different times that they specify and represent.

This could be seen as an intensification of the situation described in *Proust,* where it is argued that the mobility of the subject through time, the endless process of 'decantation' from the past to the future, makes it impossible to be fully present at any one time. But there are differences too. Time as it is described in *Proust* at least has continuity of direction, even if it is occasionally interrupted by the 'fugitive salvation' of involuntary memory. But in *That Time,* time seems no longer to have any direction; whereas in *Proust* it is the impossibility of suspending time in repetition that makes living in time so uncertain, in *That Time* it is the inescapability of repetition which produces this effect. There are in the play three different and more or less distinguishable voices, to be sure, which we may begin to identify with periods in the listener's life: A describes a visit made to his home, perhaps in Dublin, and the abortive attempt to revisit a ruin frequented as a child; B describes moments of love from youth; and C describes a number of occasions on which the man has sought shelter in public buildings, in the Portrait Gallery, the Post Office and the Library, and the climactic experience of emptiness in the vision of the dust seen in the Library. As the order of the alphabetical series suggests, these are the stages of childhood, youth and age. But things are more complicated than this, for each voice also describes reminiscence, recall, or return. A describes a return late in life to the scenes of childhood, B describes the attempts in later life to recapture the memory of scenes of love, while C describes three different episodes, each one resembling the other, though they need not necessarily belong to the same period of life. Given this over-layering of experience with recall, it is hard to be sure what chrono-logical sequence the voices form. And there is a further overlayering, introduced by the figure of the listener, who is the same person as all three voices, but identical with none of them. The problem is therefore not one of a lack of differentiation, but one of an excess of differentia-tion. Each voice exists as a problematic ratio between different, even incompatible voices and experiences. Given this multiplicity, the solid-ity of the present vanishes, for every moment of time is shadowed and inhabited by the other times which precede and succeed it.

Not only is each sequence complicated by interior repetitions, but each of the individual narratives repeats elements of the others in ways that make it difficult to sustain their separation. Each of the three se-quences involves the memory of sitting on some kind of stone — the child hiding with a picture book on a stone in the folly, the young man and his lover together on a stone in the sun and the marble slab in the Portrait Gallery. Phrases recur insistently, not only within indi-vidual sequences, but across sequences, sometimes in close proximity, as with A's phrase 'was your mother ah for God's sake all gone long ago', echoed a moment later by C (*CDW*, 389), or the phrase 'out to hell out of there', again shared by A and C (*CDW*, 389, 392). Similarly A's 'till the truth began to dawn' is echoed by C's 'thanking God ... till it dawned that for all the loathing you were getting' (*CDW*, 391, 394), B's 'not a soul abroad' is echoed by C's 'not a living soul' (*CDW*, 388, 389), B's 'no stir or sound only faintly the leaves' is repeated in C's 'not a sound only the old breath and the leaves turning' (*CDW*, 392, 395), and B's references to 'making it up' are taken up in A's 'making it all up on the doorstep' (*CDW*, 390, 394). As these examples may suggest, most of the motifs are shared between two of the voices alone, giving the sense of asymmetry, or incompleteness. The listener or reader is reminded of words and phrases by repetition and encouraged to form groupings; but these groupings always form the unstable ratio of 2:1, leaving out one of the sequences.[21] In every case, similarity is pen-etrated by difference, and absolute continuity denied. The persistence of contradiction in the repetitions resists critical attempts to see the narratives blended into the unity of a single life.[22] Age and youth, for example, are run together by the repetition of references to reading, the child 'poring on his book well into the night' and the old man in the library 'with a bevy of old ones poring on the page and not a sound'. But where the child reading until well past midnight has the adult world 'all out on the roads looking for him', the old man has slipped into the library out of the cold and rain 'when no one was looking' (*CDW*, 393, 394) — a difference which in its turn recalls A's memory that, as a child he would 'slip off when no one was looking' (*CDW*, 389). In a similar way, references to light and dark repeat and alternate. The old man in A's narrative sits in the 'pale sun' on a doorstep, reminding us of the stone 'in the sun' shared by the lovers in B's narrative (*CDW*, 394, 392). The child sits reading on the stone long after dark, just as the man in B's narrative sits 'by the window in the dark', and the old man in C's narrative sits not in the sun but in the gloom of an interior (*CDW*, 390, 394).

As with *Molloy* and the Trilogy, the effect of these two different kinds of repetition, repetition to mark continuity, and repetition to mark contrast, is to twist together sameness and difference indistinguishably, abolishing the grounds by which they may be discerned and maintained as concepts, so that every continuity may be glimpsed paradoxically as a difference, every difference as a continuity. C's narrative seems to articulate this in the passage following his description of the gallery. To return to the scene in memory is to establish that he was 'never the same afterwards,' but this unique experience, which opens up the rift between before and after, sameness and difference, turns out not to be unique, but itself to be a repeated experience: 'never the same after that never quite the same but that was nothing new if it wasn't this it was that common occurrence something you could never be the same after crawling about year after year sunk in your lifelong mess muttering to yourself who else you'll never be the same after this you were never the same after that' (*CDW*, 390). These repeated experiences of split, or difference — the repetition of non-repeatability — leads to a condition of permanent impermanence, in which it is impossible to speak reliably of sameness or difference. The speaker is 'never the same but the same as what for God's sake' (*CDW, 390*).

There is one set of verbal repetitions in the text which is shared between the three speakers, namely, the insistent references to time,

in all its senses — 'that time ... that last time, was that the time or
... was that another time ... another place another time ... like time
could go no further at closing-time ... till the time came in the end
... come and gone in no time'. This also allows the repetition through
the text of the title itself (though we might at the same time see the
title as a quotation or repetition of the text). The title's repetition of the
words 'that time' may oppose the sense that the listener is hearing these
words from a position outside or beyond time, may imply that the play
is itself the representation of a particular moment or period in time.
This would establish a continuity between the listener's position and
the position of the characters described in the the narratives of A, B and
C. 'That time' functions as a deictic, that is, it designates a particular
moment in time which varies with the context. This play multiplies the
contexts of this phrase, endlessly shifting this particularity. As with the
title of *Watt,* metonymic grafting mobilizes the fixity of metaphorical
naming.[23]

'That time' can also carry the sense of 'time in general'. This duality is not contained within a single word in the French, and, in his
translation of the play, Beckett is forced to distribute the different
senses of 'time' between the words 'fois', 'temps' and 'heure'. There
seems to be some compensation for this in the increase in frequency
of the last two words in the text, presumably to make the repetitions
more conspicuous — 'every now and then' becomes, very naturally,
'de temps en temps', 'waiting with the nightbag till the truth began to
dawn' becomes 'la besace à la main le temps de te rendre à l'évidence',
'till it was night' becomes 'le temps qu'il fasse nuit' and 'till that time
came' becomes 'le temps que cette heure vienne'.[24]

The difficulty and multiplicity of interpretation comes about because of the separation of the voice from the face, a separation which
compels us to try to unify the two, without ever offering the prospect
of complete success. Separated from immediate reference, the flood of
speech which surrounds the face takes on the condition of a writing,
in that we must all the time supply for it interpretative contexts. The
meaning of these words does not reside in them, but, as with the words
on the tape that winds off slowly at the end of *Krapp's Last Tape,* is produced from the relationship of the words to a context that subsequently
comes about, a context which is a supervention and a displacement

of the words. What is important to note is that the face itself is not exempt from these displacements, despite the problematic separation of voice and text, for the face too begins to display itself as repetition and displacement. Perhaps the most powerful of its displacements is brought about in the last words, which seem to predict the final fade-out, and at the same time to offer an interpretation of the preceding play: 'not a sound only the old breath and the leaves turning and then suddenly this dust whole place suddenly full of dust when you opened your eyes from floor to ceiling nothing only dust and not a sound only what was it it said come and gone was it something like that come and gone come and gone no one come and gone in no time gone in no time' (*CDW, 395*).

These final words allude to the breath we are to hear when they cease ('the old breath'), as well as to the opening eyes of the listener. Perhaps they also evoke the reader of this text, with the reference to the 'leaves turning' in the library. Clearly, this detail cooperates with the reference to dust to allude to the passage of time and the decay that it brings, and this conflation of writing and mutability is itself a repeated motif in Beckett's work. Reader and spectator are then offered a summary of the preceding performance: all that can be said for certain is that the voices and the listening face have 'come and gone', that formula which Beckett often returns to to express the shadowy interdependence of presence and absence. The banal phrase which follows, 'in no time', is given a new impetus by its position at the end of the play; its ordinary meaning of 'abruptly' is intensified, as we realize that the apparently interminable voices are actually coming to an end, just as every life must, and that the time which they have occupied seems both appallingly long and sickeningly brief. The words may also suggest that the audience has participated in a stretch of 'no-time', that is, the 'non-time' of dramatic representation, in which there is no real before or after, or even present tense, but only the representations of them. If we feel ourselves about to be restored to the real time of habitual experience, we may also feel for a moment the anxiety that this theatrical 'no-time' is more like our own lived time and our representations of it than we care to, or can afford to, believe.

Chapter 7

What? Where? Space and the Body

What? Where?

To challenge the prestige of dramatic speech, as Beckett's theatre does, is also to challenge one of the most powerful and recurrent oppositions between drama and writing — that opposition between the living, the embodied, the concrete on the one hand, and the abstract, the symbolic and the intangible on the other. The two alleged characteristics of drama, its phonic immediacy and its physicality, are closely connected, of course, for the critical ascendancy of voice in the theatre derives from and is reinforced by the sense of the origin of the voice in the body. If the language of the written book is distant and immaterial, then the language of the performed drama is conceived to be living and potent because it is physical. Again, Artaud's work provides a useful expression of these ideas. The mark of true and intrinsically theatrical language for Artaud is the physicality that guarantees it freedom from the tyranny of preexisiting script:

> To make metaphysics out of spoken language is to make language convey what it does not normally convey. That is to use it in a new, exceptional and unusual way, to give it its full, physical shock potential, to split it up and distribute it actively in space, to treat inflexions in a completely tangible manner and restore their shattering power and really to manifest something.
>
> ('Production and Metaphysics', *TO*, 35)

This materialization of language goes along with Artaud's stress on the immediate concreteness of the stage and the intrinsic expressiveness of the material world, *'this revealing aspect of matter,* suddenly seeming to disperse in signs, to teach us the metaphysical identity of abstract and concrete' ('On the Balinese Theatre', *TD*, 41).

Beckett's theatre indeed displays a deep and continuous concentration on the physical in all its senses, in the rigorous attention to spacing, movement and position, and emphasizes the irreducible physicality of human bodies in the spaces they actually inhabit. For Beckett's characters, the stage has its own tangible presence, usually in the sense of a limit or boundary, as, most especially, in *Act Without Words* I, where the function of the offstage area is to stress that there is no other place permitted for the actor than the stage. The limits of this available area in Beckett's theatre have tended to shrink remorselessly. Whereas in *Waiting for Godot* the two tramps range vigorously over the whole stage and even leave it from time to time, in *Endgame* only one character can move around freely, thus turning the large empty space around the characters from a functional, habitable space into a space of ironic unavailability. Though Krapp has the run of the stage and of a small offstage area, the action is effectively concentrated in the pool of light in the centre and, from this play onwards, characters are restricted to smaller and smaller spaces, either by lighting, as with the reduced area provided in *Footfalls,* or the spotlight on the face in *That Time* and on the mouth in *Not I,* or by physical restraint, as with Winnie in *Happy Days,* or the speakers in *Play.* It is as though Beckett were seeking to narrow the stage around the bodies of his actors and to abolish the difference between them, in a version of that process described in *All Strange Away,* in which the narrator 'tightens' the cube to eliminate empty space *(CSP,* 118, 120). This same process is enacted more directly in an unpublished fragment called 'Mongrel Mime', which requires the passage of an actor from right to left over the stage through three progressively smaller chambers.[1] One of the advantages for Beckett of writing for television is that it provides a mobile frame, allowing, in *Eh Joe* and in the television version of *Not I,* the exploitation of the constricting effects of closeup.

All this might seem to evidence an attention to stage space which is reflexive, in an affirmation of the limited autonomy of the theatre similar to that proclaimed by Artaud. If this is accepted, then it might stand as some more reassuring ground of certainty or limitation amid the uncertainties regarding identity or location which are manifested through the plays. Such a claim is found, for example, in Ruby Cohn's arguments for the increasing 'theatereality' of Beckett's plays, by which

she means the increasing convergence of the space that the plays represent with the actual theatre space in which they are performed. The
spotlight in *Play* is, then, primarily just a spotlight, the mouth in *Not I*
is simply a mouth, isolated in light, the space of *That Time* is the space
of playing in the theatre, and the track paced by M in *Footfalls* is 'the
place known as the Board' to which Pozzo refers in *Waiting for Godot*.[2]
Cohn retains the troubling sense of the tension maintained in the plays
between the literal stage and the representation of other spaces in the
text, but Enoch Brater carries the critical claim a stage further, in argu-
ing for the *identity* established between text and image in a play like
Rockaby, in which, he says, 'a verbal metaphor becomes concrete and
palpable. In a word it has become real'.[3]

But, as we saw in the last chapter, even if it eschews the ambition of representing anywhere else but itself, stage-space still requires
representation of some kind. Even if it represents itself alone, the stage
is still an imaginary place, which is different from the 'actual' stage
known during the day by cleaners, scene-shifters and rehearsing actors.
In order to affirm itself as elementary, irreducible stage-space, the stage
must cease to be absolutely itself. Beckett's theatre, for all its simplicity and directness with regard to stage space, time and again shows
us actual space repeating itself, or moving from the simplicity of the
concrete into the complex condition of the represented — Pozzo, hearing from Vladimir that the place they are in is 'like nothing. There's
nothing. There's a tree' decides 'Then it's not the Board' (*CDW*, 80).

Endgame, in particular, has impressed many commentators with
its apparent spatial self-sufficiency. Hugh Kenner, answering his own
question 'where is this place?' declares 'It is here, that is all we can say,
here before us, on stage. The set does not *represent*, the set is itself'.[4]
Beryl and John Fletcher affirm similarly that 'the stage in Beckett has a
particular reality. It is not a facsimile of a middle-class living room …
but a place in its own right.'[5] But this is to underestimate the complexity of what happens to conventional expectations of theatrical space
during the course of this play. *Endgame* plays notably with the audience's conceptions of inside and outside. Normally, in a play that insists
on the unity of place, we are given a sense of accessory or contingent
spaces, extending outside and adjacent to what we see before us on
stage and, in fact, we gain our sense of the solidity of the stage space

by reference to this imagined context. It is difficult to place the action of *Endgame* by means of such imaginary coordinates, because of the difference in representative status or level of the inside and the outside. Sometimes, as when Hamm declares 'Outside of here it's death', or when Clov announces that all he can see out of the window is 'Zero', the claim seems to be made that this contracted space is the whole world. But at other times we are given the opposite impression, that this is a sort of non-locality, a place where time is absent, or never gets going; to borrow the paradoxical notion of *Worstward Ho,* it might be a 'grot in the void', a fold of imaginary space within absence itself (p. 16). If this is so, then the stage-space might seem like a provisional or hypothetical space, which is less 'real' even than the reduced exterior that Clov sees. Nor should we forget Clov's kitchen. Is this part of the stage-space, part of the surrounding 'zero', or some intermediate zone? And, if the last, how do we account for this?

The point is that, in *Endgame,* we are asked to conceive of a place which is absolute in itself and at the same time exists alongside adjacent spaces. On top of this, our perception of the limiting space of the play is made ambiguous by Hamm's blind experience of it. Hamm's blindness seems to induce in him the vertigo of placelessness: 'Infinite emptiness will be all around you, all the resurrected dead of all the ages wouldn't fill it, and there you'll be like a little bit of grit in the middle of the steppe' (*CDW,* 109–10). Hamm tries to counteract this sensation by having Clov move him round the walls and back to the centre of the stage, but in neither place does he seem to achieve the sense of full occupancy. Sitting at the centre, he feels the need to confirm the limiting circumference of the room, to relish the solidity of the wall. At the wall, the feeling of eccentricity to himself overtakes him and he makes Clov hurry him back to the centre of his world — but, once there, is unable to content himself that he really is at the centre. Hamm presumably wishes to be at the centre because that is the place of least movement, and the defining place of stability. But his blindness means that the centre becomes detached in his mind from its circumference — for, obviously, a centre can only function as such when the circle of which it is a centre is also perceived, or structurally present in it. This means that, far from abolishing or canceling the circumference, the centre continually requires or internally repeats it; considered as a structural necessity as well as a perceptual function, this is as true for a sighted as for a blind person.

Hamm's centripetal movement inwards is therefore likely to be converted at any moment to a centrifugal movement outwards to his own periphery and vice versa. What makes this more complex is that whereas a circumference only has one centre, a given centre has an infinite number of possible circumferences. Hamm seems to enact this on his return to the centre: 'I feel a little too far to the left. [*Clov moves chair slightly.*] Now I feel a little too far to the right. [*Clov moves chair slightly.*] I feel a little too far forward. [*Clov moves chair slightly.*] I feel a little too far back. [*Clov moves chair slightly.*]' (*CDW*, 105). His obsessive attempts to stabilize himself actually mark out the beginnings of another circle, as any attempt to find a centre must. Hamm can never *be* in the place where movement is cancelled out, for the movement between centre and circle is continual and generic. This is perhaps the reason why Hamm is uncertain whether he wants to be 'exactly' or 'more or less' in the middle. To be 'more or less' at the centre offers the delicious prospect of more movement inwards towards the centre, while to be at the centre opens up the desire for confirming movement away from itself.

In *Quad*, a play devoted entirely to movement, a similar compulsion to oscillate between centre and periphery is found. Each of the four hooded players tramps in a series of triangles down two sides of a square and diagonally across the middle— though without actually touching the centre. As with Hamm in *Endgame*, the movement round the edge of the square seems to require or bring about a deviation into the middle, and the approach to the middle seems to project the players back out again to the edge. This seems in itself to be a refiguring in miniature of the larger oscillation of the play between movement into and movement away from the square. Like comets, the players are repeatedly drawn into the gravitational pull of the square, only to be flung off into outer darkness at the end of their courses. As with Hamm, again, the exact centre is never reached, but skirted round in a movement which, when all four players are moving at once, describes an internal circle.

Though the square seems to be a simple given — we see it empty, before the players enter — it is not long before the movement of the players seems to take over and internalize its shape. But once annexed by movement, the shape of the square becomes impermanent and has to be inscribed and anxiously reinscribed by the pacing figures. It may be that, in this, Beckett is insisting on the specificity of the TV medium, which relies not upon the presence of images before us, but on the retinal persistence of the interrupted lines of light that shuttle back and forth across the screen. Just as a still image is made up of the rapid, exactly repeated motion of these lines, so the sense of poise and completeness of design in *Quad* is made up from the repeated movements of the four players.

Quad therefore collapses and complicates the relationship of outside and inside. The players arrive in the square and, moving round it, may seem, like Dante's damned, to be the prisoners of their movement. But, since the movement they describe creates a space, they may be said to be outside it (and, in a literal sense, they describe their prison from the outside not from the inside, like the searchers in *The Lost Ones*). They are therefore, in different senses, prisoner and jailor, inside and outside. This duality may be reinforced by an interesting fact about the movement of each of the players. As Antoni Libera has observed, the movement of each player is fundamentally anticlockwise, since every turn is made to the left (this is especially apparent at the moments when all four players are circling round the centre at once, forming an anticlockwise swirl).[6] But the overall design that is paced out by each player moves him or her gradually round the square in a clockwise direction. Anticlockwise and clockwise are the directions moved by the inhabitants of the Inferno and Purgatory respectively in Dante's *Divine Comedy,* to signify movement away from and towards God, or, to put it another way, away from or towards freedom. The players in *Quad* therefore seem locked in a movement that is double, and endlessly irresolvable, since one cannot imagine even some general overall direction for the players (as one can in *The Lost Ones*). Endlessly, backwards and forwards, inside and outside, anticlockwise and clockwise, restriction and freedom, alternate and produce each other in repetitions.

In some ways, however, *Quad* is an exception. In most of his later plays, Beckett has allowed his characters less and less room, fewer and fewer opportunities to explore the space that they occupy. This means in turn that the audiences of these plays have less and less to go on in recognizing or interpreting the space which is being witnessed, and relating characters to that space. Though the three urns in *Play* are self-evidently ranged alongside each other, none of the occupants seems aware of the others speaking at his or her elbow. In *Eh Joe*, as the camera moves into tighter and tighter closeup on Joe's face, we are progressively deprived of the means of positioning him in his room. And in later plays, where the available space for viewing is reduced to that of a head, face, or mouth, we lose almost entirely the means of relating it to its stage environment. We appear to be hovering above the head seen throughout *That Time*, but are unable to provide the scale or spatial context for this, so that, in the sensory deprivation of the auditorium, we may begin to wonder whether the head is not gazing down upon us. Similarly, the mouth in *Not I* seems impossible to assign to any imaginable theatrical space, despite the shadowy figure of the listener. Hearing the description of the woman who finds herself in the dark, we may share her sense of vertigo:

> found herself in the dark...and if not exactly...insentient...insentient. [...]...feeling so dulled...she did not know...what position she was in...imagine!...what position she was in!...whether standing...or sitting...but the brain– ...what?...kneeling?...yes...whether standing...or sitting...or kneeling...but the brain– ...what?...lying?... yes...whether standing...or sitting...or kneeling...or lying...
> (*CDW*, 377)

Often, Beckett intensifies the sense of a character's uncertain relationship to the space they occupy by placing them literally off-centre. The strip of light which M paces in *Footfalls* is '*a little off-centre audience right*', the listener's face in *That Time* is '*about 10 feet above stage level midstage off-centre*', the rocking-chair in *Rockaby* is placed '*slightly off-centre audience left*' and the speaker in *A Piece of Monologue* stands '*well off-centre downstage audience left*'. To deny a solitary character the centre of the stage is to decentre the whole playing space, making it difficult to establish the actual middle or limits of the stage.

Even when Beckett provides a context of light and shadow for his character, or gives us more than one character, it is made difficult for the audience to relate them. If the listener in *Not I* is in one sense the representative of the audience, it is difficult to specify the distance between him/her and the Mouth, and their relationship to each other

in space. In a similar way, the relationship of the megaphone/voice in
What Where to the four figures of whom it speaks is difficult to specify.
(Is the megaphone life-size? What is life-size for a megaphone?) As
with ... *but the clouds* ... and *Quad*, the figures simply appear in the
playing area and give no indication of where they go to or have come
from. We cannot be sure whether the voice inhabits the same dimension as the four performers or, as seems likely, the physical stage space is
being used to designate the non-localized places of dreaming or imagination, as in the TV play *Nacht und Träume*.

Beckett's habitual use of shadow in his later plays can also undermine our sense of position and spatial relationship. If one effect of
reducing the functional area of the stage is to draw in its boundaries,
then another effect is to include on the stage the sense of an outside,
all those areas of non-space which are held at bay at the fringes of the
stage, the wings, backstage, etc. It is as though the stage were exhib-
iting openly its border with that space of nonrepresentability which
establishes the limits and possibility of the stage as representation — as
though a painting should include within it a painting of the wall that
surrounds its frame. Inside and outside are therefore brought together
in a paradoxical way that cannot be consistently conceived and the
actual playing area is made to seem arbitrary and unfixed. Visible in
its relationship to the areas of shadow which surround it, it is therefore
no longer simply, self-sufficiently apparent for the viewer, but instead
stands in a complex and shifting relationship to this equally visible
emptiness.[7]

What is even more surprising in Beckett's theatre is the assign-
ment of the stage space not to action, but to the preparation for or
preliminary to action. This is apparent in *What Where,* in which the
stage space is made into a kind of animated doodle-pad, into which
the absent author projects his first thoughts and rewrites. This process
is carried even further in *A Piece of Monologue,* in which the stage is
given over to the delivery of what sounds like the stage directions for
some other play: 'Gropes to window and stares out ... Gropes back in
the end to where the lamp is standing. Was standing. When last went
out' (*COW,* 425). The speaker also describes the stage on which he
stands: 'Lights lamp as described ... Lights and moves to face wall as
described ... Head almost touching wall. White hair catching light.

White gown. White socks. White foot of pallet edge of frame stage left' (*CDW*, 428–9).

This shows clearly how mutually implicated are the voice/text opposition and the opposition between 'real' and 'imaginary' space. Action and physical space are here supplanted by text, for the words that we hear in the theatre repeat with only small modifications the words we read in the stage directions at the beginning of the printed text of the play: '*White hair, white nightgown, white socks. Two metres to his left, same level, same height, standard lamp … Just visible extreme right, same level, white foot of pallet bed*' (*CDW*, 425). The actual space of what we see in the theatre has been turned into a mental, potential space, for which we must supply the action. This is to say that the immediacy of dramatic experience is distanced from itself, or internally framed by itself, by the possibility of repetition which its words open up.

Artaud objected to the status of the stage space as repetition, as a subsidiary emptiness, called into being by, and subordinate to the absent text which projects and controls it; he wanted the space of the stage to be 'full' and immediate, not the shadow of some other text or controlling intention. Beckett's late theatre pushes in exactly the opposite direction. Instead of closing the gap between text and enacting space, a play like *A Piece of Monologue* incorporates that gap. What is usually a structural distance *between* the script and the performance becomes a disparity which is displayed *within* the performance. But the effect of this is to gather up the script into the performance, and to affirm the unity of the two, or even the predominance of the performance over the script, for the gap persists and indeed multiplies as the audience is required to participate in the imaginative redoubling described in the play: the speaker stands motionless and describes the actions of another character, dressed identically, who stares out of the window and then gropes to light the lamp, or who stands at the window looking back into the room to watch another hand appear and light the lamp.

The gap of repetition comes about because the play describes its own staging, seeming to insist on the dual nature, the dual place of every represented idea or narrative. Of course, this repetitive structure extends beyond simple duality, for every narrative may be staged in an infinite number of ways, none of them exactly coincidental with the original. This can involve repetitions within repetitions, as when a particular production of a play is adapted for another medium, such as television. Indeed, such a double repetition is alluded to within *A Piece of Monologue,* in the passages which allude to terms used in TV or film scripts, 'seen from above … Thirty seconds. Then fade' (*CDW,* 428). This doubling of media is to be found in *Footfalls,* too, where, again, it suggests an internal doubling of speech and writing, performance and script. At one point, the play suspends its action in order to allow M to speak, and this speech mimics written forms, sometimes of narrative — 'Amy — the daughter's given name, as the reader will remember' and sometimes of theatre script:

> Amy: Just what exactly, Mother, did you perhaps fancy it was? […] … Mrs W: You yourself observed nothing…strange? Amy: No, Mother I myself did not to put it mildly. Mrs. W: What do you mean, Amy, to put it mildly, what can you possibly mean, Amy, to put it mildly?
> (*CDW,* 403)

This capacity for 'quotation' of other representational media further erodes the specificity of the stage-performance, so much so that we cannot be absolutely sure of the appropriate form or medium of the play. This sits oddly with Beckett's often-quoted strictures about the specificity of medium of his plays, and his attempts to restrain adaptations. Writing to Barney Rosset, about a proposed adaptation of *All That Fall* for the stage, for example, Beckett said that the play was:

> a specifically radio play, or rather radio text, for voices, not bodies … I am absolutely opposed to any form of adaptation with a view to its conversion into 'theatre'. It is no more theatre than *Endgame* is radio and to 'act' it is to kill it. Even the reduced visual dimension it will receive from the simplest and most static of readings…will be destructive of whatever quality it may have and which depends upon the whole thing's *coming out of the dark.*[8]

In a similar way, Beckett resisted TV adaptations of stage plays like *Waiting for Godot, Krapp's Last Tape* and *Act Without Words I,* and attempts to dramatize passages from the fiction. In another letter to Barney Rosset, Beckett's general adherence to the principle of the specificity of medium is made clear. 'If we can't keep our genres more or less distinct, or extricate them from the confusion that has them where they are, we might as well go home and lie down.'[9]

This strict control over medium is very curious when one considers the kinds of internal gestures towards other media which almost every one of his plays contains. Beckett's later writing for the theatre demands of it technicalities of lighting and staging which suggest video and film— the separation and dismemberment of the body, with isolation of faces and lips, or the effect of hovering and bird's-eye view, and consequent concentration of focus, as well as the separation of voices from bodies, giving the effect of voice-over, as in *Footfalls* and *Rockaby*. His writing for TV, on the other hand, though it is difficult to imagine it being staged in quite the same way in any other medium, retains and even highlights many of the features of the stage play — the single unchanging set, for instance, and the restriction of TV's mobility of viewpoint.[10]

In the case of *Not I*, we have a very good example of this variability of medium. Even though he had nothing to do with the making of it, Beckett actually at one time preferred the TV version, which dispensed with the figure of the auditor, in favour of a claustrophobically close focus on the mouth. The mouth in the theatre seems magically remote, as though produced in some space of illusion, and may make audiences think of something other than a physical mouth (I heard a member of one audience describe the mouth as being like a flickering candle-flame), while the mouth in the TV version is inescapably physical, enforcing a fascinated attention to the violent, erotic struggle of lips, teeth, tongue and spittle. The point is not really which version of the play is better, or preferable, or closer to its spirit, for the play includes both versions, and in a sense consists in the self-distancing movement across different media which these two versions bring about. The case is analogous to what happens with Beckett's self-translations. The two versions of a text each require the other to complete them, even though the 'other' version never does complete, but instead introduces complexity or discrepancy.

This inhabitation of texts by other media, by the possibility of their reappearance in other spaces, is characteristic of Beckett's later dramatic writing, though not confined to it. In *Waiting for Godot*, there are hints of other kinds of theatrical context, like the circus and the music hall, in which the play might be staged. This duality even affects *All That Fall,* which, as we have seen, Beckett thought of as intrinsically a radio play 'for voices rather than bodies', for it is the most spatially concrete of radio plays, requiring of the viewer or reader a staging in some interior mental space, even as it parodies the conventions which allow the construction of this mental space. If one had to imagine what a mixture between a radio play and a stage play would be like, however, it would probably be something like *Krapp's Last Tape,* written shortly after *All That Fall* and perhaps stimulated by the experience of working for radio, or *That Time. Krapp's Last Tape* is a kind of 'staging' (rather than an adaptation) of a radio play, for it mingles, without attempting to unify, the visibility of bodies on the stage and the placeless voices 'coming out of the dark' of the radio play.

In later years, Beckett extended this principle of transferability to his prose work, which to a steadily greater degree suggests continuities with his writing for the stage, radio and TV. The close attention to details of space and position in the related texts *The Lost Ones, Ping, Imagination Dead Imagine* and *All Strange Away,* as well as the theatrical language often used in these works, suggests a certain variability or doubling of medium, as though the texts included within themselves the possibility of their staging in some other form. Among the most striking of these is *Company.* The voice which 'comes to one in the dark' throughout this text has many of the qualities of the voices 'coming out of the dark' of radio drama and the details of the listener's position remind us remarkably of the listening face of *That Time,* a stage play that itself uses some of the properties of radio drama. The careful attention to the physical space of the listening, and the division of this physical space from the imaginary spaces of quotation/remembering, suggests the simple insistent physicality of some of Beckett's late drama, while the use of intercutting and flashback, as well as the close visual attention paid to certain items in the narrative, such as the watch face, suggests continuities with visual media.

These internal allusions to a plurality of different places for staging make *Company* typical of Beckett's late writing (and especially his dramatic writing), rather than an exception to it. It is in the metaphor of boundary as well as the metaphor of centre that we define identity or unity— a country asserts its territorial and ethnic integrity most emphatically in its capital city, often buried deep in the country, and at its borders, the place where the movement of outsiders is carefully regulated and the strict line between inside and outside clearly sustained. If it remains true that Beckett's dramatic works assert the specificity of their media, it is because they are placed at the representative edges of those media, rather than at their centres. It is these boundaries which constitute the specificity of the medium, even as they mark the dubious place where they touch and perhaps cross into different media. Beckett's plays trace this tenuous place of difference, stimulating a sense of the repetitions within any structure of identity.[11]

All this poses problems for the theory of immediate dramatic presence in Beckett's plays. We rely upon the written or spoken text to tell us where we are, what we are looking at, but it is precisely this text which prevents us from identifying the place with certainty, or, rather, suggests the haunting of the space we see before us by other spaces. Krapp's den, for example, remains unchanged in physical terms yet, as we listen to the tape of his earlier self, we feel the introduction of a difference in what the space means, to Krapp, and to us. The place is the same, but no longer coincides with itself.

In later plays, like *That Time, Footfalls, Rockaby* and *Ohio Impromptu,* the situation is more complex, for in each case the text that we hear suggests a number of different locations which the stage space may represent. In *That Time,* we appear to be offered a position outside or beyond the chaos of memory and representation. Unlike *Company,* where we are reminded all the time that the one on his back in the dark listening to the voice may just be a 'figment', we seem to have, in the listener's face, evidence of some irreducible presence. Set against the voices that surround the face, we hear throughout the slow, regular sound of his breathing, and, most strikingly, see the listener's smile (smile of recognition, relief, celebration?) after the last voice has faded away with its evocation of dissolution. It is as though the listener has been freed, if only temporarily, from the voices which beset it. As often in Beckett's theatre, then, the permanence or self-evidence of physical form seems to be eroded by the impalpability of voice. But even this is undermined by another kind of repetition in the text. For the three voices not only recall each other, but recall for the audience the experience of the dramatic spectacle itself. The account of the child in the shelter of his folly, 'talking to yourself who else out loud imaginary conversations ... making it up now one voice now another till you were hoarse and they all sounded the same ... making up talk breaking up two or more talking to himself' (*CDW*, 390, 393), strikes the audience forcibly as an anticipation of the position of the listener, except that, of course, the voices he hears no longer seem to be of his own devising, but instead speak to him independently and arbitrarily.

In a similarly reflexive movement, the appearance of the face that we see before us is evoked in A's description of the old man on the step, 'drooling away out loud eyes closed and the white hair pouring out from under the hat' (*CDW*, 393–4), which in turn recalls another memory described by B: 'suddenly there in whatever thoughts you might be having whatever scenes perhaps way back in childhood or in the womb worst of all or that old Chinaman long before Christ born with long white hair' (*CDW*, 390). These details obviously link the disembodied narrative with the face that we see before us in the theatre, but in oblique and partial ways; the figure we see doesn't have hair pouring out from under a hat, for instance, but 'long flaring white hair as if seen from above outspread' (the French suggests a little more about his position in specifying 'longs cheveux blancs dressés comme vus de haut étalés sur un oreiller').[12] Other details in the text seem designed to remind the audience of the face that it sees before it, with its opening and closing eyes; B's references, for example, to the lovers 'gazing up at the blue or eyes closed blue dark blue dark' (*CDW*, 392), or A's and C's references to being looked at, looked through, or slipping in or away when no one is looking.

All these not only establish the 'action' on stage before us as an imitation or re-enactment of what we are being told in the narrative, but implicate the audience in the play of reminiscence and recall. Something similar happens in *Rockaby* where the references in the taped monologue to the woman 'at her window/quiet at her window/ only window/facing other windows/other only windows/all eyes/all sides/high and low/for another/another like herself/a little like/another living soul' (*CDW*, 438) keep the audience unnervingly aware that they are equally being looked at or looked for. In *That Time*, there is one passage in particular which establishes this reflexive repetition, the passage in which C describes the face suddenly seen by the man in the portrait gallery:

> till you hoisted your head and there before your eyes when they opened a vast oil black with age and dirt someone famous in his time same famous man or woman or even child such as a young prince or princess some young prince or princess of the blood black with age behind the glass where gradually as you peered trying to make it out gradually of all things a face appeared had you swivel on the slab to see who it was there at your elbow.
>
> (*CDW,* 389)

It is uncertain what is being described here. There seem to be at least four possibilities; peering at the blackened portrait, the man may suddenly make out the face that is painted, or may see his own face reflected in the glass, or he may see the face of someone else who is sitting beside him, also looking forwards (like the lover sitting beside the young man in B's narrative), or he may simply be experiencing an hallucination. The details of the description suggest that the face is a temporal composite, for, though it is 'black with age', it may represent a child. As such it is a visual analogue for the overlayerings of youth and age in the voices of A and B, and may therefore suggest a way of 'reading' the face that we see before us in the theatre, a face that is both old and young, a tissue of visual citations. This reading of the face in the portrait is reinforced a little later by the passage in which the uncertainty of the portrait's identity is run together with the voice's uncertainty about which time he inhabits: 'was that the time or was that another time there alone with the portraits of the dead black with dirt and antiquity and the date on the frames in case you might get the century wrong not believing it could be you till they put you out in the rain at closingtime' (*CDW,* 391).

As well as reminding the audience of the face they see before them, this scene may also remind them of their own spectatorship. Like the man in the gallery, the audience peering at the tiny face on the stage may succeed in making out their own features reflected back at them, or — more shockingly, somehow — the features of the person sitting at their elbow. The simplicity and directness of face-to-face looking is split and multiplied by the repetitions set up in this passage and the playas a whole.

There are similar redoublings of position in other late plays. In *Ohio Impromptu* we may be in the very room that is spoken of in the reader's narration, the room to which the listener, if he is indeed the subject as well as the addressee of the story, has retired, or we may be in some other location altogether, earthly or unearthly. In *Footfalls*, we may be watching May, first of all 'stark, with her face to the wall,' and then pacing up and down in 'the old home', or may be watching some other (May again? her mother? Amy?) after her death walking up and down the north or south transept of a church. And, as with *A Piece of Monologue*, we cannot always be sure whether what is taking place is actually taking place in front of us, or elsewhere, in some ghostly off-stage doubling. In the first part of the play, the voice asks us to 'watch her move, in silence' (*CDW*, 401), while M does, indeed, walk up and down. But then, in the sequel, M herself enjoins us to watch the 'tangle of tatters' pass before us; though she resembles the creature that she describes, she is at this moment standing still, in the same way as the speaker in *A Piece of Monologue* during his descriptions of the movements of another resembling himself.

The person M is referring to must be elsewhere, in one of two senses: she must be elsewhere in the physical sense, in some other location expressible within the terms of her story but in fact unexpressed, or elsewhere in a structural sense, in the 'other place' of memory, imagination or narrative. If what she says is a story, then it must wait to be performed or staged in some other context. We are uncertain whether this elsewhere is physical or metaphorical, since we are similarly uncertain whether the physical space that we are watching is physical or metaphorical. This is not to imply that all is dissolved into utter impalpability; that might be a philosophical and emotional relief. This play, perhaps more than any other of Beckett's, draws us into the tangled relationship of claustrophobic presence and shifting impalpability. A now-famous story told by Billie Whitelaw about rehearsals for *Footfalls* seems to bear this out. Billie Whitelaw asked Beckett whether the character she was playing was dead, and says that he replied 'Let's just say you're not quite there.'[13] It is precisely the agony of not being there that the play seems to present, or almost represent. Beckett's remark alludes to the story that M tells (about herself?) in the sequel section of the play, in which Amy tells her mother that despite appearances, she was 'not there' in the church. The mother's urgent questions leave the issue undecided of how it is possible to be present and absent at the same time, but *Footfalls* itself seems to provide one demonstration of this. At the end of the play, when M ceases to discriminate between the persons speaking at the end of her narrative, the effect is less that of a dissolution or merging of persons, than of a multiple enveloping, in which her voice quotes, or is quoted by, other voices (the voice of her mother, the voices of the characters in the story), without ever being fully identified with them: 'Amy [*Pause. No louder.*] Amy. [*Pause.*] Yes, Mother. [*Pause.*] Will you never have done? [*Pause.*] Will you never have done ... revolving it all? [*Pause.*] It? [*Pause.*] It all. [*Pause.*] In your poor mind. [*Pause.*] It all. [*Pause.*] It all' (*CDW*, 403).

In a similar way, *Rockaby* shows us a woman who is not altogether there, despite the fact that we see her seated so undeniably in front of us. As with M, her absence from herself is a matter not so much of a failure or lack of definition, as of her inhabitation by multiple selves, and of multiple locations. The rocking text describes her gradual movement inside from the street, to her upstairs window, to her chair in the basement of her house, and we naturally assume that the last of these positions is the one that she occupies 'now'. But the insistent repetitions of the text suggest that she may be imagined as occupying different spaces. Even in the street, when not seated, she is still said to be 'going to and fro/all eyes/all sides/high and low' (*CDW*, 435). Similarly, when she sits at her window looking out (as she looks out at the audience) she is not in a rocking-chair, but the same words used to describe her looking suggest rocking — 'all eyes/all sides/high and low', as does the motion of the blind, which is alternately 'let up' and 'let down'.

Fundamental Sounds — Language and the Body: *Not I, Acts Without Words, Quad*

Many of the claims made for the theatre of presence rest upon the fact of the visibility of the human body, and of course, the authenticating claims of the voice and the body are linked closely; the immediacy

and truthfulness of the voice is based upon its origin in and issue from
the body, just as the menace and treachery of writing consist in its intrinsic separability from the body. Again, Artaud provides a convenient
reference point. For Artaud, modern man is painfully divided between
utterance and expression, between the immediate speech of the body
and the separateness of external writing; and he sees classical theatre
as in the grip of the model of speech and writing which opposes, in
Derrida's words, 'clear and willing thought' to 'writing that represents
representative speech' ('La Parole Soufflée,' *WD*, 191). Artaud's absolute theatrical language is designed to explode this paralysing distinction, and to reassert the primary language of the body, which is
projected not in articulate forms, but in the breath. As Derrida argues
again, this is an attempt to rescue the uniqueness of the theatrical experience from the structures of repetition and commentary that divide
and mutilate it:

> Artaud attempted to destroy ... the duality of the body and the soul
> which supports, secretly of course, the duality of speech and exis-
> tence, of the text and the body, etc. The metaphysics of the com-
> mentary which authorised 'commentaries' because it *already* governed
> the works commented upon: nontheoretical works, in the sense un-
> derstood by Artaud, works that are already deported commentaries.
> Beating his flesh in order to reawaken it at the eve prior to this depor-
> tation, Artaud attempted to forbid that his speech be spirited away
> from [*soufflé*] his body.
>
> ('La Parole Soufflée', *WD*, 175)

This stress upon the physical origin of language means that, for
Artaud, words must be treated, not as conductors of meaning, but as
concrete manifestations in their own right; he aimed to give language
in the theatre a 'full, physical shock potential' and to 'treat inflexions
in a completely tangible manner' ('Production and Metaphysics', *TD*,
35). The result of this will not be the blocking of communication,
but rather the capacity to communicate directly, with and through the
anatomies of the audience; Artaud compared the effect of this theatrical language on the audience to the effect of musical vibrations trans-
mitted through the ground to the body of a coiled snake ('No More
Metaphysics', *TD*, 61).

Beckett's theatre has often been seen in a similar way. Where the prose up to and including the Trilogy had tended to denigrate the corruption of the body and to enact its disgust with it by the progressive deportation of the physical from the arena of the text, with the gradual decay of the body in *Molloy* and *Malone Dies* until it is only present as memory, trace or supposition in *The Unnamable,* the theatre shows a new awareness of the expressive potential of the body. This is an awareness which it imparts to the later prose, with its close and sustained attention to the body in its material locations. Partly this has to do with Beckett's exploration, as a director as well as a writer, of the expressive potential of gesture and posture, alongside that of language, for they seem to offer the prospect of images which can concretize meaning or emotion in a way that abstracted text cannot. This stress on the external or the objective seems to have affected Beckett's ideas about language itself; it is surprising to read that the writer who once protested that English was 'abstracted to death' later thought it 'a good theatre language because of its concreteness, its close relationship between thing and vocable'.[14]

This desire for a concrete language connects with a close attention to the origin of language in 'human bodies', rather than merely 'coming out of the dark'. Beckett seems to draw upon the notion of the language of the body when attempting, like Artaud, to rescue his theatre from commentary; in the famous letter to Alan Schneider about *Endgame,* he reinforces his claim about the 'extreme simplicity' of character and situation by affirming that it is a matter of 'fundamental sounds (no pun intended)' (*Disjecta,* 109). Whether or not we credit Beckett's coy denial of the allusion to the body, it seems clear that he is here affirming the physicality of language in the same way as Artaud. If the fundamental sounds are not the language of the body, then they are at least the body of language. Beckett is even less given to explicit considerations of audience response than to critical elucidation of his work, but in one of his rare remarks about this, he matches Artaud's ideas about anatomical communication with his audience: 'I am not unduly concerned with intelligibility. I hope my piece may work on the nerves of the audience not on its intellect.'[15]

This latent affirmation of the body can be found even in a radio play like *All That Fall,* a play which, as we have seen, paradoxically requires of its listener an energetic fleshing-out of the voices heard from the dark. Despite her longing to be 'in atoms', Mrs Rooney is affirmed as a solid and palpable physical presence, particularly in her struggles to climb into Mr Slocum's car:

> Mr Slocum: [In position behind her.] Now, Mrs Rooney, how shall we do this?
> Mrs Rooney: As if I were a bale, Mr Slocum, don't be afraid. [*Pause. Sounds of effort.*] That's the way! [*Effort.*] Lower! [*Effort.*] Wait! [*Pause.*] No, don't let go! [*Pause.*] Suppose I do get up, will I ever get down?
> Mr Slocum: [*Breathing hard.*] You'll get down, Mrs Rooney, you'll get down. We may not get you up, but I warrant you we'll get you down. [*He resumes his efforts. Sound of these.*]
> Mrs Rooney: Oh!...Lower!...Don't be afraid!...We're past the age when...There!...Now!...Get your shoulder under it... Oh!...[*Giggles.*] Oh glory! Up! Up!...Ah!...I'm in!
>
> (*CDW*, 178)

The comedy of a passage like this is of the kind described by Bergson, in which the body is experienced as weight, matter and comic impediment. In this it has much in common with the passages of clowning and clumsy effort in *Waiting for Godot*. But at the same time, there is an affirmation of the life of the body, if only in the sense of immediacy that is gained in the absorption of the language in its subject. With the sounds of panting and exertion, we feel the struggles of the body enacted in the language. At moments like this, it is no longer a matter of the dissociation of self and body, as expressed in the last lines of *From An Abandoned Work* — 'just went on, my body doing its best without me' (*CSP*, 137) — for the character is sunk absolutely in the life of the body.

Critics have responded gratefully to this apparent return of the body in Beckett's drama. Pierre Chabert, for instance, argues for the seriousness of Beckett's attention to the body, his 'deliberate and intense effort to make the body come to light, to give the body its full weight, dimension, and its physical presence'. This produces a renewal and intensification of the forms and possibilities of drama itself, for Beckett uses the (often defective) human body 'to systematically explore theatrical space, to construct a physical and sensory space, filled with the presence of the body, to affirm cruelly (as Artaud would have said) a space invested by the body'. In this concentrated theatre 'word and gesture are restored to a primal expressive function.'[16]

So the affirmation of the body in the theatre has a reflexive dimension as well. For the drama doesn't merely present bodies on stage; rather the metaphor of body and soul is what constitutes and sustains the drama, even calls it into being. Traditionally the stage is the physical manifestation of some absent idea or intention (the script, the text, the ideal play 'in itself') and the interdependence of text and performance is often expressed in terms of a body/soul synthesis: if the body is the stage or frame within which the soul moves, so the performance on the physical stage is the bodying or incarnation of the soul of the play. Just as the soul is different and absent from the body, and yet inconceivable without it, so the 'play' is different from every particular production of it, and yet to be apprehended nowhere but in actual production. This blending of the material and the immaterial is an important metaphorical element in conventional constitutions of the relationship of language and intention too. So, within any affirmation of the body *in* the theatre, we may see the affirmation of the body *of* the theatre:

> Beckett's aim is not, in other words, to reduce the stage to words alone, but rather to concentrate upon those words that are incarnated and pronounced by the body. His is a theatre of elementary things, of words and bodies, words in a body, words expulsed by a body, words epitomized by a body. The immobility peculiar to the Beckettian stage is, then, paradoxical: in eliminating all the customary properties pertaining to the body Beckett reaffirms the irreducibility of the body, and reminds us that it remains an agent of disclosure ... It is out of these unprepossessing raw materials that Beckett generates a dramaturgy of which the smallest detail may possess significance, thereby restoring to the stage its exceptional potential as a corporeal medium without parallel.
>
> (Chabert, 27–8)

The body is here used to affirm the powerfully unified, non-repetitive structure of the theatre itself, in which the body or the 'corporeal medium' of the form closes the gap between meaning and performance. Though Chabert sees the body as 'agent of disclosure', this does not mean that it is merely accessory to or different from what it discloses; the theatre is, above all 'words in a body'. We can see, therefore, how the local affirmation of the body allows a number of congruous affirmations of the blending of the virtual and the actual, the blending of meaning and form, signifier and signified, text and performance, soul and body themselves, each of these couples acting as confirming metaphor for the others. In his resounding claims for the theatre of presence in *Rockaby*, Enoch Brater restates these confirming metaphors in paradigmatic fashion:

> With each contraction of sound, light and movement ... the audience's 'famished eyes' gradually focus on an image free of all nonessentials. For each loss in *Rockaby* progressively validates the purity of Beckett's condensed image. With every softening sound, every fading light, every decrease in stage movement, the image unexpectedly expands as we study in production its simplicity and authenticity. Technology wears a human face, the face, if not of tragedy, then of dramatic poetry. The performance, moreover, is the poem. Language art and theater art have finally become one.[17]

But in ways that are important and striking, Beckett's theatre often fails to confirm the metaphors and models of the self-evidencing body. Just as space and location are made progressively less and less reliably self-evident in Beckett's drama, so the body, inhabitant of the theatre's physical space, itself becomes a problematic space.

This is brought about particularly by the failure of Beckett's drama to affirm consistently the language of the body and the body of language against the inauthenticity of writing. In Beckett's drama, voices consistently fail to be located in the bodies from which or to which they speak. In *Krapp's Last Tape*, as we have seen, the only way in which Krapp can preserve his voice is to separate it from its origin in his body. In plays like *That Time*, and *Rockaby*, the voices of the characters, far from being 'words in a body', come from some unlocatable point outside their actual bodies. This split is enacted in other plays, like *Footfalls* and *A Piece of Monologue*, by separating speech and motion, and in the TV plays *Eh Joe*, *Ghost Trio* and *... but the clouds ...*, by separating voice-over and perceived action. If the speaking body cannot be in motion, then this somehow suggests an inverse ratio be-tween bodily presence and language. The same split can be found in earlier plays, though in less sustained ways: Clov is not confined to a wheelchair, and seems for this reason to be less linguistically pro-ductive than his master Hamm. For Hamm, immobility is both an imprisonment in the body and an alienation from proper physical life; his position is therefore like that of the bedridden authors of the books in the Trilogy, for whom the retreat from the body seems to bring on a compensatory surfeit of speech. Lucky, in *Waiting for Godot,* similarly never speaks while on the move, and when he does speak, the effect is of a language which possesses him, like a medium at a séance, rather than speaking naturally 'from' his body.

Beckett's work in different media similarly refuses or complicates the sense of the physical as natural or given. This arises from the un-expected uses to which he puts these different media. Often, as we have seen, it is the TV which requires of the viewer of Beckett's plays a concentration upon the forms of the physical (Joe's face, the mouth in *Not I*), while in the theatre the audience is often disturbed by images that seem remote, placeless and disembodied. This duality enforces the sense of the body as inhabiting spaces of representation, rather than being part of a tangibly physical world. The camera in *Eh Joe,* for ex-ample, could move closer and closer to Joe's face without the possibil-ity of ever touching him; eventually the face would dissolve into the insubstantial lines that make up the image.

What is more, both in the theatre and in TV plays, Beckett re-fuses one of the most important features of the body as traditionally projected, its wholeness, or unity. Time and again the body is dismem-bered, fragmented, or reduced grotesquely to its parts, whether it is Winnie, whose body gradually disappears before us, or Joe, reduced to his face, and then less than his face, or the listener in *That Time,* the face of the rocking woman in *Rockaby,* the players in their long cowls in *What Where* and *Quad,* the protagonist in *Catastrophe* (whose gradual exposure seems to fulfil the function of a dismemberment), the disem-bodied hands seen or imagined in *A Piece of Monologue* and *Nacht und Träume,* or, most memorably, the mouth in *Not I.*

Undeniably, this narrowing down of the body could be seen as a powerfully metonymic device, since it requires of the viewer an imaginary filling-out of the missing body; but it is the narrowing down that changes the status of the visible portion of the body into that of a sign. The body can never be witnessed in its palpable wholeness; rather that wholeness will always be the result of a retrieval or reconstitution, lying somewhere between what the stage or screen makes present, and what it leaves out. The frame which the spotlight or the TV screen draws around the segment of the body, hand, mouth, or face, always remains part of the reconstitution, as an interior deficiency in its wholeness.

Sometimes, the fragmentation of the body in Beckett's work is achieved not by amputation but by concentration on one position, gesture, or movement. The effect of M's relentless pacing in *Footfalls* is of a metonymic intensification, even as it gnaws at the assurance of the physical for the viewer. The physicality of M's pacing has a representative status, too, enacting as it does the desire for presence which is at the heart of the play. The desire to *be* there, a desire which surely anticipates — or repeats — the audience's desire to place or define the action, is expressed, or staged, in M's urgent pacing up and down and her desire to have this confirmed in the sound of the feet 'however faint they fall'. In the theatre, it is the sound of the feet and M's tatters sliding over the floor which seems to attest to the physical solidity of this ghostly figure before us. But, like all compulsions to repeat, her walking up and down can never complete itself, can never succeed in producing that full sense of being which she seems to seek. And since the pacing up and down is projected and understood as part of a repetitive series which includes May, Amy and M, it offers no guarantee of self. M paces to 'be there', but it is pacing that carries her inevitably away from herself. This double signification is hinted at in the English title 'Footfalls', in which the second half of the word suggests declension, or falling away into impalpability, but this is much improved in the grim auto-negation of the French title, 'Pas'.

In M's case, as with other Beckett characters on the stage, the narrowing down of the body to one portion or function focuses the immediacy of the physical while making its wholeness difficult to restore. As many have observed, the effect of the transition from stage to screen of *Not I* is to focus attention on the furious movement of the mouth itself, and it has seemed to some that this gives a sense of physical presence that mitigates or compensates for the alienation from the self and body that is spoken of in the text. But it might just as easily be said that the hypnotized, fetishizing concentration upon the speaking mouth interrupts the imaginative effort to supply the whole absent body. After a while, the mouth seems to draw up the whole of the speaker's body into it — 'as if the mouth had eaten the body', in Chabert's words (p. 27) — in a displacement which is profoundly alienating.

One of the most disturbing things about using a mouth to represent the body is that it contradicts habitual metaphors of the body as somehow projective, convex, solid, and 'full'. In *Not I,* the mouth is both a presence, and an enclosing absence — performs the function, in fact, of a miniaturized stage, in which light and shadow, hard and soft, space and solidity, alternate. In other words, this is not an organ that exists solidly in space, but is itself the space in which solidity and vacancy are produced and reproduced. If this mouth may seem to some viewers to suggest a vagina, with its lips and teeth alternately vulnerable and ravening, then, in its ceaseless movement, it suggests other bodily orifices, particularly, with the faecal eruptions of its language, the anus: 'sometimes sudden urge ... once or twice a year ... always winter some strange reason ... the long evenings ... hours of darkness ... sudden urge to ... tell ... then rush out stop the first she saw ... nearest lavatory ... start pouring it out ... steady stream ... (*CDW,* 382). Allusions to birth at the beginning of the monologue also suggest the ambiguity of the physical, poised between shadow and substance, solidity and emptiness: the girl is born, 'before her time', but this movement is not as customarily conceived from void or vacuum into fullness, but from one 'hole' into another 'godforsaken hole'. Far from fixing the topography of the self, in its movement from an enclosing inside to the 'outside' world, this endlessly mobile mouth, which, with its teeth and tongue includes phallic fullness and vaginal hollowness, enacts the insoluble inter-involvement of inside and outside — 'out ... into this world ... this world ... tiny little thing ... before its time ... in a godfor– ... what? ... girl? ... yes ... tiny little girl ... into this ... out into this' (*CDW,* 376).[18]

If the body is enacted not as presence, but as a spatial process which itself creates space, then this has implications too for our sense of its relationship to its language. In a sense, the whole of *Not I* might be seen as an attempt to subject to scrutiny the proposition that speech comes 'from' the mouth, or the body. For, although we are clearly being forced to contemplate the physical struggle involved in producing language, this very intensity of focus is what prevents us from identifying language and the body; we cannot say where language comes from, or where it is in relation to the furious physical contortions that we see before us. All we have are the metaphors we inherit about voice and the body, as well as those metaphors suggested in the spoken text, and none of these metaphors proves to be continuously sustainable.

Sometimes, for example, the voice, or the words it speaks, is pictured as a solid, or projective presence — imaged, as it were, in the tongue, within the mouth. This is language that subordinates or eclipses the body:

> yes...the tongue in the mouth...all those contortions without which...no speech possible...and yet in the ordinary way...not felt at all...so intent one is...on what one is saying he whole being... hanging on its words ...
>
> (*CDW*, 379)

A being which is 'hanging on its words' suggests impalement on some penetrating, solid projection. (Pierre Chabert repeats this metaphor with a more explicitly phallic variation when he speaks of the 'words which literally seem to pierce the aperture through which they are emitted' [Chabert, p. 23].) At other times, though, the body is conceived as *more* solid than its language, which issues from it in a 'steady stream' — imaged for the viewer of the TV version, perhaps, in the pools and strings of saliva produced by the mouth.

The birth/excretion metaphors that are repeated through the play, initiate another spatial contradiction; for the mouth seems to speak frequently of a language which it encloses, and wishes to try to expel, even as it complains of the way that language speaks through it, and endlessly eludes capture. This brings into play yet another bodily orifice, the ear, which is necessary to complete the circuit of self-understanding, of 's'entendre parler'.[19] In *Not I*, the distance between ear and mouth splits the short-circuit:

all this...all that...steady stream...straining to hear...make some-thing of it...and her own thoughts...make something of them... all–...what?...the buzzing?...yes...all the time the buzzing...so-called...all that together...imagine!...whole body like gone...just the mouth...lips...cheeks...jaws...never-...what?...tongue?...yes... lips...cheeks...jaws...tongue...never still a second...mouth on fire... stream of...words...in her ear...practically in her ear... not catching the half...not the quarter...no idea what she's saying...imagine!...no idea what she's saying!...and can't stop...no stopping it...

(*CDW*, 380)

The sense that language cannot ever securely be imaged as residing within the body, or coming from it, is enacted here in the play between different constituents of the body, lips, cheeks, jaws, tongue and ear, which refuse to join in self-identity.

In all these ways, *Not I* suggests that there may be no comfort for the viewer weary of the dissolving or divided self in the sheer presence of the body or the language of the body. The moment that the body is displayed on the stage or the screen, it reveals itself as representation, constituted by unstable metaphors. The body is 'staged' in metaphor just as much as the self, and attempts to know it are liable to just the same problematic self-reflections and redoublings.

The same seems to be true even of the three plays in which Beckett gives us nothing but the body in action in space, the three mimes, *Act Without Words* I and II and *Quad*. Critics have not spent much time on these works, understandably perhaps, given the difficulty of dis-cussing nonverbal action in words; but they occupy an important and representative place in Beckett's work in their absolute refusal of lan-guage — or, rather, in their refusal of anything but corporeal language. Beckett himself described *Act Without Words* I as 'primitive theatre' and stressed its immediate physicality, saying that 'the play requires that this last extremity of human meat — or bones— be there, think-ing and stumbling and sweating, under our noses.'[20] Sidney Homan uses another implicitly physical metaphor to discuss the mimes. The mime is characterized above all by visibility, he writes, the mime being a form in which 'nothing can remain inner or conceptual'. The poverty of the mime artist's resources is the source of the sense of complete-ness which his or her performance gives — '*All* must be shown; the

mime has nothing but his body.'[21] This uncompromised externality
is what in turn brings about the unity of general and particular, action and meaning. Once again, we have the claim for a self-sufficient
theatre, whose smooth surface offers no crevice in which commentary
may get a grip: 'The play either "is" as a whole or it is not. The paradox,
then, is that mime is at once intensely immediate theater and, since all
inner thoughts, emotions and states are manifest in action, the most
purely philosophical ... in the mimes, the abstract and the literal are
the same.'[22]

Other writers have not been so comfortable with Beckett's mimes.
Where Homan sees fullness and concentration, John Fletcher and
John Spurling find the mimes thin and 'over-explicit'; what they lack
is precisely Beckett's voice, without which, they say, 'what is left is de-
cidedly too little.'[23] My point is not so much to try to decide which of
these two attitudes to the mimes is right or preferable, but to consider
the structure of ideas which they share. For Homan and Fletcher and
Spurling, the mimes provide an image of unsatisfactory repleteness
of being. For Fletcher and Spurling, the plays are 'overexplicit,' even
as they lack voice; while, for Homan, the bald self-sufficiency of the
mimes is precisely what stimulates interpretation. There seems to be
something in the very plainness, accessibility and unity of the mimes
which strikes the critic as deficient; it is as though the flat visibility
of the play's surface suddenly hollowed itself into problematic depth,
transforming its repletion into lack: 'If we are an active audience in
Beckett's work, no matter what medium he chooses, here in the mimes
we are even more so. There are no words; we must supply the silent
commentary. The actions are devastatingly physical, especially in *Act
Without Words* II, and yet we cannot resist the self-imposed drive toward symbolism and meaning.'[24]

Commentary is an interruption of the serene unity of the mime
performance, because it stages or repeats the action elsewhere, in the
space of interpretation; and commentary itself seems to rely upon the
trope of repetition to stabilize it. Nor are the three mimes really independent of written texts in the first place; despite the appearance
that they give of self-sufficiency, in performance all three plays are repetitions or reworkings of preexistent scripts. Or, at least, the two *Acts
Without Words* are; *Quad* is a slightly more complicated example, be-

cause the written form of the performance is not a script so much as a piece of software. If the scripts of the two *Acts Without Words* function in some way as present-tense narration, as though the script were witnessing and describing the play as it is performed, then the written form of *Quad* seems no more than a projection, which offers suggestions for some future production, rather than describing an action in the present. However, the 'script' of *Quad* also does something more than this, for it incorporates remarks about the television production with which Beckett had already been involved when the script was published. The effect of this is to complicate considerably the relationship between text and performance. In one sense, as Enoch Brater has observed, the performance of *Quad* is its own text, and has, if anything, a higher status than the actual written form which in some ways it modifies and supersedes.[25] But if this written form comes before *and after* the performance, then both text and performance repeat and perhaps displace each other, the text being one 'original' for the production, just as the production is another 'original' for the text.

Though the situation is somewhat simpler in the *Acts Without Words,* the relationship of repetition between text and performance has its own complexities. If the texts of the two mimes seem subordinated to the corporeal reality they describe, then the verbal forms of the two plays exercise a very particular influence over the performance. There is nothing in the texts, for example, to indicate explicitly that the performer should perform the various repeated actions in the same way each time, but, as Cesare Segre points out, the patterns of exact repetition in the text of the plays begin to function as a rule or indicator that the accompanying actions should also be exact repetitions.[26] The doubling is now multiple, for each repeated gesture or movement not only repeats an initiating gesture or movement in the performance, but also repeats the condition of repeatability of the verbal text. Quite apart from the control exercised by this text, there may be other kinds of citation at work in the play — both text and performance seem to quote, for instance, the stylized clowning of the circus, music-hall and silent screen and these contexts define and control the movements to a large extent.

Most important of all is the context supplied by Beckett's oeuvre and reputation. The plays form part of this oeuvre and demand to be understood in its terms. Even their wordlessness is a term to be understood in relation to Beckett's verbal output. The titles do not specify mimes, but 'acts without words', in a refusal of language which is in some ways a reassertion of it. The mimes do not escape language, because their corporeal immediacy is constituted all the time as a lack of or refraining from language, so that, though there may be no words spoken in the drama, the phrase 'without words' seems to resound through it in just the same way as the only word spoken in *Film,* the word 'Shh', establishes that we are not watching a film without a soundtrack, but a film with an empty soundtrack. There is a similar differentiation of silences in *Krapp's Last Tape,* where the presence of the tape recorder allows us to distinguish 'live' silence, or the absence of language, from the recorded silence on the tape, which is a sort of absence *within* language. In all these texts, therefore, the withdrawal or censoring of language operates as a linguistic term, within structures of meaning which are themselves linguistic.

All this has been to demonstrate that the body in Beckett's plays is a 'scene of writing', even though it may seem to affirm the pre-linguistic immediacy of physical presence. It is not that the body is simply unknowable, but rather that it comes to be known and experienced as immediate presence only by virtue of the mediations of structures of difference and repetition which compromise that presence.

Though we cannot abstract ourselves as viewers, readers or critics from the problematic redoublings involved here, it is nevertheless possible to measure some of the subversive effects of these paradoxes. For metaphors and representations of the kind that we have been discussing here embody power, power that certainly does not end with the text, the performance, or even the institutions of theatre or criticism. It is hardly without significance, for example, that *Not I,* and a number of Beckett's later plays centre on a woman. Traditionally, of course, oppositions between presence and difference, control and hysteria, intellect and body, reason and emotion, have been sustained by, and have helped to sustain, gender differences between male and female. It might be argued with some justice that Beckett's theatre falls in with at least one of these conventional opppositions, that which puts woman in the place of nature and the body, as opposed to man's association with culture and the spirit. It may even be that there is a homological association of woman, as the bodily, with the theatre, or the stage itself — certainly women characters seem to be placed in more intimate proximity than men with the physical substance or surface of the stage, with Winnie's imprisonment, or M's relentless pacing. There may be a more general association, too, between 'female' qualities and the theatre. Beckett paid serious attention to women characters only after his turn to the theatre, his turn to what some critics have seen as a more intuitive, emotional and 'human' kind of art, after the ratiocinative aridities of the prose. As some have argued, this association of woman and the body is reduplicated by an opposition between two different conceptions of the body itself, in which the male body is seen as full, projective and phallic, while the female body is a place of absence, orifice, lack and uncertainty.

But at different levels, Beckett's writing and theatrical practice confirms *and* undermines such notions. The woman's body in *Not I* is an absence, but not an absence that can be identified simply with lack, and fixed at the opposite pole to fullness and masculine potency. It is a 'complex' rather than a 'simple' absence, and is identified with the process of signification by means of which such opposites are established. Woman is placed at the point of merging and separation between gender positions, like the voice in *The Unnamable,* which imagines itself as a membrane or tympanum between inside and outside, self and other, and, as such, is both free and fixed, inside and outside the metaphors that produce texts and sustain readers in their constitution of those texts.

It seems impossible after viewing *Not I* to hold to the systematic oppositions which frame it, and frame criticism and interpretation of it. Surprisingly this is not to say that Beckett's texts actually do induce this kind of self-reflection in readers or viewers. Indeed, just the opposite seems to be the case. If Beckett's plays resist the notion of the innocent self-evidence of the body and its language, demonstrating instead that the body is knowable only in repetitions and representations, then this is an apprehension which seems in its turn to have been resisted by most criticism of Beckett, which has been content to reproduce these metaphors and representations. It is not so much that criticism is simply in error in misrepresenting the intensity of Beckett's challenge to conventional placings of the body and the self, and the projection of this in the theatre. Rather, it is that Beckett's texts, his practice as a director and the constitution of these in and by criticism, exist in a complicated inter-involvement which prohibits a simple oppositional relationship of the object and critical knowledge of it. This inter-involvement involves complex relationships of power and resistance, and repetition and displacement, relationships that are in some ways reduplications of issues of power and control that exist elsewhere than in theatre and theatre criticism. The purpose of the final chapter will be to examine these lines of inter-involvement.

Chapter 8

Repetition and Power

Beckett might seem, at first sight, an author for whom the issue of power has little relevance. Rather than representing power, control or success, it is often said, his works are concerned with suffering, powerlessness and endurance. Beckett himself provided an often quoted formulation of this in his interview with Israel Schenker:

> With Joyce the difference is that Joyce was a superb manipulator of material — perhaps the greatest. He was making the words do the absolute maximum of work.... The kind of work I do is one in which I'm not master of my material. The more Joyce knew the more he could. He's tending towards omniscience and omnipotence as an artist. I'm working with impotence, ignorance. I don't think impotence has been exploited in the past.[1]

As Alan Astro has observed, the important thing about Beckett's formulation is that it allows us to see him not only as working with impotence, but also *working with* and 'exploiting' impotence.[2] It will be the argument of this chapter that, just as the slave or masochist does not escape the nexus of power merely by making himself the object of power, so Beckett's texts do not escape or cancel out questions of power merely by resigning interest in its conspicuous attainment or exercise. Impotence is not a simple condition, for it exists in a complicated relationship to questions of power. Impotence is always failure under certain specific conditions. To 'work with' impotence is to enter into a reordering of the relationships of power and powerlessness, because it is an attempt to take possession of one's poverty, to neuter impotence by affirming it, to resist subjugation by embracing it.

Beckett's works compel a sense of the complexities of power relationships as they are established and replicated, not only in the individual's relationship to his or her social world, but also in the deepest, most inaccessible solitudes of the self. If *Murphy* seems to announce a retreat from the 'big world' in which the exercise of power plays such a conspicuous part, and to initiate that exploratory movement inwards to the unconditioned and perhaps incommunicable private self, then that involves only superficially a break with questions of power. The closer one penetrates to the self, the more insistently relations of power and resistance, freedom and authority are reproduced. These may not be exact or paradigmatic reflections of structures of power in the social world, but they are not wholly separate from them either.

The interrelations in Beckett's work between power, control, authority, surrender, subversion and resistance are not easily to be understood with a simple, binary model in which power is set strictly and symmetrically against powerlessness. The psychological terrain which his work brings into being can be better understood with more complex models like Hegel's master/slave dialectic, with its stress on the mutual dependence of master and slave, or, even better, Michel Foucault's notion of 'immanent' power, power which 'is everywhere; not because it embraces everything, but because it comes from everywhere'. Power, for Foucault, does not reside in fixed points or conditions, for 'power means relations, a more-or-less organized, hierarchical, co-ordinated cluster of relations.'³ Beckett's work not only 'shows' these relations, but enters into them, for it is in the very activity of writing that questions of authority, control and resistance are most intensely posed. The encounter with language and writing is never a private or pre-social encounter, and so the apparent retreat from the 'big world' of power usually succeeds only in displacing or reinstating its structures at different levels. Beckett's turn to the public art of theatre in the 1950s intensifies the struggle of writer and medium which had been so much a part of the prose work that preceded it. Beckett's subsequent work for stage and page begins more and more to include the question of its relationship to the forms of critical knowledge that represent it. Even Beckett's obstinate refusal to be involved in critical explication of his work comes to be a term or moment within the practices of interpretation with which his work increasingly meshes. To speak of Beckett's texts or Beckett's oeuvre is, more than with any other writer except Shakespeare, or possibly Dickens, to speak of a large and powerful ensemble of discourses, divided and constituted in the relationships of power and authority which expression and interpretation irresistibly bring about.

Textual Power

The break with the big world can be placed more accurately not between *Murphy* and *Watt,* but at the beginning of *Watt* itself. The world of external restraints is represented by the policeman who is summoned by Mr Hackett to protect public decency, but this external authority is quickly forgotten in the struggle to establish the more intangible and fugitive authority of reason and knowledge. Subsequently, the book establishes a clear allegorical pairing of power and knowledge. Watt's search for knowledge is inseparable from the terms of his service to Mr Knott and, though Mr Knott's authority is largely absent and impersonal, it nevertheless provides a frame for the little that Watt comes to know and the forms of his knowledge. The important thing about Watt is, in one respect, his passivity, for it is this passivity that allows him to bear the well-nigh intolerable intensity of ratiocination that is his life in Mr Knott's house. One way of seeing the compendiousness of *Watt* is as an absolute dependence on and surrender to the forms and objects of knowledge or enquiry. Watt is so little himself a source of being or power that there is nothing to resist or distort his endless researches. The account of Watt's service of Mr Knott (given to Sam in reverse order) makes the association between absolute obedience and absolute narrative fidelity very clear:

> Shave, he'd say. When had got things ready to shave, the bowl, the brush, the powder, the razor, the soap, the sponge, the towel, the water, No, he'd say, Wash, he'd say. When had got things ready to wash, the basin, the brush, the glove, the salts, the soap, the sponge, the towel, the water, No, he'd say, Dress, he'd say. When had got things ready to dress, the coat, the drawers, the shirt, the shoes, the socks, the trousers, the vest, the waistcoat, No, he'd say.
>
> (p. 165: quotation reconstructed)

If much of the reasoning in *Watt* concurs with this unprotesting servility, then there is clearly another sense in which the language and narrative style of the book is aggressively self-assertive. Watt's reasonings are ordered by the discipline of repetition and yet also relentlessly impose that discipline. When Watt considers the number of solutions to the problem of Mr Knott's dog and the number of objections to these solutions, he orders them in the form of a table, which is reproduced in the text (p. 95). The effect is to remove the problem from the realm of the independently external world and make it the theoretical possession of Watt, or at least of the reader. Even the various forms of Watt's backwards narrative assert a kind of power, by deliberately denying the forward movement of time, and the endless loss which this brings about, to make time ultimately possessible by representation.

Repetitive language dramatizes the dichotomy between surrender and control. Repetition, and especially repetition in the form of listing, seems to establish a language deprived of inhibiting corporeal substance and therefore capable of obedient adherence to its original. A list seems the least stylized, the most inert of linguistic forms, for a list appears to 'do' nothing to its objects except name them. But, at the same time, a list is the most conspicuously unnatural form of language, for, in problematically displaying itself in all its alien bulk, it may seem like an imposition or supervention of language upon its objects. This is why, in the long and distinguished history of the literary list, in Rabelais, Sterne, Swift, Dickens and Joyce, it so often appears as a comic device for affirming the monstrous primacy of language over life. In Beckett's use of the list in *Watt,* there is a particularly intense exposure of the power relationships involved in representation, for, in *Watt,* the list is at one and the same time master and servant, the mark of control and the threat of endless openness.

Mathematics, too, often provides the consolation of order in *Watt.* If the language of the book is mathematical in the sense that it enforces a rigorously faithful relationship between word and thing, then mathematics also provides a different promise of control; for mathematics can have the function of a metalanguage, which can place and subordinate the more slippery, perishable forms of verbal language. To resort, as *Watt* does, to diagrams and calculations is to attempt to master the imperfections of ordinary language in the most visible way. One of the best examples of this movement towards the control of metalanguage is to be found in a draft version of the passage in Arsene's address to Watt, in which he protests that it would be no use beginning his life all over again, since the result would always be the same. The manuscript version specifies what this result will always be, a 'lamentable tale of error, waste, folly and ruin', and then proceeds to restate the proposition in two mathematical formulae:[4]

> Let L be the life, E the experience and ltewfr the lamentable tale of error, waste, folly and ruin — then
>
> ltewfr = L = L + E = L + 2E = L + 3E = L + (n–1)E = n(2L + (n–1)E
>
> or perhaps better
>
> ltewfr = L = LE = LE^2 = LE^3 = … LE(n–l) = L(En–l) E–1

Each repetition of the material translates and simplifies the relationship between its elements, in a way that exercises a progressively greater degree of control over it. This struggle between form and content repeats itself in various ways in *Watt,* but most notably in the relationship of the different narratives. As only becomes clear some way into the book, everything in it is being conveyed to us, not by Watt himself, but by Sam, his intimate at the asylum. Consequently, we have no way of knowing whether this narrative is a faithful representation, or whether it is Sam's madly methodical mind which is in control, or, rather, which struggles all the way through to *assert* control.

The adaptation which this requires on the reader's part repeats the structure of subordination and mastery. Just as Sam, like anyone in the grip of a compulsion, is both controller of it, and also controlled by it, so the reader is likely to be both repelled by the outlandishly ungenerous narrative of the book, and tempted by the prospect of subduing it, rendering it knowable and pleasurable. The narrative of *Watt* simultaneously excludes the reader and offers him or her the prospect of a control which is actually more thoroughgoing than anything a novel-reader has a right to expect. Reader and author bend themselves to the same arduous discipline, and thereby encounter the same duality of control and surrender.

These issues continue to dominate Beckett's work, even though the object of enquiry is no longer the form of the external world, but the more intangible nature of the interior self. In *Molloy,* the problematic relationship between the two narrators brings about a complex shifting of power positions. Moran seeks continually to exercise power, both outwards in his treatment of his son and the material world ('When a thing resists me, even if it is for my own good, it does not resist me long' *[T,* 166]), and inwards, in his angry self-discipline. Molloy, on the other hand, has no such desire for control, and seems throughout his narrative to have nothing of the vexed relationship with authority that Moran does. These different attitudes are reproduced in the narratives of the two men and their attitudes towards the writing of them. Moran gives his report under duress, almost as a confession, and, as such, his narrative is a complex mixture of servility and surliness; grimly he holds himself to his commission to write his report even though he clearly produces something other than a strict and literal account of his adventures. He repeatedly breaks off to insist that his report will not be a full or accurate one, since he does not know any more than he did when first setting out what lies in store for him. Moran thus accepts the burden of 'this relation that is forced upon me ... this petty scrivening which is not of my province' (*T,* 132), but refuses to take responsibility for it. But in refusing the position of author or editor of his own life, he also asserts a kind of stubborn resistance in incapacity: 'it would not surprise me if I deviated, in the pages to follow, from the true and exact succession of events. But I do not think even Sisyphus is required to scratch himself, or to groan, or to rejoice, as the fashion is now, always at the same appointed places' (*T,* 133).

In his rages, compulsions and habits, Moran internalizes authority, subduing himself as he subdues his son. For Moran, authority exists in repetition, even in the way that he repeats structures of authority within himself. His narrative is the place where these repetitive structures of control, freedom and self-discipline enact themselves. Progressively, however, a different source of power asserts itself, in the mysterious voice that he begins to hear. The voice exhorts him 'to continue to the end the faithful servant I have always been, of a cause that is not mine, and patiently fulfill in all its bitterness my calamitous part, as it was my will, when I had a will, that others should. And this with hatred in my heart, and scorn, of my master and his designs' (*T,* 132). The voice slowly grows in authority, while Moran gradually subordinates himself to it. It is a voice that, by the end of the novel, he is beginning to understand. We learn now that it was in obedience to this voice that Moran wrote his report, not directly at the instigation of Youdi. It may perhaps be the voice of Molloy, or the same voice that Molloy hears at the end of his narrative; or may be an early version of that voice that most of the narrators in the Trilogy and later texts say they hear, and sometimes, like the narrator of *How It Is,* claim to quote. But even in Moran's patient attention to this voice, the dialectic of freedom and authority persists. The last words of his narrative are a complex overwriting of command, acquiescence and denial; the voice tells him to write the report, and presumably also tells him to write the final words of the narrative, words which displace the authority of that report, and assert control in a different place: 'It told me to write the report. Does this mean I am freer now than I was? I do not know. I shall learn. Then I went back into the house and wrote, It is midnight. The rain is beating on the windows. It was not midnight. It was not raining' (*T,* 176).

Molloy seems to have inherited something of Moran's final passivity, though he is no freer than Moran, required as he is to produce his pages as he lies in his bed in his mother's room. However, Molloy seems to inhabit his passivity, *passively,* as it were, without witnessing or possessing it for himself. He does not reread his pages after he has written them or when they are returned to him (and Malone seems similarly unable or unwilling to reread what he has written). This means that his narration is almost entirely out of his hands, edited and assembled, we may assume, by the mysterious 'others'. His carelessness about the details of his narrative is a similar resignation of authority.

But authority is not entirely abolished, even in Molloy's narrative, for there are moments when it reasserts a Moran-like will-to-knowledge and will-to-control. The account of the disposition of the sucking-stones, for example, shows a rage for method and orderliness, not only in what it describes, but in the way it describes it, which may remind us of Moran, or even Sam in *Watt.* The compulsive rhythms of freedom and control become evident as Molloy feels that he must recount every stage of his calculations, in order to free himself from the anxiety that a lack of method and less than complete solutions bring him. His narrative exhibits the characteristic double structure of a compulsion: he and the reader are in the grip of the repetition-compulsion, even though the symptom of this is a dictatorial control over the narrative, a control which is signaled archly in the showman-like display: 'Good. Now I can begin to suck. Watch me closely … Do I have to go on? No …' (*T,* 72). Even Molloy's self-abandonment at the end of his narrative brings about something other than an absolute dissolution of the self. The move to the third person, corresponding to Moran's self-distancing at the end of his narrative, relinquishes the authority of the speaking 'I' but assumes a different, more distant authority: to assert that 'Molloy could stay, where he happened to be' is to suggest that the writer is already somewhere else, already somebody else.

The next two books in the Trilogy present the reader with an intensification of the dichotomy between surrender and control. Malone's narrative is in one sense a blending of Moran's and Molloy's, for it combines helplessness with unbending authority. Malone's is a willed surrender of self, in which, paradoxically, continuous vigilance is required to keep down its resurgence. His ambition to die in his narrative, or to have his narrative die with him, is at once a surrender of narrative to the utmost of contingency and an outrageous attempt to use narrative to master death. As with Molloy's narration, Malone's last words repeatedly assert impotence — 'Lemuel is in charge … he will not hit anyone … never he will never or with his pencil or with his stick' (*T*, 289) — even though the repetitions in themselves assert the powerful demand to continue speaking. To speak one's own death is to speak the moment of absolute incapacity, to attempt to extend the control of the self even as it vanishes into non-being.

In the reduced world of *The Unnamable* the opportunities for the exercise of power might again seem to be terminally diminished. In the absence of a material form, a place, or body to inhabit, there seems nothing for the self to speak of, and therefore nothing to control in narrative. The only response to this impasse is, nevertheless, to begin to speak, with the certainty that this brings of a split between the self and what the self is speaking of, a division of the self into *pour-soi* and *en-soi*. This split is the source of pain and also of narrative opportunity. To speak is to project a substitute self, Basil, or Mahood, which the enunciating self can then stand aside from and even repudiate. This repudiation is the strenuous means by which the tenuous *pour-soi* asserts itself, even if only as a Sartrean negation, or 'nothingness'. The realm of the not-self which the speaker rejects includes 'innate knowledge … like that of good and evil', as well as 'the low-down on God' and love, intelligence, even reason, all of which are derived from the 'reliable authority' of God's agents at Bally (*T*, 300). Knowledge and culture are seen unequivocally as the exercise of power:

> There were four or five of them at me, they called that presenting their report. One in particular, Basil I think he was called, filled me with hatred. Without opening his mouth, fastening on me his eyes like cinders with all their seeing, he changed me a little more each time into what he wanted me to be. Is he still glaring at me, from the shadows? Is he still usurping my name, the one they foisted on me, up there in their world, patiently, from season to season? No, no, here I am in safety, amusing myself wondering who can have dealt me these insignificant wounds.
>
> (*T,* 300)

The formation of the self and its knowledge is here presented as a product of the fierce attempt to subdue and control the self, to 'usurp' its name. But it is hard to know where this preexisting self is, that is harried and subdued by these 'external' forces, if the self is also no more than the sedimentation of these external forces. This is why the speaker can conceive of Basil as both interrogator and surrogate. Basil both foists a name on the nameless speaker, and yet, at the same instant, usurps that inauthentic name. So, although the self may resist the invasions of the not-self, this is not because it knows of any essential or verifiable core of being. Rather, the notion of the essential self, and its resistance, is itself a product of the structure of opposition.

Every attempt after this to assert the self against the not-self — even the attempt to assert its impotence or nothingness — repeats this structure of power relations. The voice resists identification with the simulacra that it brings into being in the very act of speaking, and attempts continually to exclude them from its narrative — 'Let them be gone now, them and all the others.' But if the voice continually seeks to exercise power by this sort of exclusion, then it also seeks a kind of release in submission to power, for its dominating attitude towards these simulacra is also the evidence of its submission to the will of the 'masters', the 'college of tyrants' who seem in some way to be the origin of its obligation to speak its 'pensum', in order to be free. The voice is suspended between the two alternatives of exercising the power of denial over its creatures and obeying the will of its masters. Like Moran, it is required to narrate, and yet resists that requirement all the way through. Obedience and dissidence alternate, as the voice wonders how best to fulfil its obligation to speak of itself; and sometimes the two dimensions of this power relationship invert, changing the places of creature and master, as the voice even takes pity on its master, 'the unfortunate brute, quite miserable because of me' (*T,* 315) and begins to wonder whether he is 'solitary like me, not free like me' (*T, 316).*

What this means is that, even in the most inaccessible interior of individual being, the self remains inhabited by the 'other' of social life. The search for being consists in the endless struggle to separate the self from what constitutes it, a struggle of resistance and recoil which continually reasserts the interdependence of self and world. This is why *The Unnamable,* the novel in which Beckett explores the self in the last extremity of deprivation, is also the most aggressive, the most vigorous in its alternations between desire and control, subordination and resistance; full of 'the little murmur of unconsenting man, to murmur what it is their humanity stifles' (*T, 328).* The phrase suggests that even the essential 'self' of species is stifled and falsified, by the 'self' of humanity, or the ways in which 'humanity' is invented and reproduced. Rather than setting out simply to produce archetypal image of the 'human condition', Beckett's work consists of an obstinate struggle with the very question of humanity, and against the definitions that control and produce ideas of 'the human'.

Seen in this way, the move from the fiction back into the 'big world' of the drama may seem like a break that is structurally predictable. The drama moves from the recognition that the attempt to escape structures of power only reinstates them at another level, to a much more explicit concern with power and power relationships. The absent Godot, in Beckett's first performed play, who is saviour and tyrant at once, seems the origin and reference point of all power in the play, even though that power is never visible in itself. Instead, the manifestations of Godot's power are partial repetitions of or substitutes for transcendent power — Vladimir's and Estragon's strange sense of compulsion, the unpredictable status of day and night, the boy who is sent as emissary and, most particularly, Pozzo, who is first of all mistaken for Godot. The absence of transcendent principles underlying Pozzo's power means that it is uncertain in its operations. Pozzo identifies himself with God, saying that Vladimir and Estragon are 'Of the same species as myself [*he bursts into an enormous laugh*] Of the same species as Pozzo! Made in God's image!' (*CDW*, 22–3), but is jealous of Godot and dependent upon Vladimir and Estragon to verify his existence by their subservient attention to him — he doesn't like 'talking in a vacuum' (*CDW*, 29). In this he resembles Hamm in *Endgame*. The suggestions of a transcendent power are even more perfunctory in this play and, as a result, the self-enclosure of structures of power and relationship is clearer to see. Hamm and Clov are locked together in a nightmare of mutual subjugation, in which each is exploiter and victim of the other.[5]

In later plays, this relationship is taken away from the stage and extended outwards to include the audience and readership. In *Happy Days*, what keeps Winnie enclosed and having to talk is being in the theatre itself, in front of an audience; the bell that rings to wake her up is like the bell that summons performers on to the stage and the lights that blaze down so unremittingly on her seem simply and frankly the lights of the theatre. The enactment of power through looking and being looked at is even more forcefully apparent in *Film*, in which the visual medium of the play is torn by a struggle for possession and escape. The analogue to the pursuing gaze of *Film* in the theatre is the mobile, inquisitory spotlight of *Play*, which duplicates the audience's attempts to make sense of and analytically to control the related narratives of the three characters.

Play, in particular, shows the close relationship of repetition and power. The characters are trapped in a hell of repetition, because they must go through their stories again and again in obedience to the remorseless probing of the light. Even though, each time through, the characters seem able to break off from their narratives to reflect on the nature of the light and their subordination to it, this access of self-consciousness seems to be cancelled as they are forced by the repetition to move back into narrative. And the effect of the repetition is to reveal that the light is no freer than they are, but is itself forced to repeat the inquisition, having learned nothing, or with no more knowledge than its victims of what has already passed. The comments Beckett applied to Winnie in his production notebook for *Happy Days* might seem to apply just as well to the characters in *Play* — 'time experience incomprehensible transport from one inextricable present to the next, those past unremembered, those to come inconceivable', for they live, not in repetition, but in a hell of non-repeatability, or unrecognized repetition, denied even what Moran calls the satisfaction of seeing themselves doing the same thing over and over again.[6]

The audience are therefore crucial to *Play,* for it is they, and they only, who realize what is happening, as the light, identified as scrutineer in the first half of the play, becomes the object of scrutiny the second time through. This transfer of position is not a permanent transfer of power, because the self-consciousness induced by the awareness of repetition may also bring about an embarrassed sense in the audience that they themselves are being observed, perhaps by some other audience. In each case, the reversal of perceptual positions brings about a spasm in the relations of appraiser and appraised. The effect is not to elide or abolish power. Rather, it is to point to power as centreless and unfixed, as consisting in exchange rather than in permanence. This alteration is evidenced in *How It Is,* in which the three stages of domination, before Pim, with Pim and after Pim, open out to the prospect of a whole universe of mutual tormentors, moving slowly across the mud, 'martyring and being martyred' (p. 138). In *How It Is,* as in *Play,* the torment consists in making one's victim speak, and this is doubled by the fact that it is overheard and transcribed by a series of unseen interlocutors, Krim, Kram, etc. 'up in the light'. The alternating structure of power is found, too, in *What Where,* in which Bim, Bem, Bam and Bom (names which recall those in *How It Is)* are merely positions in a circulation of power and control, in which each participant plays the role of torturer and victim, master and servant. Unlike *How It Is, What Where* seems to offer no prospect of escaping this circle of power, since Bam, the narrator, is both devisor and devised, narrator and participant. When he counsels 'Make sense who may' at the end of the play, he draws the audience and critic into the grim game of torture, for understanding the play means 'giving it the works', to make it render up a sense, make it 'say what.'

Such a concern with power and the representation of its operations might seem to be self-abolishing. If everything is power, and if power is infinitely reversible, then this might be to say that there is no real power lodged anywhere. There are ways, however, in which Beckett's work for the theatre does reflect upon and engage with specific hierarchies of power and control. One of the most important of these is that of gender, and Beckett's later works bring to light in complex ways the gendering that inflects even the most abstruse philosophical concepts and representations.

It is not merely the fact that Beckett's characters tend to be such fierce misogynists that defines the female position in his early fiction. Throughout the early work, the figure of the female tends to concentrate the constrictions of bourgeois domesticity and the absurd falsities of routine, as well the blind will of the natural — it is women who urge the claims of regular employment in *Murphy* and force other narrators unwillingly into sexual congress. Beckett's early work reproduces faithfully the traditional double insult to women, that they are both absurdly spiritual (Lousse) and disgustingly physical (Ruth, Molloy's mother). It seems that women, in Beckett's early work as in the writing of the Schopenhauer he admired, simply do not have the largeness of mind to encompass the kinds of anxiety and despair experienced by male characters. (Criticism tends to reproduce the privative opposition when it speaks of the way that male characters 'explore' their predicament, while female characters like Winnie merely 'endure' theirs.)[7]

Beckett's interrogation of the self in his later fiction also reproduces gender hierarchies, in identifying woman as the *en-soi,* as being in itself, as matter, and as the false objectifications of ideology, while man occupies the pole of the questing, heroic *pour-soi,* the spark of consciousness endlessly seeking to detach himself from incarceration in the inauthentic *en-soi.* What underlies this perhaps is a metaphorology of the phallus, the attempt to assert 'male' singleness or self-identity of being against the muddling multiplicity of vaginal woman; and it may be that Beckett's work reproduces something of the hierarchical gendering in Sartre's *Being and Nothingness,* in which the *en-soi* is characterized by a threatening and repulsive stickiness, whose ambiguity of being threatens the solidity of the male self.[8]

However, Beckett's move into the theatre seems slowly to have brought with it an awareness and exploitation of the power relations built into representations of gender. Certainly, women characters come to occupy more attention in the drama, since there are, quite simply, more female characters to be seen in central roles — Winnie, Maddy, May, the woman in *Rockaby.* However, this should not be seen simply as the ceding to woman of the franchise of a full and visible identity which was previously denied. Rather, it is the result of an awareness that the power relations inherent in the loss of presence and identity are concentrated in a particularly intense way when it is a woman who is the object of scrutiny on the stage. We can say that Beckett's drama increasingly engages with the power structures inherent in gender rather than (and sometimes as well as) unconsciously reproducing them.[9]

Crucial to this is the foregrounding of sight and seeing which the theatre allows and requires. Where characters in the fiction tend to rely on being heard or understood for the confirmation of their being, characters in the drama displace this anxiety into the need to be seen: 'You're sure you saw me', Vladimir says to the boy, 'you won't come tomorrow and say that you never saw me before?' (*CDW,* 85); 'Am I as much as — being seen?' wonders M in *Play* (*CDW,* 317). The shift from hearing to seeing is made even clearer in *Film.* Here, it is no longer a matter of ensuring the confirming gaze of others, but of escaping a gaze which is now experienced as predatory, even though it turns out that the structure of looking is constitutive of the self, since being consists in observing oneself in consciousness.

The particular appropriateness of having female characters on the stage is that it can induce a sense of the complex gendering of looking. Conventionally, woman is constituted as object to be looked at by the male. This asymmetry results in a doubling. If this structure gives the male as the origin of the gaze, with the fixity of position which this offers, the woman must occupy the position of looker and looked-at at once. What she sees, in the eyes of the male, is herself being looked at. The security of the male position is ensured by his invisibility to himself, for his gaze is directed aggressively outwards; but the woman is forced to inspect herself all the time, with a gaze that imitates the gaze of the male.[10] This structure of redoubling is to be found in Beckett's early work, in Murphy's sight of himself reflected, though unseen, in Mr Endon's eyes; but in the presentation of characters, and especially women characters, on the stage, an awareness of the operations of power is added to this structure, not least because of the ways that the viewer is drawn into this looking.

Perhaps the most extended exploration of the ironies of woman as spectacle is *Happy Days.* At first sight, Winnie might appear to be the very embodiment of the female as restricting materiality. Her immurement in the ground seems to express the sense of the closeness to the natural (even though hers is an unwilling immurement), and her addiction to meaningless routines to express a 'typically' female incapacity to attend to the actual conditions of her existence. Even the fact that Winnie feels drawn up out of the element that is consuming her, so that one day she might 'simply float up into the blue' (*CDW,* 151) might be seen as a conventional dramatization of the female as the place where the spiritual and the earthly commingle — and, in fact, this is acted out a moment before in the play, when Winnie professes horror at Willie's dirty postcard but subjects it nevertheless to prolonged scrutiny through her magnifying glass.

　　But if Winnie is the object of the audience's scrutiny, then she also sees herself as such, as the story about the Shower/Cooker (German, *schauen* and *gucken,* 'staring', 'gawping') couple indicates.[11] Different kinds of self-consciousness converge in this story. At the same time as being an object of enquiry and interpretation for the male viewer, Winnie is a sexual object: 'What's she doing? he says — What's the idea? he says — stuck up to her diddies in the bleeding ground — coarse fellow — What does it mean, he says — What's it meant to mean? — and so on — lots more stuff like that — usual drivel' (*CDW,* 156). But in incorporating and retelling this story, Winnie is both reproducing her position as spectacle and also taking control of it, as it were returning the gaze of the male.

　　As a woman, Winnie allows the dramatization of the observation as both violation and necessity. Winnie needs the gaze of another to confirm her sense of being, just as she needs to know that Willie is still there listening to her, or 'conceivably on the qui vive' (*CDW,* 148). In the second act of the play, she is reduced to looking at what little of herself remains visible to her, in an effort to supply the gap in her being, and, as she strives to make out the features which Willie has once admired, her desperate squinting still reduplicates the male gaze: 'that curve you once admired [...] ... the tongue of course ... you once admired' (*CDW,* 161–2). But to emphasise this activity of looking, as the play does, is also to disturb the imaginary, commodity status of the theatre spectacle, as an object that is simply out there, available for consumption. Here, the female spectacle looks at itself, and watches the audience look at it.

The representation of woman seems, in a number of later plays, to be a crucial factor in the reflection on representation as power. In *Footfalls* and *Rockaby,* there is a particular advantage gained from the foregrounding of endless watching: in *Rockaby,* the aggression of the audience's watching is contrasted with the woman's helpless attempts to see 'one other living soul', and failing to see it still, as she looks out at the audience. In *Footfalls,* we are never sure what it is that we are being asked to watch so intently, never left secure in our position as spectators, because of the movement in the different narratives between spectatorship and spectacle. In both these plays, woman is projected as extrinsic to herself, the condition of being 'not quite there' appropriate for 'ce sexe qui n'en est pas un'.[12]

The most elaborated form of this collusion between the figure of the woman and the anxiety of self is in *Not I*. Here, the extreme dismemberment of the woman makes the spectator participate in an uncomfortably aggressive voyeurism, while at the same time unsettling that position. The mouth appears as pure object, because it is deprived of the means of its seeing, even of seeing itself being looked at. But this uncomfortable blindness of the mouth, especially in the TV version, and its failure to return the viewer's gaze, is itself a threat. The dismemberment of *Not I* is not one which allows an unequivocal 'male' celebration of the power to mutilate and disperse the female body, for it is a dismemberment which fails to confirm the presence or entirety of the watcher.

This is not simply to rescue Beckett's works from the myths of humanism, or voluntaristically to assert its absolute freedom from such myths. Beckett's work, and the criticism which reconstitutes it, remain deeply implicated in the structures of power which, in certain senses, his work undermines. The figure of woman as passive sufferer survives, even as it is modified, and the relationship of director and actress reproduces the opposition of artist and medium, stylus and receiving surface; Billie Whitelaw, for example, speaks repeatedly of the ways in which Beckett speaks through her as writer and director, poses and constructs her as though she were a painting or sculpture.[13] This shift into the visual arts reproduces a conventional opposition between the artist as creator, and woman as his inert and receptive medium.

Producing Power

It is tempting to see tensions of this kind, between authority and openness, as simply interior features of individual texts. But in dramatic writing it is clear that such questions are often activated by the process of production which takes place subsequent to or outside the texts. The dependence of dramatic texts upon production means that their meaning is always produced out of a kind of grappling, in which the production seeks to accommodate itself to the text, while also unavoidably pulling against its influence. That Beckett's power and prestige as a writer have come after his turn to the theatre means that his reputation is established within a discourse underwritten by a network of power relations, in which the authority of the author is always to some degree pitted against his medium.

The underlying struggle in drama and its production is in fact between the two forms of repetition which have recurred through this study; Deleuze's 'naked' repetition, repetition as faithful and exact copy — which is to say, repetition as the servant of presence — and 'clothed repetition' — repetition as reproduction, or repetition-with-difference, which tends to disrupt presence. It is an opposition that structures most criticism of Beckett, as one might expect, since it also underlies most cultural criticism. This question has a wider reach than the relationship of Beckett's dramatic texts to their productions, for it involves also Beckett's relationship as author to the criticism which stages, or mediates all of his texts. Beckett seems to try to absolve himself from the dangers of interpretative reproduction by affirming that, as an artist, he has nothing to do with interpreting his own work. This is an attempt to discredit interpretation in advance, and to harness it to the idea of origin in the artist. It implies that the only acceptable sort of interpretation is transparent or tautologous doubling of the original work of art, for any other kind of criticism will inevitably be a betrayal of its real nature.

This mastering of repetition is instanced more tangibly in Beckett's own work in the theatre. It is as though the discrediting of interpretative repetition were not enough, and Beckett needed to be able to control as director the play of repetition in the theatre, to police the post-textual afterlife of his plays. If all authors fear the breaks, ruptures and discontinuities that reading, interpretation and production bring, then to direct one's own plays is a way of extending authorial control into the act of reading or consumption, and bringing idea and embodiment, script and performance together. If a performance of a play is exactly what is 'meant' by its script (and how could a play directed by its author be anything else, we might wonder?), then it is as if nothing intervened between original and copy. The intense work of repetition required to keep the production in line with the 'original' text ends up paradoxically turning repetition into mere superfluity, since it asserts the absolute authority of the original. Clas Zilliacus is probably right to suggest that the reason for Beckett's attraction to radio and television is the opportunity for increased control offered by these media.[14] Once it has been recorded, a radio or TV play or a film, especially one which has the author present as director or consultant, collapses text and performance together in a way that guarantees its absolute authority. The self-identity of the resulting work seems to render it immune from all the disruptive dangers of reproduction, since it reduces reproduction to the exact repetition of re-broadcast, a kind of repetition which can only reconfirm endlessly the integrity of the original.

Of course, Beckett continued to write for the stage as well as for electronic media, but his work for these media seems to have kindled a desire to replicate the structures of control that they offer. The conventional opposition between the reproducible text and the unique and transitory performance is upset by plays like *Rockaby* and *That Time,* in which the actual performance consists largely of a recording. Once again, repetition is associated with control; for what is legally controllable is that which can be repeated. If I were illegally to record a performance of either of these two plays, what I would be stealing would in fact already be a recording. If I were then to mount the plays without permission, using a different actor or actress, but using my bootleg copy of the original recording, then I would be able not just to perform the text of the play, but also, very nearly, to perform the performance of the play; my performance could be an exact repetition of the play in a way that is only possible when the play is already a recording. So, for the original performance to consist in a recording is to make it vulnerable to theft in a way that a normal performance is not. But its vulnerability conceals a strength, too; for what I steal, I can only ever perform by reproducing it intact, or restoring it to itself. In effect, the play would steal itself back from me.

Even in texts that do not use recorded material in this way, Beckett attempted in later years to extend his control over the text and performance. His stage directions became more and more detailed and consequently left less and less room for the intervention of the director. It may be that, as Pierre Chabert puts it, Beckett is writing as director in the first place, to constrain in advance the director's reproductive activity.[15] As such, the text reaches out jealously beyond itself to predict and monitor the form of its theatrical embodiment. This can sometimes mean that the script becomes a commentary on the performance, as in *Quad,* where, as we have seen, the script is able to draw on the experience of the Stuttgart TV production of the play, or, more problematically, in *Film,* where the script speaks in advance of elements of the performance as though they had already been performed, with the description of the expression on O's face or that of the couple and flower-seller — 'the expression gradually comes over their faces which will be that of the flower-woman in the stairs scene and that of O at the end of film, an expression only to be described as corresponding to the agony of perceivedness ... [an expression] impossible to describe, neither severity nor benignity, but rather acute *intentness'* (*CDW* 325, 329). This commentary on an image that does not yet exist corresponds to the passage at the beginning of the text in which Beckett not only describes the film, but also interprets it (*CDW* 323).

Another way in which the power of the authorial text is extended is through the production notebooks that Beckett was in the habit of compiling before directing one of his plays. These notebooks serve as a rereading and rewriting of the play, as, prior to rehearsals, Beckett tried to imagine the play spatially and visually. This seems to have been particularly important for a play such as *Waiting for Godot,* for which the notebook is, as Walter Asmus describes it, an 'attempt to give a scenic outline — a structure — to a play that has been regarded as "not visualized"'.[16] As such, the production notebook attempts, *in the form of a text,* to master and control all of the variations which performance might introduce, rewriting the distance between text and performance as the distance between two texts, the original play and the 'metabook' with which Beckett supplements it. Accounts of Beckett's direction make it clear that the production notebook, or 'regie-book', exerted considerable influence during rehearsals, although this 'notebook immanence', as Ruby Cohn describes it, was not total (*Just Play,* 265). The text had always still to be realized in concrete production, that necessary supplement which fills out the text, at the same time as it advertises its incompleteness. But, as Asmus's description of the writing of the notebooks makes clear, even this space between page and stage is anticipated in the text: 'When Beckett made the attempt — sitting at his desk — to visualize his play, he knew of course why he always left the left-hand page in the regie-book blank. The practice on the stage during the rehearsals led — if only occasionally — to corrections. Without these additions (in red) the regie-book is no longer complete.[17]

But with the addition of these corrections, derived from the experience of the play, the production notebook is, presumably, 'complete'. Once the experience of mounting the play has looped back and been inscribed in the text, that text stands both before and after the performance; it is both blueprint and record, a self-fulfilling prediction of the form that the play will have taken. Undeniably the production notebooks are an important resource for the student of Beckett's plays and practice as a director, but some writers have claimed for them an even greater significance; James Knowlson, for instance, feels that the notebooks supersede the performance texts, just as thoroughly as if Beckett had revised his earlier texts.[18] But to accord the notebooks this status is once more to assert the power of unity of intention, grounded in the figure of the author, and to close the gap between text and embodiment, so as to control in advance the form of every conceivable production.

What is at issue here is something much larger and more significant than Beckett's own personal attitudes towards his plays and their staging. Beckett's work as writer, self-translator and director meant that he was drawn into public structures of representation, and forced to play a part in them (sometimes, it seems, a very subsidiary part). There simply was no space for Beckett to withdraw into which was not already prepared for him by this public world of discourse. His very silence on interpretative matters became and remains a crucial term in the system of critical values which mediates his work, and Beckett's withdrawals from interpretation are reproduced, circulated and interpeted as feverishly as anything else in his writing. This was brought out in peculiarly striking ways when Beckett was directing his plays, because the refusal to comment on meaning becomes part of a directorial style or signature.

One story in particular bears out the complex relationship between Beckett's practice and the criticism that reconstructs it. Enoch Brater tells how, when Alan Schneider questioned Beckett as to whether the Auditor in *Not I* was a death figure or a guardian angel, Beckett shrugged his shoulders, lifted his arms and let them fall to his sides, just like the Auditor in the play. This story is retold by James Knowlson and Bernard Beckerman, both of whom take care to reproduce Brater's words, especially his last judgment that Beckett's gesture left 'the ambiguity of the figure wholly intact'.[19] The story is a delicious one and, in the way of such stories, gets better the more it is told. We can never now be sure how much Beckett meant to tease by reproducing the 'gesture of helpless compassion' of the Auditor within the play, but it hardly matters; the story will continue to do this work of redoubling as it is retold. Beckett's detachment from interpretation is here enacted through a withdrawal that is also an act of control. If Beckett had merely said 'Search me', then it might have left the field for interpretation more open than it does; but the fact that the story has Beckett mimicking the action of the play in fending off interpretation of it, confers textual sanction on the gesture of helplessness. Failure to understand is the essence of the play, the gesture seems to say, and one cannot comprehend or interpret this failure from the outside; all one can do is replicate it. This kind of 'naked' repetition asserts the solidity of the play which precedes it, and discredits the inauthentic supplement of interpretation, opposing an authority which is inward with the play 'itself' to a critical activity which is made to seem violently alien to it. Similar stories have been told about Beckett's direction, to indicate that actors too must stifle their impulses to fill out the plays with superfluous character motivation: when Jack MacGowran asked him how as Clov he should say the line 'If I knew the combination of the refrigerator I'd kill you', Beckett is said to have told him simply to think that if he knew the combination of the refrigerator he would kill Hamm.[20]

If the story of hermeneutic impotence in the face of *Not I* were one that Beckett himself was fond of telling, then the matter could be left there, as a simple allegory, or wish-fulfilling fantasy of authorial power. But who does tell the story? Like most of the legends about Beckett, it is told time and time again by critics themselves, in books, in lectures, in interviews, in seminars, in the bars at conferences. Why do critics enjoy and reproduce such a story of their own discomfiture? The truth is, of course, that, every time the story is repeated, it actually increases the authority of the critic, and, in some respects, of the institution of criticism in general. The repetition of the story about a repetition reappropriates it, and subtly re-angles the story to the critic's advantage; for it shows how humanely and humbly self-aware he or she is. The critical repetition of the story aligns itself with, instead of against, Beckett's own repetition within the story, and therefore associates itself with the line of integrity connecting play and commentary. In other words, we need to understand the assertions of the impossibility of interpretation that the story and the glosses on the story make as a performative rather than a constative utterance; what matters is not so much the truth or falsity of the proposition in itself, so much as the unspoken claim to authority which underlies it. If repeatability is in the nature of every utterance, since every utterance can be lifted out of its originating context and spliced into new contexts, then what counts is not the infinite play of these possible contexts, but the actual contexts of reiteration; who speaks, to whom, in what place, and for what purpose?

The stratifications of power that make up Beckett's texts in their relationship to criticism are therefore extremely complex, and not the least important consequence of this complexity is the difficulty that it produces in separating text from interpretation. Beckett's texts, his comments on those texts, his own criticism, his practice as a director, and the many different kinds of criticism and interpretation which his work has elicited, not to mention all the other, more 'unofficial' kinds of Beckettian writing, reviews, blurbs, interviews and exhibition catalogues, are knit together in a web of discursive inter-reference. The distinctions between author and text, and text and interpretation, are carefully defined and continually reaffirmed within this web of discourse, but in ways that actually tend to blur or transgress those limits. Criticism borrows the gesture of Beckett's shrug, to assert humbly its own limits, but in the very act defies those limits, affirming the possibility of speech and commentary even where these are denied.

Beckettian discourse has now reached such a pitch of productivity and influence that it can almost be thought of as a 'discursive formation' in its own terms, an ensemble of representational practices, unified around the name of Samuel Beckett, but engaged in continual redefinition of what that founding name means, and how far its authority extends. It would be wrong to conceive of the formation itself as necessarily possessing absolute coherence. What holds it together, indeed, is the intensity of its internal divisions, the struggle not only of competing interpretations of Beckett's work, the humanist, existential, religious and structural-linguistic, but of definitions of what criticism is, and where it stands in relation to its object.

We can say, then, that it is not the actual figure of Beckett himself, which unifies this discursive field, but rather that 'Beckett' who is its complex projection. For, in fact, what gives Beckett criticism such importance and cultural centrality is the continued reassertion in that critical discourse of the myth of the author as creator, source and absolute origin. Criticism has the curious task of representing for its publics Beckett's disclaimers of the public aura and prestige of the writer, while at the same time ceaselessly reconstituting this willed-away mystique in its own operations; after all, what could be more recognizably 'artistic' than Beckett's scrupulous aloofness from the public world and the marketplace? All this is made even more complicated by the fact that, despite his withdrawals, Beckett was forced to collaborate with the criticism that speaks around and within his name; reluctant though he may have been to talk about his work, Beckett seemed increasingly willing to let slip cryptic hints about his work and intentions, and he even wrote the blurb for one of his books.[21] Comparisons with the practice of Joyce are irresistible. Joyce was not given to public discussions of his work and its meaning, but devoted a great deal of time to publicizing it in indirect ways, and superintending the ways in which it was represented and explicated — Beckett was, of course, one of the contributors to the volume of studies on *Work in Progress* which Joyce seems unofficially to have edited.

Certain preconceptions about the nature of the theatre cooperate with and sustain the insistent narrative of origin and authorship. Just as the theatre seems to show us characters who are simply, elementally 'there', so, despite the obvious contradiction which this involves, the theatre can be read as a naked confrontation with the forms of the author's consciousness. No drama has ever been so 'authored' in its impersonality as Beckett's — except perhaps Shakespeare's, and that, as we shall see, is an association that is not without its significance. The insistence on the authored drama takes quite sophisticated forms, of course, and one would expect this of an Anglo-American criticism that has struggled to digest the anti-Romanticism of James and Eliot, the evacuation of intention required by the New Criticism and the death of the author announced in postmodernism. If the fiction presents us with an art of claustrophobic inwardness, a recession into the self which is ultimately an undermining of the author's 'presence', then the drama offers opportunities for an altogether more familiar narrative of mutual engagement and self-definition between self and 'the world'. Beckett's drama repeats the Yeatsian myth of descent from the tower into the grimy activity of 'theatre business, management of men', in which the private self must struggle with the recalcitrantly objective forms of the public world. We should not be surprised that it is in the drama that Beckett's authoriality has been so triumphantly asserted, for it is here, in the concrete forms of a visible art, rather than in the shifting dimness of narrative prose, that Beckett's authorial presence can leave its imprint, on a material that, because of its initial resistance, can bear that imprint permanently.

It is not just in metaphors of visibility that this myth of authorial presence asserts itself, but also in the metaphor of the voice. Billie Whitelaw is not alone in saying that she needs to hear Beckett's voice speaking the lines of his plays before she can understand them. The closeness of Beckett to his actors seems sometimes to imply that his plays cannot be satisfactorily performed except by someone who, literally as well as figuratively, knows his voice. This famous voice is everywhere, but also nowhere to be heard, for Beckett refuses to allow his voice to be recorded; this refusal exists in strange, erotic complicity with the dependence on this voice of those with whom he works. This metaphor of voice may account partly for the extraordinary power which is invested by Beckett and Beckettian discourse in a small number of authorized actors and actresses, who have dominated all the 'important' performances of Beckett's plays; Jack MacGowran, Patrick Magee, Max Wall, Madeleine Renaud and David Warrilow as well as, most notably, Billie Whitelaw. Surely such a small group of performers have never before had such power over an author's work, a power that is the more remarkable since Beckett's works are more often performed than those of any other living playwright. Authority is added to this by the often-repeated claim that Beckett heard in these performers the voice that speaks to him when he is writing. The metaphor of voice here sinks to a deeper, and more mystical level; the actors' voices are no longer repetitions of Beckett's own voice, but rather of that deeper more authentic voice that speaks through him and his writing. The result of this is that all the (considerable) differences between the actual voices of his actors can be forgotten, in order that there should always be as little difference as possible between the performing voice and the voice that, prophet-like, it transmits.

The relationship of the metaphor of voice to notions of origin and integrity is illustrated well in the remarks of a reviewer of Beckett's *How It Is,* who like other reviewers had received from a canny John Calder, with his copy of the book, a record of Patrick Magee reading passages from it: 'Magee's marvelously phrased realizations — they have a subtle intimacy and inwardness with the text that makes them seem more like a musical interpreter's work than an actor's were what an ideal reader would have in mind'.[22] As Calder and others have realized, the promise of intimacy and inwardness which the drama offers could be used to reclaim the more intractably impersonal form of the fiction, to ground it in speech and presence. With the growth in Beckett's reputation, dramatic readings of his prose works have multiplied, from MacGowran's *Beginning to End,* a performance which was, to a certain extent, 'directed' by the author, to Patrick Magee's BBC readings of the Trilogy and the later prose works, *Company* and *Ill Seen Ill Said,* and Billie Whitelaw's (unaccountable) promotion of the story *Enough* into a triple-bill, along with *Rockaby* and *Footfalls.*

The effect of this is to eliminate the difference between the different areas of Beckett's writing, and to suggest that all his works are equally infused with the aura of his writerly personality. If it is to make the individual work the possession of an individual actor's voice, the critically constituted interchangeability of Beckett actors also helps to restore the texts to the ownership of its central authorial voice. This effect of interchangeability is reinforced by the doubling of these actors in each other's parts. When David Clark and Katherine Worth came to remake *Eh Joe* for the University of London Audio-Visual Centre there could be no more natural choice for the part originally played by Jack MacGowran than Patrick Magee, and, in David Clark's *Film*, Max Wall stepped neatly into the place of Buster Keaton in a similar way. The differences between the actors are plain to see, but turn out to be much less important than the fact of their interchangeability as embodiments of Beckett's presence.

The tautologous relationship between actor and author results at its most extreme in an absolute doubling, in which the actor's individuality neither submits to nor supervenes on the play, but simply reproduces it in himself or herself. Bending themselves to the unselfing discipline of the text, the actors are led slowly back to a sense of themselves and, at the same time, closer and closer to Beckett. In the words of John Russell Brown:

> Performance reveals, without fuss or confusion, living concomitants for Beckett's words. In both fleeting and deep-set impressions, the singular beings of the performers become absolutely present as they fulfill selflessly the technical requirements which are as rigorous and demanding as those of any text that I can call to mind ... when inhabiting these fictions, an actor becomes close to Beckett's mind, and that brings into play the actor's most secret and most individual responses — I think that is why the best actors of Beckett's plays become his friends and associates.[23]

Other testimonies to the relationship that Beckett establishes with his actors stress this structure of doubling. It is possible to represent this, as Walter Asmus does, as an 'unauthoritarian' relationship, though it is perhaps only in a superficial sense that this is true.[24] The accounts of Beckett's relationship with actors frequently take the form of a theological narrative, in which the individual actor is left free in ways that lead inevitably to the discovery, at the heart of his or her freedom, of the imprint of Beckettian necessity.

As well as this identification of actor and author, Beckettian discourse has promoted another kind of authorial Doppelgänger, in the person of the director Alan Schneider, who was for so long the authorized interpreter of Beckett's works in the USA. Despite his close relationship with Beckett, Schneider directed his plays largely in the author's absence, so that, as he says, his account of working with Beckett might more accurately be labeled' "Not Working With Beckett" or "Working With Beckett's" or perhaps the most precisely "Working on Beckett", ('"Any Way You Like, Alan"', 27). This absence of the author proves to be the crucial element in fixing Schneider's determination to maintain absolute control, on Beckett's behalf, over his work. Again, religious metaphors exert a powerful influence in Schneider's account of the immanent presence of Beckett:

> I agree with my friend and Sam's, the late Jack MacGowran, that most of the time we seem to be trying to keep the author out, but with Beckett we feel just the other way round: we want him in. To hold our hands through the darkness. To illuminate the dots, interpret the ellipses and explain the inexplicable. To hover and fume (though he'd never let us see). So, although he's never actually been there, I've always rehearsed as though he were in the shadows somewhere watching and listening, ready to answer all our doubts, quell our fears, and share our surprises and small talk. Sometimes, without sounding too mystical or psychotic, I've felt that he was indeed there, and that I might easily be talking to him. (ibid., 28)

A little later, Schneider acknowledges the religious sense behind his account when he says that he has been 'more faithful than [sic] the Pope himself' and speaks of going to Paris, his 'Rome', to get the author's words at first hand. Like a priest or member of the church, Schneider is free, but under conditions that require the absolute subjection of faith. The fierceness of this faith was evidenced in a jealous determination to save Beckett's work from what he saw as adulteration or misrepresentation, convinced as he was of the unity of Beckett's work ('Almost any page of Beckett can be immediately identified as his') and of the need to safeguard the plays from performances in seventeenth-century armour or space-suits; this extends even to the casting of actors, for Schneider would cast 'only those whom I felt to be suitable and agreeable to Beckett's world and not cast those who would destroy or deny that world' (ibid., 35). This can have embarrassing consequences. One of the ideas for staging *Not I* that Schneider congratulates himself for resisting was the suggestion that the mouth be blown up on to television screens during the performance, an idea which, in the light of Beckett's admiration for the TV version of his play which does precisely this, no longer seems so absurdly, and self-evidently contrary to the author's intentions (ibid., 30).

If the notion of presence demands a certain dream of intimate contact with the author, then, as might be expected, actual personal intimacy between actor, critic and author is an important component in Beckettian mythology. Just as the faithfulness of an actor to Beckett's intentions is rewarded by friendship or association with the author, so critics too can penetrate to this mystical presence and advertise this validating friendship in books and lectures. What is strange is the way in which these stories of close contact go along with the repeated accounts of Beckett's mysterious privacy and aloofness. Actually, if Beckett really counted as close friends all those who hint deliciously at close and continuous intimacy with him, then the most celebrated literary recluse of the twentieth century would have a social diary to rival Nancy Mitford's. But my point is not really to sneer at these friendships (as though critics should never fraternize with the enemy), or indeed, to dispute the accounts of Beckett's personal qualities — Beckett always responded kindly and helpfully to my own enquiries. But when narratives of personal intimacy come to have such a central place in a public discourse, and to cooperate so strikingly with other ideological purposes, then they have a different status from garden-fence gossip. They become part of a myth, which can be articulated drearily around mysticisms and the sterility that they can enshrine.

Personal contact with Beckett is clearly a valued commodity because it is not available to all in the same way as texts are. As one might expect, Beckettian discourse has actually generated substitutes for this personal intimacy. If one cannot be in the presence of the celebrated Beckettian voice, for example, then the physical presence of his equally famous handwriting may be an acceptable substitute. The enormous amount of manuscript material relating to Beckett which has been deposited in libraries all over the world make available to anyone able to scrape together a research grant that sense of physical closeness to the author that turning over the pages of a manuscript can give. It might also have been anticipated that this private manuscript material would begin to enter the public domain, as it has with the publication of facsimiles of the production notebooks, and the frequent reproduction of manuscript facsimiles in works on Beckett. This is evidence of the recurrent contradiction between identity and repetition which is to be found in Beckettian discourse; the discourse is magnetized around the image of the writer, and seeks to approach ever more closely to this authorial 'presence' at its core, but the very intensity of this demand calls into being many different kinds of substitution for authorial presence, all of which tend to draw the discourse away from its hidden centre. If manuscripts take us into the presence of the artist, allowing us to perceive the creative mind at the very moment of its creation, then the multiplication of knowledge about manuscripts seems to work against this, for by making them publicly manifest and available, it desecrates the auratic privacy of the process of creation. This in turn creates a demand for more and more 'authentic' evidence of the process. Ruby Cohn, for instance, describes the manuscript of *En Attendant Godot,* which she says 'flows across the page with few changes and few hesitations' and therefore (unaccountably) 'reveals the work's fluidity'.[25] The reader anxious to enjoy for himself or herself the fluidity of the *Godot* manuscript is in for a disappointment, for it is one of the few manuscripts which is still not available for consultation; the fact that the knowledge of this manuscript is privileged seems to make it more authentic, and closer to its origin.

Beckett is not the only writer, of course, whose manuscripts can provide this thrill of intimacy, nor is there necessarily anything wrong in this fetishism. But what is significant is the way in which the representation of Beckett's manuscripts within critical discourse cooperates with the drive to affirm notions of origin and integrity in the literary productions. If reproduction always poses a threat to unity and essence, then the manuscript is a powerful countering image of permanence and self-possession, because there can only ever be one manuscript for each particular stage of a work's evolution. This parallels and helps to confirm the recurrent narrative that underlies manuscript studies themselves. The priority in such studies is always to establish the teleological drift of the scattered drafts and fragments, so as to be able to tell the story of the work's gradual evolution towards the integrity of its final form.[26] This is a narrative which, in its stress on the gradual purging of the auxiliary or inessential, corresponds, of course, to representations of Beckett's work as a whole; we are often told how Beckett has progressively 'pared down' his plays and fictions, in the search for essential form. Surprisingly, this narrative of evolution is also reversible; one 'goes back' to the 'original' manuscripts to observe the move towards completeness and definition, but since this move involves the discarding of the superfluous, it is also, in a sense, a gradual return to a point of origin, an 'excavation', to use Beckett's word, of the original inspirational secret of his work. The fetishization of Beckett's manuscripts, therefore, cooperates with a number of powerful myths of origin, presence and interiority.

At its worst, this kind of manuscript fetishism can be both absurd and rather sinister:

> *Watt* is a whale of a manuscript — a white whale. Among the thousands of modern manuscripts in the Humanities Research Center, it glows like a luminous secular relic. It is, at moments, magnificently ornate, a worthy scion of the Book of Kells, with the colors reduced to more somber hues. The doodles, cartoons, caricatures, portraits *en cartouche* include reminiscences of African and Oceanic art, the gargoyles of Notre Dame, heraldry, and more. Beckett's handwriting is at its most deceptively cursive. *Eppur si legge!* And it 'reads' in other ways, too. Jorge Luis Borges, examining *Watt* tactilely, along with manuscripts by Poe and Whitman, Baudelaire and other favourites of his, sensed something of its extraordinary qualities which, obviously, must transcend the visual. He asked his companion to describe it to him. This she did in detail, Borges nodding 'Yes, yes', with a happy smile throughout her description.[27]

If I were the curator of the Humanities Research Center I wouldn't be too happy about the incitement this passage offers to the erotic fondling of manuscript materials. However, the passage suggests other important things. The manuscript has here attained the status of an icon, or holy relic, which, rather than being vulgarly legible like normal texts, reveals its aura only to the faithful. The icon repels the unitiated curious ('Beckett's handwriting is at its most deceptively cursive') offering itself only to the receptive intuition, in an inspirational unveiling which, since the work 'reads itself', requires nothing from the reader. The manuscript is therefore a perfect image of the aura of a work of art, as something which is both fugitive and captive, an unseizable essence which is nevertheless always mysteriously there.

What is more, the manuscript asserts its own place within a tradition of such holy objects. The description of *Watt* hints discreetly at the vast resources of the Humanities Research Center (though the Book of Kells is not among them), the infinite riches in a little room gathered with Texan oil profits. *Watt* does more than advertise its place in that tradition, for its manuscript sums up the universality of human culture in itself, with its reminiscences of the Book of Kells, African and Oceanic art, the gargoyles of Notre Dame, heraldry. So it is that this urgent activity of metaphor and connotation takes a book which marks the collapse of the values of Western rationalism and culture, and restores it incontestably to continuity with that tradition.

This more general cultural claim is what underlies much of Beckett criticism, though it does not often come to light in quite so unguarded a way as this. For all of its alleged challenge to the notion of 'the human', and the decisive breaks which Beckett's work makes with history, Beckettian critical discourse has devoted itself energetically to reforging the continuities between his work and the traditions of Western literature and culture. So the story of Beckett's acceptance within literary culture is more than just a repetition of the familiar classicization of the avant-garde, for Beckett's work comes to stand for the power of tradition itself. One striking way in which this representative status is confirmed is by the increasing tendency to compare Beckett with Shakespeare. Beckett is, like Shakespeare, the representative writer of his age, and yet also the spokesman for the eternal human spirit. Like Shakespeare, Beckett is an artist who finds and confirms his solitary selfhood finally in the public art of the drama, and in the dialectical mingling of self and other which this requires. And like Shakespeare, Beckett is the representative of a whole cultural patrimony, an inherited tradition that, despite Beckett's disgusted turn away from his 'mother' tongue, is identified with the power and prestige of 'English' as a language.

The importance of the extraordinary universe of discourse that has formed around Beckett lies precisely in the fact that it allows an affirmation of the values of literature and culture themselves, and, at the same time, an assertion of the power of criticism as the privileged

mediator of that culture. The necessity of this affirmation is particularly great at a time when criticism and its institutions in Britain and the
USA have been increasingly drawn to the centres of state-based power
while being simultaneously stripped of their cultural and ideological
effectiveness. Against this, the discourse of Beckett criticism has a special, representative place within discourses of culture as a whole, for it
is a site in which cultural values of great importance may be repeated
and recirculated with authority. What is extraordinary is that all the
breaks which Beckett's writing practice makes, or attempts to make,
with these traditions and the power relationships they encode can be
so effectively contained and rewritten as repetitions.

But, as this study has argued, Beckett's works also suggest the
dangerous openness of repetition, and his practice as a director, as well
as his willingness to be involved in direct and oblique ways with interpretative activity in general, put some parts of the Beckettian myth
under strain. To speak of one's work within a critical discourse may
seem to reinforce the control and centrality of the artist, but it is also
to consent to a certain structural distancing from oneself. As author,
one speaks from an originating centre which, because it is within interpretation, is no longer exactly central in its circle, no longer exactly
its origin. In the same way, to direct one's own work is simultaneously
to evidence the proprietorial power of the author and to move into
something other than an authorial relationship to the work, since the
priorities of a director can never be exactly coincidental with those of
an author, if only because of the specific material questions attending
every individual production, the size of the budget, the personalities
of the actors, the dimensions of the stage, etc. Attempts to protect the
integrity of a text are therefore always liable to be upset by the differences which production brings about, and, time and again, Beckett
productively failed to make the productions of his plays exact replicas
of their 'original' natures, failed to let repetition stifle the possibilities of reproduction. And, as with the changes introduced in his self-
translations, Beckett seemed curiously reluctant to revise his originals
to bring them into line with the subsequent productions. Even in the
case of work for electronically reproducible media, where, as we have
seen, there is the unparalleled opportunity for 'definitive' versions of
a work to be produced, Beckett succumbed to the temptations of re-

production. He sanctioned David Clark's remaking of *Film,* which worked from the original script but introduced important changes, like the introduction of colour and sound.[28] Beckett himself has been involved with two productions of *Ghost Trio,* one in English for the BBC, for which he was a consultant, and the other in German, which he directed, and James Knowlson has highlighted the interesting differences between them.[29]

Beckett also directed a TV version of *What Where,* again for German television, a production that radically reworks his stage version by dispensing with the megaphone and the figures of the actors. Martha Fehsenfeld unnecessarily resorts to metaphors of origin and essence to account for the relationship of the two versions of the play. The TV version, she says, is not a disruption or distortion of the original; rather, it is the final stage in a movement towards unity, intensity and concentration, in which the stage play is only an intermediate point. It is as though the TV play lay concealed inside the stage play and has only now been brought to light; so that we can now see that in certain respects, *What Where* was really a TV play all along.[30] But Fehsenfeld's account of Beckett's work in Stuttgart suggests less this remorseless drive towards final form than a freely-ranging *bricolage,* in which Beckett, collaborating with Jim Lewis and other technicians, searched among alternatives for staging the play right up to the last minute, in a work of inquisition which uncannily resembled that in the play.

It is not necessary, in the face of Beckett's self-distancing as director, to resort anxiously, as Pierre Chabert does with his claim that 'Beckett as writer and director is one and the same person', to notions of the persistence and integrity of the authorial self (Chabert, 41). Beckett's work in the theatre need not be read as the sterile compulsion of repetition. Instead, it might be seen as enacting the condition of the texts themselves, as work rather than embodiment, practice rather than commodity. If, in one sense, Beckett's works have tended more and more to signal their condition as sealed, emptily formalized artifacts, then that exists in tension with the sense that they give of work which is always still in progress. As Claude Bernard suggests, Beckett's work can be thought of as dominated by *expolition,* that rhetorical figure which denotes the open demonstration of revision, reworking, and approximation.[31] It is a figure which suggests the ways in which Beckett's practice in fiction and in the theatre poses questions about the nature of repetition and the kinds of control and freedom which it allows. It is a practice which instances the powerful possibilities of reproduction over the sterile compulsions of replication.

Notes

Chapter 1 Difference and Repetition

1. John Pilling, review of *Company,* in *Journal of Beckett Studies,* 7 (Spring, 1982), pp. 129–31.

2. Some, like Gilles Deleuze, have celebrated the coming of the age of the simulacrum: see 'Plato et le simulacre', in *Logique du Sens* (Paris: Editions de Minuit, 1968), pp. 347–61. Jean Baudrillard similarly charts the movement from 'a theology of truth and secrecy' to 'an age of simulacra and simulation', but views it with a mixture of elation and horror: see 'The Precession of Simulacra', in *Simulations* (New York: Semiotext(e), 1983), pp. 1–79. See, too, the discussion of the relationship of mimicry and repetition between text and criticism in Gregory L. Ulmer, 'The Object of Post-Criticism', in *Postmodern Culture,* ed. Hal Foster (London: Pluto Press, 1985), pp. 83–110.

3. Jacques Derrida, 'Signature Event Context', in *Margins of Philosophy,* trans. Alan Bass (Brighton: Harvester Press, 1982), pp. 309–30.

4. 'Theatrum Philosophicum', (review of *Différence et Répétition)* in *Language, Counter-Memory, Practice: Selected* Essays *and Interviews,* ed. Donald F. Bouchard, trans. Donald F. Bouchard and Sherry Simon (Oxford: Basil Blackwell, 1977), p. 184.

5. This duality forms the basis for J. Hillis Miller's valuable *Fiction and Repetition* (Oxford: Basil Blackwell, 1982), pp. 5–9.

6. *Beyond the Pleasure Principle,* first published, 1920, reprinted in *The Standard Edition of the Psychological Works of Sigmund Freud,* trans. James Strachey, Vol. 18 (London: Hogarth Press, 1955), p. 36. References in the text hereafter are to *BPP.*

7. Charles Juliet, *Rencontre Avec Samuel Beckett* (Paris: Editions Fata Morgana, 1986), p. 39.

8. Ibid.

9. Rubin Rabinovitz, *The Development of Samuel Beckett's Fiction* (Urbana and Chicago: University of Illinois Press, 1984), p. 74.

10. Ruby Cohn, *Just Play: Beckett's Theater* (Princeton, N.J.: Princeton UP, 1980), p. 105. (References in text hereafter are to *Just Play).* John Pilling, too, writes of the centering force of repetition, which, he says, emphasizes the integrity of each organizational system in Beckett's texts: 'repetition fixes the system in our minds, amplifies it, gives it body and relevance', *Samuel Beckett* (London: Routledge and Kegan Paul, 1976), p. 31. An exception to the prevailing attitude towards repetition in Beckett's work is S.E. Gontarski's 'Molloy

and the Reiterated Novel', in *As No Other Dare Fail: For Samuel Beckett on his 80th Birthday by his Friends and Admirers* (London: John Calder, 1986), pp. 57–66. Gontarski sees reiteration as part of Beckett's assault on coherence, with his 'undoing of Joyce in particular and the Modernist text in general' (p. 99).

11. Bruce F. Kawin, *Telling It Again and Again: Repetition in Literature and Film* (Ithaca and London: Cornell UP, 1972), p. 33.

Chapter 2 Economies of Repetition

1. Roman Jakobson, 'Linguistics and Poetics: Closing Statement', in *Style in Language,* ed. Thomas A. Sebeok (Cambridge, Mass.: Harvard UP, 1960), pp. 353–7.

2. See Jacques Derrida, 'Signature Event Context', in *Margins of Philosophy,* trans. Alan Bass (Brighton: Harvester Press, 1982), pp. 315–18.

3. *Murphy* (Paris: Editions de Minuit, 1965), p. 7.

4. The French version of the text seems to make up for the loss of the easily-identifiable reference to Ecclesiastes by another religious reference; the mew is named 'l'Impasse de l'Enfant-]ésu' (p. 7), a reference which is arguably the more effective for being a refusal of the redemptive possibilities of the new dispensation.

5. For a much more extended account of verbal, episodic and thematic repetitions in *Murphy,* see Rubin Rabinovitz, *The Development of Samuel Beckett's Fiction* (Urbana and Chicago: University of Illinois Press, 1984), pp. 71–3, 185–222.

6. Jonathan Culler, *The Pursuit of Signs: Semiotics, Literature, Deconstruction* (London: Routledge and Kegan Paul, 1981), pp. 191–2.

7. What happens here resembles the effect of displacement brought about by the unruly intrusion of metonymy into the metaphorical economy of Proust's writing, as it is described in Paul de Man's *Allegories of Reading* (New Haven and London: Yale UP, 1979), pp. 57–78.

8. Culler, *Pursuit of Signs,* p. 189.

9. *Watt,* p. 27; *Watt* (Paris: Editions de Minuit, 1968), pp. 30–1.

10. Derrida has suggested that this economic duality is built into the structure of Western ideas about representation itself. Representation gives us the repetitive double of a thing either by being nothing in itself — in which case it is 'less' than its original, and so potentially an inauthentic or inadequate repetition of it, a threatening negativity — or by trying to be something in itself, standing in for its original — and so may seem like a problematic, distorting excess over that original. These two possibilities form an economy, or 'logical machine', says Derrida, the terms of which have predicted and controlled

debates about representation. See 'The Double Session', in *Dissemination*, trans. Barbara Johnson (London: Athlone Press, 1981), pp. 186–7.

11. 'Watt' becomes 'tav' in reverse, 'quelle' becomes 'lek', 'pour' becomes 'rop.' In one set of reversals, in which 'Mais faim. Pas sur. Mais repas. Sais pas' is rendered as 'Miaf siam? Rus sap. Saper siam? Sap sias', ignorance is allowed to generate an allusion to knowing 'sapience': see the Minuit edition of *Watt*, pp. 171–3.

12. The French version, though it achieves a similar phonemic echoing, loses the repetition of names: 'tout cela/Watt Le dira/mais quel cela ... c'est ce cela/que Watt dira/tout ce cela' (pp. 262–3).

13. This is not all, however. As Ann Beer suggests, the word 'pot' in English summons up the ghost of the French 'sourd comme un pot': see *'Watt*, Knot and Beckett's Bilingualism', in *Journal of Beckett Studies*, 10 (1985), p.63.

14. See the discussion of the relationship between title and text in Jacques Derrida's 'Devant la loi', in *Philosophy and Literature*, ed. A. Phillips Griffiths (Cambridge: Cambridge UP, 1983), pp. 173–88.

15. Michael Robinson writes that 'the "I" that speaks [in *The Unnamable*] ... is the voice of the creature who has been concealed behind and spoken through Murphy, Watt and Malone from the beginning', *The Long Sonata of the Dead: A Study of Samuel Beckett* (NY: Grove Press, 1969), p. 191. The designation 'Q' is given to the archetypal and unique form of the Beckett protagonist by Josephine Jacobsen and William R. Mueller, in *The Testament of Samuel Beckett* (London: Faber and Faber, 1966) p. 21.

16. See, for example, Kenneth and Alice Hamilton, *Condemned to Life: The World of Samuel Beckett* (Grand Rapids: Eerdman's, 1976), p. 149 and Frederick J. Hoffman, *Samuel Beckett: The Language of Self* (Carbondale: Southern Illinois UP, 1962), p. 115.

17. Frederick J. Hoffman, *Samuel Beckett: The Language of Self*, p. 115. See, too, Ludovic Janvier's discussion of Beckett's 'M' in *Pour Samuel Beckett* (Paris: Editions de Minuit, 1966), pp. 271–4.

18. *Molloy* (Paris: Editions de Minuit, 1951), p. 187.

Chapter 3 Repetition in Time: Proust and Molloy

1. For a discussion of Heideggerian parallels in Beckett's works see Lance St John Butler, *Samuel Beckett and the Meaning of Being: A Study in Ontological Parable* (London: Macmillan, 1985), pp. 17–38.

2. Michael Robinson writes that Molloy 'includes within himself the whole human experience and is ... a powerfully poetic and mythopoetic creation', *The Long Sonata of the Dead: A Study of Samuel Beckett* (NY: Grove Press, 1969), p. 155. Ruby Cohn discusses the mythical qualities of Molloy's

narrative in *Back to Beckett* (Princeton, NJ: Princeton UP, 1973), pp. 83–4. Edith Kern, in 'Moran-Molloy: The Hero as Author', in *Twentieth-Century Interpretations of Molloy, Malone Dies and The Unnamable: A Collection of Critical Essays,* ed. J.D. O'Hara (Englewood Cliffs, NJ: Prentice-Hall Inc., 1970), pp. 35–45, sees Molloy as a Dionysian force.
3. *Remembrance of Things Past,* trans. C.K. Scott-Moncrieff and Terence Kilmartin, 3 vols (London: Chatto and Windus, 1981), II, 86. Beckett refers explicitly to this paragraph in *Proust,* though, as often, his paraphrase is a significant reangling of the original:

> There is no great difference, says Proust, between the memory of a dream and the memory of reality. When the sleeper awakes, the emissary of his habit assures him that his 'personality' has not disappeared with his fatigue. It is possible (for those who take an interest in such speculations) to consider the resurrection of the soul as a final piece of impertinence from the same source. (*PTD,* 33)

The last phrase is a bitter reworking of Proust's neutral comment that 'perhaps the resurrection of the soul after death is to be conceived of as a phenomenon of memory' (II, 86).
4. John Fletcher, for instance, sees Moran and Molloy opposed and identified in Jungian complementarity, in 'Interpreting Molloy', in *Samuel Beckett Now: Critical Approaches to the Novels, Poetry and Plays,* 2nd edn, ed. Melvin J. Friedman (Chicago and London: University of Chicago Press, 1975), pp. 157–70. See, too, David Hayman's essay in the same volume, 'Molloy or the Quest for Meaninglessness: A Global Interpretation', which sees the two narratives as 'a complementary or an ironic couple contributing to a fascinating portrait of the universal man and an ingenious satire of his aspirations and accomplishments', pp. 140–1. Michael Robinson sees Molloy as a continuation of Moran, and the novel as a reconciliation of the two, in *The Long Sonata of the Dead,* pp. 162–3.

Chapter 4 Centre, Line, Circumference: Repetition in the Trilogy

1. J.E. Dearlove sees the whole of Beckett's work as a movement towards the 'incoercible absence of relation' between the artist and his occasion; *Accommodating the Chaos: Samuel Beckett's Nonrelational Art* (Durham, NC: Duke UP, 1982).
2. In the attempt to 'write death' in this way, Beckett's work reproduces the transgression which is described in Barthes's analysis of Poe's 'The Strange Facts in the Case of M. Valdemar', a story in which a man is hypnotized just before the moment of his death to enable him to continue speaking

posthumously; 'Textual Analysis of Poe's Valdemar', in *Untying the Text: A Post-Structuralist Reader,* ed. Robert Young (London: Routledge and Kegan Paul, 1981), pp. 133–61. See, too, Derrida's analysis of the denial/supplementation of death by writing in Maurice Blanchot's *Arrêt de Mort (Death Sentence),* in Derrida, 'Living On: Borderlines', in Harold Bloom et. al., *Deconstruction and Criticism* (London: Routledge and Kegan Paul, 1979), pp. 107–76.

3. See Derrida, 'The End of the Book and the Beginning of Writing', in *Of Grammatology,* trans. Gayatri Spivak (Baltimore and London: Johns Hopkins UP, 1976), pp. 6–26.

4. The exercise book is in the manuscript collection of the Humanities Research Center at Austin, Texas. See Admussen, p. 66.

5. Compare Eric P. Levy's discussion of the story 'Enough', in which he suggests that the two characters are personifications of the pen and the hand; *Samuel Beckett and the Voice of Species: A Study of the Prose Fiction* (Totowa, NJ: Barnes and Noble, 1980), pp. 113–15.

6. H. Porter Abbott draws attention to the dialogic structure in which Malone's narrative itself, though intended to answer and negate those of Molloy, ends up repeating them; *The Fiction of Samuel Beckett: Form and Effect* (Berkeley: University of California Press, 1973), pp. 110–15.

7. Reported in Charles Juliet, *Rencontre Avec Samuel Beckett* (Paris: Editions Fata Morgana, 1986), p. 49.

8. The sense of transitionality that the image of the eardrum suggests has been discussed by Derrida. In 'The Double Session', Derrida finds in the word 'hymen' in Mallarmé's prose-poem 'Mimique' an enactment of the instability of meaning in the poem. The word 'hymen' not only signifies a point of division and connection in the poem, but also divides and connects different meanings in itself, including sexual desire and prohibition. The hymen stands for the principle of difference itself, difference which 'inscribes itself without any decidable poles, without any independent, irreversible terms ... the hymen "takes place" in the "interim", in the spacing between desire and fulfillment, between perpetration and its recollection. But the medium of this *entre* has nothing to do with a centre' *(Dissemination,* trans. Barbara Johnson (London: Athlone Press, 1981), pp. 210, 212.

9. Derrida's discussion of the supplement is to be found in *Of Grammatology,* pp. 147–64, 269–316.

10. See John Fletcher, *The Novels of Samuel Beckett,* 2nd edn (London: Chatto and Windus, 1972), p. 129.

11. 'It has always been thought that the center, which is by definition unique, constituted that very thing within a structure which, while governing the structure, escapes structurality. This is why classical thought concerning

structure could say that the center is, paradoxically, within the structure and outside it. The center is at the center of the totality, and yet, since the center does not belong to the totality (is not part of the totality), the totality has its center elsewhere. The center is not the center', 'Structure, Sign and Play in the Discourse of the Human Sciences', *WD*, 279.

12. Richard Admussen writes that the paragraph was added after the completion of the novel on 1 November 1947 (Admussen, pp. 68–9).

13. Levy, *Beckett and the Voice of Species*, p. 106.

14. J.E. Dearlove sees the novellas as 'an embryonic trilogy ... they like the novels blend into a single image into [sic] diverse versions of the same basic story' (*Accommodating the Chaos*, p. 56).

15. See Bair, p. 304, and Ruby Cohn, *Back to Beckett* (Princeton, NJ: Princeton UP, 1973), p. 70 .

16. Michael Robinson, *The Long Sonata of the Dead: A Study of Samuel Beckett* (NY: Grove Press, 1969), p. 137).

17. It may be that *La Fin* was written before any of the others. The earliest surviving mss for *L'Expulsé* and *Le Calmant* are dated 6–14 October 1946 and 23 December 1946, while the first part of *La Fin* appeared in *Les Temps Modernes* on 1 July 1946. There may, of course, be other mss of the two stories that are earlier than these (Admussen, pp. 25, 47–8, 83).

18. Though Beckett has expressed doubt about this; see Raymond Federman and John Fletcher, *Samuel Beckett: His Works and his Critics* (Berkeley and Los Angeles: University of California Press, 1970), p. 6.

19. Hugh Kenner, *Samuel Beckett: A Critical Study* (Berkeley and Los Angeles: University of California Press, 1968), p. 63.

20. Eugene Webb, *Samuel Beckett: A Study of His Novels* (London: Peter Owen, 1970), p. 84; Dearlove, *Accommodating the Chaos*, p. 72; Raymond Federman, *Journey into Chaos: Samuel Beckett's Early Fiction* (Berkeley: University of California Press, 1965), p. 204.

Chapter 5 Repetition and Self-Translation: Mercier and Camier, First Love, The Lost Ones

1. When this book first appeared, there had not been many sustained studies of Beckett's self-translations, but among the best essays on the topic was Hugh Kenner's 'Beckett Translating Beckett: *Comment C'est*', in *Delos: A Journal On and Of Translation*, 5 (1970), pp. 194–211. Kenner comments interestingly on certain aspects of the translation of *Mercier et Camier* in *A Reader's Guide to Samuel Beckett* (London: Thames and Hudson, 1973), pp. 83–91. Also of interest and importance are Ruby Cohn's 'Samuel Beckett, Self-Translator', in *PMLA*, 76 (1961), pp. 613–21; Ludovic Janvier, 'Combinaison et

Liberté', in *Pour Samuel Beckett,* pp. 224–30; Harry Cockerham, 'Samuel Beckett, Bilingual Playwright', in *Samuel Beckett the Shape-Changer,* ed. Katherine Worth (London: Routledge and Kegan Paul, 1975), pp. 139–59; John Fletcher, 'Ecrivain Bilingue', in *L'Herne Beckett,* ed. Tom Bishop and Raymond Federman (Paris: Editions de l'Herne, 1976), pp. 212–19; Erika Ostrovsky, 'Le Silence de Babel', ibid., pp. 206–11; Ann Beer, 'Watt, Knot and Beckett's Bilingualism', in *Journal of Beckett Studies,* 10 (1985), pp. 37–75. I have also learnt much from two unpublished dissertations, A.R. Jones's 'Samuel Beckett's Prose Fiction: A Comparative Study of the French and English Versions', PhD, Birmingham, England, 1972, and Yolande Cantù's 'Samuel Beckett Self-Translator', MA, Birkbeck College, London, 1984.

2. Tom Bishop, 'Samuel Beckett: Working Multilingually', in *Centerpoint: A Journal of Interdisciplinary Studies,* 4:2 (Fall, 1980), p. 142.

3. *Positions,* trans. Alan Bass (London: Athlone Press, 1981), p. 20.

4. There is evidence from the mss that this happened in the case of *Comédie* and of *Va et Vient;* there are signs, too, that the rendering of *Company* into French resulted in changes in the original version. See Admussen, pp. 30, 87.

5. A.R. Jones, 'The French Murphy: From "Rare Bird" to "Cancre": *Journal of Beckett Studies,* 6 (Autumn, 1980), pp. 37–50.

6. *Mercier et Camier* (Paris: Editions de Minuit, 1970), pp. 151–2; omitted in the English *Mercier and Camier,* p. 90. References hereafter are to Minuit and Calder and are incorporated in the text.

7. Ruby Cohn, *Samuel Beckett: The Comic Gamut* (Brunswick, NJ: Rutgers UP, 1962), pp. 97–8.

8. This quotation is taken from Beckett's drafts for the translation of *Mercier et Camier.* The Samuel Beckett Collection in the Reading University Library holds what seems to be a complete run of the manuscripts and typescripts of Beckett's translation of this text, consisting of a first manuscript draft in a series of notebooks, a second draft in typescript, which is heavily corrected and in which much of the material which is now absent from the final translation is first struck out, and a final typescript, which is very close to the printed version of the text.

9. John Fletcher, *The Novels of Samuel Beckett,* 2nd edn (London: Chatto and Windus, 1972), p. 115.

10. *Sunday Times,* 13 October 1974, p. 34.

11. *Premier Amour* (Paris: Editions de Minuit, 1970): *First Love* (London: John Calder, 1977), reprinted in *CSP,* pp. 1–19. References hereafter are to Minuit and *CSP,* and are incorporated in the text.

12. The French text occupied Beckett from October 1965 to May 1966, when it was 'abandoned because of its intractable difficulties.' Beckett did not begin

his translation until September 1971 and it was completed by May of the following year (Admussen, pp. 35–9, 63–4).

13. *Le Dépeupleur* (Paris: Editions de Minuit, 1971), pp. 10–11; *The Lost Ones* (London: Calder and Boyars, 1972), reprinted in *CSP*, 160. References hereafter are to Minuit and *CSP*, and are incorporated in the text.

14. The drafts of Beckett's translation of *Le Dépeupleur* are held in the Berg collection in the New York Public Library. They consist of two notebooks containing Beckett's ms first draft and two typescripts. References in the text and notes hereafter are to ms, tsl and ts2. This phrase is translated in ms as 'in the fiery shadow of the ceiling the fiery zenith guards its legend'. As will be seen, Beckett's translation in the ms draft is a faithful and rather literal translation and it is in tsl that many of the important changes are introduced.

15. Kenner, *Reader's Guide*, p. 89.

16. 'The Measure of Translation Effects', in *Difference in Translation*, ed. Joseph F. Graham (Ithaca and London: Cornell UP, 1985), p. 41.

17. A.R. Jones reports that Beckett urged Elmar Tophoven, his German translator, 'to use a vocabulary of low emotional intensity, and a syntax as unemphatic and as unelevated as possible' ('Samuel Beckett's Prose Fiction', p. 5).

18. Beckett's remark that 'en français c'est plus facile d'écrire sans style' is quoted in Niklaus Gessner, *Die Unzulänglichkeit der Sprache: Eine Untersuchung über Formzufall und Beziehungslosigkeit bei Samuel Beckett* (Zürich: Junis–Verlag, 1957), p. 32. Charles Juliet records Beckett's remark about English having become a foreign language for him again in *Rencontre Avec Samuel Beckett* (Paris: Editions Fata Morgana, 1986), p. 49.

19. The drafts of *Premier Amour* are held in the Humanities Research Center of the University of Texas at Austin.

20. A. Alvarez, *Beckett* (London: Collins, 1973), p. 128.

21. See, for example, Fletcher, 'Ecrivain Bilingue', in *L'Herne Beckett*, pp. 212–19, and the discussion of the leakage between French and English in Ann Beer, '*Watt*, Knot and Beckett's Bilingualism'.

22. Walter Benjamin, 'The Task of the Translator', in *Illuminations*, trans. Harry Zohn, ed. Hannah Arendt (London: Collins, 1973), pp. 80–1.

23. Beckett wrote in a letter of 1973 to Barney Rosset that the translation of *Mercier et Camier* was not going well and that he was 'bogged down through loathing of the original' (quoted in Bair, p. 634.)

24. See discussion above, pp. 88.

25. 'Des Tours de Babel', in *Difference in Translation*, p. 184.

26. 'Taking Fidelity Philosophically', in *Difference in Translation*, p. 146. Paul de Man, discussing Walter Benjamin's views on translation, also stresses the way in which a translation subverts the canonical authority of its original. In this, he says, translation resembles other linguistically 'secondary' activities,

such as philosophy and literary theory: 'They disarticulate, they undo the original, they reveal that the original was always already disarticulated. They reveal that their failure, which seems to be due to the fact that they are secondary in relation to the original, reveals an essential failure, an essential disarticulation which was already there in the original. They kill the original, by discovering that the original was already dead' ('Conclusions: "The Task of the Translator"', in *The Resistance* to *Theory* [Manchester: Manchester UP, 1986], p. 84).

27. Erika Ostrovsky remarks that 'dans les reformulations bilingues d'un oeuvre, les deux versions se poursuivent en gardant toujours un léger écart et révélant un itinéraire aussi frustrant que celui de Mercier et Camier qui rend impossible tout rencontre mais nécessite une quête continuelle' ('Le Silence de Babel', *L'Herne Beckett*, p. 210).

28. See Michael Haerdter, 'Samuel Beckett inszeniert das Endspiel', in *Materialen zu Becketts Endspiel* (Frankfurt: Suhrkamp Verlag, 1968), p. 36.

29. Niels Egebak, *L'écriture de Samuel Beckett* (Copenhagen: Akademisk Forlag, 1973), p. 120.

Chapter 6 *Presence and Repetition in Beckett's Theatre*

1. 'Moody Man of Letters', *New York Times,* Sunday, 6 May 1956, section 2, p.3.

2. Michael Robinson, *The Long Sonata of the Dead: A Study of Samuel Beckett* (NY: Grove Press, 1969), p. 230.

3. Quoted in Michael Haerdter, *Materialen zu Becketts Endspiel* (Frankfurt: Suhrkamp Verlag, 1968), p. 88.

4. 'Samuel Beckett, or Presence on the Stage', in *Snapshots and Towards a New Novel* (London: Calder and Boyars, 1965), p. 119. References in the text hereafter are to *TNN.*

5. See the discussion in Bruce Morrissette, 'Robbe-Grillet as a Critic of Samuel Beckett', in *Samuel Beckett Now: Critical Approaches to the Novels, Poetry and Plays,* 2nd edn, ed. Melvin J. Friedman (Chicago and London: University of Chicago Press, 1975), pp. 59–72.

6. 'Beckett's Actor', in *Modern Drama* 26:4 (December 1983), p. 420.

7. Sidney Homan, *Beckett's Theaters: Interpretations for Performance* (London and Toronto: Associated University Presses, 1984), p. 49.

8. See the discussion of drama and art in general as historical 'play' in Hans-Georg Gadamer, *Truth and Method* (London: Sheed and Ward, 1981), pp. 104–7. Joel Weinsheimer summarizes Gadamer's views on the relationship of play-text and performance in the following terms:

> When something is imitated, when it is represented and recognised as something (else), it becomes something more than what it was, and that

'more' is that it becomes itself more fully. Gadamer suggests that the same happens when anything is transformed into a Gebilde — that is, when it becomes repeatable by being repeated (other-wise) in an artwork. Performance is not something ancillary, accidental, or superfluous that can be distinguished from the play proper. The play proper exists first and only when it is played. Performance brings the play into existence and the playing of the play is the play itself ... Thus, the work cannot be differentiated from the representations of it since it exists only *there*, only in the flesh. It comes to be in representation and in all the contingency and particularity of the occasions of its appearance.

(Gadamer's Hermeneutics: A Reading of 'Truth and Method' [New Haven and London: Yale UP, 1985], pp. 109–10)

9. 'Production and Metaphysics', in *The Theatre and its Double,* trans. Victor Corti (London: Calder and Boyars, 1970), p. 27. References hereafter in the text are to *TD*.

10. Vivian Mercier, 'The Uneventful Event', in *Irish Times,* 18 February 1956, p.6.

11. *The Complete Works of Lewis Carroll* (London: Nonesuch Press, 1939), p.680.

12. Quoted in Haerdter, *Materialen zu Becketts Endspiel,* p. 46.

13. A full account of the verbal repetitions in *Endgame* can be found in Ruby Cohn's *Just Play: Beckett's Theater* (Princeton: Princeton University Press, 1980), pp. 107–15.

14. There has been some dispute about the origin of the millet-grain metaphor. Some writers have identified it with Zeno's heap of grain which is endlessly divisible in two, though it is hard to see the application of this to the situation in *Endgame.* Hugh Kenner's attribution of the metaphor to Sextus Empiricus the Pyrrhonist seems the most satisfactory (*A Reader's Guide to Samuel Beckett* [London: Thames and Hudson, 1973], p. 123). It is confirmed by Alice and Kenneth Hamilton in *Condemned to Life: The World of Samuel Beckett* (Grand Rapids: Eerdman's, 1976), p. 220.

15. 'Rockaby Baby', interview with John Connor in *City Limits, 24–30* January 1986.

16. J.L. Austin, *How To Do Things With Words,* 2nd edn, ed. J.O. Urmson and Marina Sbisa (Oxford: OUP, 1976).

17. 'Signature Event Context', in *Margins of Philosophy,* trans. Alan Bass (Brighton: Harvester Press, 1982) p. 320.

18. *La Dèrniere Bande* (Paris: Editions de Minuit, 1959), p. 13.

19. As such, Beckett's plays might seem to exemplify Walter Benjamin's view that mechanical reproducibility brings about a dispersal of 'auratic' presence in the work of art; see 'The Work of Art in the Age of Mechanical

Reproduction', in *Illuminations,* trans. Harry Zohn, ed. Hannah Arendt (London: Collins, 1973), pp. 219–53. For a politically more optimistic reading of Beckett's work in the light of Benjamin's and Marcuse's ideas about mass-cultural forms, see George Szanto, 'Samuel Beckett and Dramatic Possibilities in an Age of Mechanical Reproduction', *Theater and Propaganda* (Austin: Texas UP, 1978), pp. 145–77.

20. See discussion of *Ill Seen Ill Said* above, ch. 1, pp. 11.

21. This ratio seems to be confirmed by the French version of the play, in which, although the actual words and phrases which are repeated are different from the English, and are also distributed differently, each repeated word or phrase is still usually shared between two speakers only; see *Catastrophe et Autres Dramaticules* (Paris: Editions de Minuit, 1982), pp. 9–25.

22. Katherine Worth, for instance, feels that the play 'seems in the end a triumphant "weaving" of a life, an achievement' (*The Irish Drama of Europe from Yeats to Beckett* [London: Athlone Press, 1978], p. 264). See, too, John Fletcher and John Spurling, *Beckett the Playwright* (London: Methuen, 1972), p. 126.

23. See discussion above, ch. 2, pp. 43–5.

24. *CDW,* 388, 394–5, 394, 395; *Catastrophe et Autres Dramaticules,* 10, 24, 23, 24.

Chapter 7 What? Where? Space and the Body

1. 'Mongrel Mime for One Old Small' is the heading for this abandoned sketch for a play, held in the Humanities Research Center at Austin, Texas.

2. *Just Play: Beckett's Theater* (Princeton: Princeton University Press, 1980), pp. 27–33; *CDW,* 80.

3. 'Light, Sound, Movement, and Action in Beckett's *Rockaby*', *Modern Drama,* 25:3 (September 1982), p. 345.

4. Hugh Kenner, *A Reader's Guide to Samuel Beckett* (London, Thames and Hudson, 1973), p. 121.

5. *A Student's Guide to the Plays of Samuel Beckett* (London: Faber and Faber, 1985), p. 93.

6. Antoni Libera made this observation during a discussion of *Quad* at the International Beckett Symposium held at the University of Stirling, 11–15 August 1986.

7. See James Knowlson's discussion of the function of shadow in *Light and Darkness in the Theatre of Samuel Beckett* (London: Turret Books, 1972).

8. Quoted by Clas Zilliacus, *Beckett and Broadcasting: A Study of the Works of Samuel Beckett for and in Radio and Television,* (Åbo: Åbo Akademi, 1976), p. 3.

9. Letter of 27 August 1957, quoted by Linda Ben-Zvi, 'Samuel Beckett's Media Plays', in *Modern Drama,* 28:1 (March, 1985), p. 24.

10. In fact, Beckett authorized a number of transpositions of his work from one medium to another. For details of some of these, see 'The Plays Out of Their Element', in Zilliacus, *Beckett and Broadcasting,* pp. 169–82, and 'Jumping Beckett's Genres' in Ruby Cohn's *Just Play,* pp. 207–29.

11. Other writers have used the metaphor of the limit or borderline in discussing Beckett's writings for different media, though without relinquishing the belief that Beckett's plays remain intrinsically for their specified medium. Cf. Linda Ben-Zvi, 'Samuel Beckett's Media Plays', p.25, and Martha Fehsenfeld, 'Beckett's Late Works: An Appraisal', *Modern Drama,* 25:3 (September 1982), p. 361. James Knowlson and John Pilling record that Beckett himself thought that *That Time* was 'on the very edge of what was possible in the theatre', *Frescoes of the Skull: The Later Prose and Drama of Samuel Beckett* (London: John Calder, 1979), p.219.

12. *Catastrophe et Autres Dramaticules,* p. 9.

13. 'Rockaby Baby', interview with John Connor in *City Limits,* 24-30 January 1986.

14. *Our Exag,* p. 15; Zilliacus, p. 30.

15. Letter to Jessica Tandy, quoted in Enoch Brater, 'Dada, Surrealism and the Genesis of *Not I', Modern Drama,* 18.1 (March 1975), p. 53.

16. 'The Body in Beckett's Theatre', *Journal of Beckett Studies,* 8 (Autumn 1982), pp. 23, 27. References hereafter in the text are to 'Chabert'.

17. 'Light, Sound, Movement, and Action in Beckett's *Rockaby',* p. 348.

18. Paul Lawley's excellent discussion of *Not I* suggests other ways in which a fragmented and placeless body is produced by the text and performance. Particularly striking is his discussion of the way that the text runs together the mouth and the eye, making us see the mouth as an eye, and the eye as a mouth-like orifice ('Counterpoint, Absence and the Medium in Beckett's *Not I', Modern Drama,* 26:4 [December 1983], pp. 407–13, especially p. 409).

19. For the 'system of 's'entendre parler'—'(over)hearing oneself speak'—see Derrida, *Of Grammatology,* trans. Gayatri Spivak (Baltimore and London: Johns Hopkins UP, 1976), pp. 7–12 and Jonathan Culler, *On Deconstruction: Theory and Criticism After Structuralism* (London: Routledge and Kegan Paul, 1983), pp. 107–10.

20. Letter to Barney Rosset, quoted in Zilliacus, p. 3.

21. Sidney Homan, *Beckett's Theaters: Interpretations for Performance* (London and Toronto: Associated University Press, 1984), p. 153.

22. Ibid.

23. John Fletcher and John Spurling, *Beckett the Playwright* (London: Methuen, 1972), p. 118.

24. Homan, *Beckett's Theatres*, p. 155.

25. Brater sees an Artaudian triumph over the structures of repetition in the collapsing together of text and performance: 'In these wordless plays there is no real script, only the pretext of one. There is, however, a performance, one, moreover, which is meant to be regularized and fixed forever on videotape. The performance we see on television is the text, for in *Quad I* and *II* the verbal element has been ultimately suppressed. The only final statement the permutations within this medium offer is the impermutability of screened presentation' (Towards a Poetics of Television Technology: Beckett's *Nacht und Triiume* and *Quad'*, *Modern Drama*, 28:1 (March 1985), p. 53). Where Brater speaks of *Quad I* and *II*, I have subsumed both acts of the mime in the title *Quad*.

26. 'The Function of Language in Samuel Beckett's *Acte Sans Paroles'*, in *Structure and Time: Narration, Poetry, Models*, trans. John Meddemen (Chicago and London: Chicago UP, 1979), pp. 225–44.

Chapter 8 Repetition and Power

1. 'Moody Man of Letters', *New York Times*, Sunday 6 May 1956, section 2, p. 3.

2. I am indebted in the discussion that follows to Alan Astro's excellent discussion of Beckett's relationship to his native and adopted languages, 'The Language of the Master and the Mastery of Language in Joyce and Beckett', paper delivered at the James Joyce International Symposium, Copenhagen, Monday 16 June 1986. Astro drew on Hegel's master/slave dialectic to explore the complex mingling of authority and subordination in Beckett's use of French.

3. Michel Foucault, *Power/Knowledge: Selected Interviews and Other Writings 1972–1977*, ed. Colin Gordon, trans. Colin Gordon, Leo Marshall, John Mepham and Kate Soper (Sussex: Harvester Press, 1980), p. 197; *The History of Sexuality: Vol. 1: An Introduction*, trans. Robert Hurley (London: Allen Lane, 1979), p. 93.

4. *Watt*, notebook II, held in the Humanities Research Center at Austin, Texas. See description in Carlton Lake, *No Symbols Where None Intended: A Catalogue of Books, Manuscripts and Other Material Relating to Samuel Beckett in the Collections of the Humanities Research Center* (Austin, Texas: Humanities Research Center, 1984), p. 57; Admussen, 90.

5. See Victor Carrabiro, 'Beckett and Hegel: The Dialectic of Lordship and Bondage', *Neophilologus* 65 (1981), pp. 32–41.

6. Quoted from Beckett's production notebook for the production of *Glückliche Tage*, at the Schiller-Theater Werkstatt, Berlin, 1971, p. 62, in *Happy Days:*

Samuel Beckett's Production Notebook, ed. James Knowlson (London: Faber and Faber, 1985), p. 150.

7. Michael Robinson, for example, speaks of the 'endeavour' of the male narrators of the Trilogy as opposed to the passive 'condition' of Winnie in *Happy Days, The Long Sonata of the Dead: A Study of Samuel Beckett* (NY: Grove Press, 1969), pp. 163, 190,290. It might justly be argued that some of Beckett's later writing does seem to distinguish between passive female suffering and anxious male exploration (for example, *Ill Seen Ill Said*). It is interesting to note, however, that on the one occasion that Beckett seems to have used a female narrator in his fiction, critics have felt the need to displace or deny female authorship. Eric Levy argues that the narrator of *Enough* is only a 'persona' adopted (invisibly in my view) after the framing male narrative of the first paragraph of the story, *Samuel Beckett and the Voice of Species: A Study of the Prose Fiction* (Totowa, NJ: Barnes and Noble, 1980), p. 114. J.M. Dearlove finds herself misquoting the last words of the story in order to protect her hypothesis of a sexless or non-female narrator - 'Enough my old breasts feel his old hand' (*CSP*, 144) becomes 'Enough my old breast feels his old hand', *Accommodating the Chaos: Samuel Beckett's Non Relational Art* (Durham, NC: Duke UP, 1982), p. 55.

8. See Jean-Paul Sartre, *Being and Nothingness: An Essay in Phenomenological Ontology,* tr. Hazel E. Barnes (London: Methuen, 1977), pp. 607–14. Toril Moi discusses the gendering of Sartre's *visqueux* and its problematic repetition in the work of Simone de Beauvoir in 'Existentialism and Feminism: The Rhetoric of Biology in *The Second Sex', Oxford Literary Review*, 8: 1–2 (1986), pp. 88–95. Roger Scruton explores the idea of Sartrean slime in Beckett's work in 'Beckett and the Cartesian Soul', in *The Aesthetic Understanding: Essays in the Philosophy of Art and Culture* (London: Methuen, 1983), pp. 235–7, and uncritically reproduces the gendered opposition of self and other: 'the slime of the other, which defiles the Cartesian self is (speaking not philosophically but in terms of the real state of mind conveyed) the slime of the vagina' p. 237).

9. My argument in the pages that follow is congruent with much that Peter Gidal says in *Understanding Beckett: A Study of Monologue and Gesture in the Works of Samuel Beckett* (London: Macmillan, 1986).

10. There is now a large and intimidating body of work on the importance of the visual in gendered power relations, much of which draws from Jacques Lacan's analysis of 'the gaze' in *The Four Fundamental Concepts of Psycho-Analysis* (London: Hogarth Press, 1977), pp. 67–119. See, Laura Mulvey, 'Visual Pleasure and Narrative Cinema', *Screen,* 16:3 (Autumn 1975), pp. 6–18 and 'On *Duel in the Sun:* Afterthoughts on Visual Pleasure and Narrative Cinema', *Framework,* 15–17 (1981), pp. 12–15 along with the discussion of

photography and the conventions of pornography in Annette Kuhn, *The Power of the Image: Essays on Representation and Sexuality* (London: Routledge and Kegan Paul, 1985), pp. 40–3; and the chapters 'The Mirror With a Memory' and 'The Look' in Rosalind Coward, *Female Desire: Women's Sexuality Today* (London: Paladin Books, 1984), pp. 47–54, 73–82. Jane Alison Hale, in her study of Beckett's use and abuse of perspective, *The Broken Window: Beckett's Dramatic Perspective* (West Lafayette, Indiana: Purdue UP, 1987), has disappointingly little to say about the relations of gender and power in structures of looking.

11. Ruby Cohn points out the associations with looking of these names in *Back to Beckett* (Princeton: Princeton UP, 1973), p. 182.

12. Luce Irigaray, *Ce sexe qui n'en est pas un* (Paris: Editions de Minuit, 1977).

13. In discussing her work for Beckett, Billie Whitelaw has said 'What it means I'm in no way interested in … Beckett blows the notes … I just want them to come out … to create a theatrical feeling' (documentary film on the making of *Rockaby*, April 1981, dir. D.A. Pennebaker and Chris Hegedus; videotape held in New York Public Library Performing Arts Research Center, NCOX 298). In another interview, Whitelaw has said 'In *Footfalls* I felt like a moving Edvard Munch painting … When Beckett was directing *Footfalls*, he was not only using me to play the notes, but I almost felt he did have a paintbrush out and was painting, and, of course, what he always has in the other pocket is the rubber, because as fast as he draws a line in, he gets out that enormous indiarubber and rubs it out until it is only faintly there' ('What … Who … No … She!', video interview with James Knowlson; transcript published as 'Extracts from an Unscripted Interview with Billie Whitelaw by James Knowlson', *Journal of Beckett Studies*, 3 (September 1978), p. 89.

14. Clas Zilliacus, *Beckett and Broadcasting: A Study of the Works of Samuel Becket for and in Radio and Television*, (Åbo: Åbo Akademi, 1976), p. 202.

15. 'Beckett is already the director long before he takes charge of the rehearsals and works with the actors. In this way he is unique in theatrical history, imposing an ultimate limitation on the work. The direction is always written into his texts in the most literal way' ('Beckett as Director', *Gambit*, 7:28 (1976), p. 41). Beckett's attempts and, following his death, those of his Estate, to control interpretation of his plays on the stage have sometimes gone beyond the legislation of the text. When the American Repertory Theatre departed from his stage directions for their production of *Endgame* at the Loeb Drama Centre in Cambridge, Mass., in December 1984, Beckett, through his publishers Grove Press, resorted to law to try to make the ART conform to his wishes for the play. See 'Playwright-Director Conflict: Whose Play Is It, Anyway?' in *New York Law Journal*, 192 no. 123 (28 December 1984)

and *The Beckett Circle: Newsletter of the Samuel Beckett Society,* VI:2 (Spring 1985), pp. 1–3.

16. Walter Asmus, 'Beckett Directs *Godot', Theatre Quarterly,* 5:19 (September-November 1975), p. 25.

17. Ibid., p. 25.

18. 'State of Play: Performance Changes and Beckett Scholarship', *Journal of Beckett Studies,* 10 (1985), pp. 108–20.

19. Enoch Brater, 'Dada, Surrealism and the Genesis of *Not I', Modern Drama,* 18.1 (March, 1975), p. 50; James Knowlson and John Pilling, *Frescoes of the Skull: The Later Prose and Drama of Samuel Beckett* (London: John Calder, 1979), p. 197; Bernard Beckerman, 'Beckett and the Act of Listening', in *Beckett at 80/Beckett in Context,* ed. Enoch Brater (Oxford: OUP, 1986), p. 149.

20. Story told by Alan Schneider, in' "Any Way You Like, Alan"', *Theatre Quarterly,* 5:19 (September-November 1975), p. 32. References hereafter in text.

21. *Lessness* (London: Calder and Boyars, 1970). The description of the text that appears on the wrapper for this volume is to be found among the drafts for Beckett's translation of *Sans* in the Yale University Library, MS Vault Uncat SI, Section II, p. 1.

22. Quoted unattributed in Zilliacus, p. 66.

23. John Russell Brown, 'Beckett and the Art of the Nonplus', in *Beckett at 80/Beckett in Context,* p. 37.

24. See Asmus, 'Beckett Directs *Godot',* p. 20.

25. 'Growing (Up?) With Godot', in *Beckett at 80/Beckett in Context,* p. 15.

26. S.E. Gontarski, in the most extensive study of Beckett's manuscripts to have appeared so far, sees the evolution of Beckett's work as a simultaneous process of self-effacement and concentration. Gontarski therefore enlists Beckett as a Derridean anti-logocentrist, while clinging on to an idealist commitment to essence and universality: 'The creative struggle is to undo the realistic sources of the text, to undo the coherence of character and to undo the author's presence.... Beckett's struggle in composition is to undo the layers of the physical world, to reveal this thing-in-itself, the metaphysical, essential, recurrent form', *The Intent of Undoing in Samuel Beckett's Dramatic Texts* (Bloomington: Indiana UP, 1985), pp. 4, 185.

27. *No Symbols Where None Intended,* p. 76.

28. See Richard Cave, review of David Clark's remaking of *Film,* in *Journal of Beckett Studies,* 7 (Spring 1982), pp. 134–8.

29. 'Ghost Trio/Geister Trio', in *Beckett at 80/Beckett in Context,* pp. 193–207.

30. '"Everything Out But the Faces": Beckett's Reshaping of *What Where* for Television', *Modern Drama,* 29:2 (June 1986), pp. 229–40, especially p.

235, where Fehsenfeld writes that the TV version 'is a work carved out of the stage work.'

31. 'Un Mal Pour Un Bien', review of *Catastrophe et Autres Dramaticules, Critique,* 42:473 (October 1986), pp. 1022–3.

Index

19426710R00138

Made in the USA
Lexington, KY
19 December 2012